D0531857

FIVE FOREIGNERS IN JAPAN

FIVE FOREIGNERS
IN JAPAN

By

HERBERT H. GOWEN, D.D., F.R. As.S.

Professor of Oriental Studies, University of Washington
Seattle, Washington

DS
836
G6
1967

Essay Index Reprint Series

BOOKS FOR LIBRARIES PRESS, INC.

FREEPORT, NEW YORK

Copyright 1936, Renewed 1963
By Sylvia Gowen Wells Henderson

Reprinted 1967, by arrangement with
Fleming H. Revell Company

LIBRARY OF CONGRESS CATALOG CARD NUMBER:
67-28735

PRINTED IN THE UNITED STATES OF AMERICA

FOREWORD

THE following sketches are designed to do two things. First, they are intended to bring into some relief the personalities of five illustrious foreigners whose fortunes touched at certain critical moments the story of Japan. Secondly, they are meant to show the influence of these men upon the history of the Far East in general and of Japan in particular. Both intentions coalesce in some desire to illustrate the influence of personality in history, a doctrine which, stressed by Carlyle and Emerson in the mid-nineteenth century, has suffered some eclipse in our own day.

The story of Pinto must, through the manifest unreliability of much of his narrative, compare somewhat unfavourably with the rest. Nevertheless, the mendacious Mendez may well be taken as typical of those hardy and picturesque Lusitanians who, in the early sixteenth century, drove their adventurous prows into the uncharted eastern seas, thus inaugurating the modern period of Oriental history.

Xavier is without doubt the great example of that unshadowed faith which did so much, as the Roman Catholic would put it, to repair the ravages of the Protestant Reformation and add new realms to an expanding Christendom. In his weakness as well as in his strength, St. Francis has been a very potent factor in determining the currents of Far Eastern history.

Will Adams is a particular favourite of mine and marks the beginning of one of the great periods in

5

Japanese history, while his failure to convince the representative of the London *East India Company* of the prophetic character of his visions brought about one of the most significant transitions in the story of the country which claimed him in death and in life.

The story of Ranald MacDonald is the romance of a young American—American in more than a single sense—who dreamed intuitively of sympathetic relations with the land and people of Nippon, and vindicated his faith in a desperate adventure which had not a little to do with preparing for the new epoch for which conditions in Japan were then ripening.

And in Townsend Harris, the New York merchant, we have illustrated the unswerving confidence and indomitable patience which, almost unsustained by support from home, tided over the most difficult transition of all and blazed the way for an intercourse which, while it has brought its problems, has brought also the increasing determination to solve these problems in the spirit of America's first representative.

So, to the outsider anxious to catch an idea of the main currents of Japanese history during these past four centuries, these five foreigners will, it is believed, stand as representative individuals, and suggest much that should aid in bringing closer understanding and accord between the great Pacific Powers.

H. H. G.

CONTENTS

I

FERNANDO MENDEZ PINTO

THE first European reference to Japan is the oft-quoted passage in Book III of *The Book of Ser Marco Polo* which commences as follows: " Chipangu is an Island towards the east in the high seas, fifteen hundred miles distant from the Continent; and a very great Island it is. The people are white, civilised and well favoured. They are Idolaters, and are dependent on nobody. And I can tell you the quantity of gold they have is endless; for they find it in their own Islands and the King does not allow it to be exported. Moreover, few merchants visit the country because it is so far from the mainland, and thus it comes to pass that their gold is abundant beyond all measure."

This is not quite an accurate description. The Chinese name, *Jih-pên-kuo*, which Polo renders as *Xipangu*, is perhaps as near to the Japanese *Ni-hon-koku* (kingdom of the Rising Sun) as one could expect a foreigner living in China to employ. The Venetian's estimate of the wealth of Japan, a country notoriously lacking in the precious metals, is exaggerated. Yet it may be regarded as a piece of good fortune that when Marco's Genoese fellow-prisoner transcribed the reminiscences of the Venetian traveller, any mention at all was made of the Far Eastern Empire, which at this time no European had visited, and of which we only hear in

9

this rather roundabout fashion. For the glamour of the Far East, which from the fourteenth century onwards so touched the imagination of the West, was in very large part the creation of this famous story. Marco Polo had many successors but the travel stories of men like Carpini and De Rubruk had no comparable influence in keeping alive the lure of the Orient, after the closing of the land routes.

It is not exactly correct to say that the immediate cause of finding a route by sea to the East was the rise of the Ottoman Turk and the consequent closing of the continental roads. As late as the fifteenth century there were travellers to the Far East through Ottoman territory and there were efforts made to find highways by sea considerably before the rise of the Turk. Nevertheless, as a generalization, the statement is in substance accurate that the dominance of Ottoman power eventually spelled the doom of the trade which had hitherto flowed along the ancient highways of continental Asia towards the ports of the Mediterranean. The barriers placed by the Turks across these highways slowly strangled the traffic which had gone on, for the most part unimpeded, for several thousand years. First, at the beginning of the fifteenth century, was closed the route to the north of the Black Sea. Then, soon after the driving of the Knights Hospitalers from Tunis to Rhodes in 1403, the prowess of Timur Leng brought a like fate upon the highway which ran through Syria. In 1483 followed the closing of the road by the Black Sea itself. There now remained only the old Indo-Egyptian highway which had been of importance long before the Mediterranean was turned into a Roman lake. It is this which was im-

perilled and ultimately barred by the growth of the
Ottoman navy and the siege of Rhodes in 1480, though
it continued to be used until the conquest of Egypt by
Sultan Selim in 1516. The immediate consequence of
this resounding success was that Venice and Genoa saw
ruin staring them in the face, while the cities of the
Hanseatic League also felt the change. " Grass grew
in the fair and pleasant streets of Bruges and seaweed
clustered about the marble halls of Venice." [1]

It is thus that the old traffic with the East was
halted in the familiar channels. It became clear that
it must perish unless some new way was discovered
whereby the road to Cathay might be kept open. It
is not strange that under such circumstances a manifest destiny was arousing into wakefulness the nation
which providence and geographical situation had already pointed out as the pioneer of the new adventure. It was at the same time preparing the man who
was to make possible and usher in an entirely new era
of human history.

The elect nation was the little kingdom of Portugal,
the classic Lusitania (so named from its supposed first
colonist, the Lusus of Vergil's *Æneid*), a country
which had maintained a precarious existence, between
the Moors and the Kingdom of Castile, in the territory about the mouth of the Douro. In 1095 Alphonso
VI, of Leon and Castile, in gratitude for services
rendered against the Muslim, had conveyed to Count
Henry, the younger brother of Hugh, Duke of Bur-
gundy, the frontier provinces of Oporto and Coimbra
(recently wrested from the Moor), together with the
hand of his natural daughter, Theresa, and the title of
Portocalensis. This title was derived from Porto Cale,

that is, Oporto, and has given us the name Portugal, which superseded that of Lusitania.

Henry's son, Don Alphonso, was the actual founder of the Kingdom of Portugal. In 1139 he gained a great victory over the Moors and was crowned king soon after 1147. With the help of English mercenaries, he then besieged and captured Lisbon in 1158. This city, supposedly founded by Ulysses and originally known as Ulyssipo, thus became the capital, as it has remained to the present day. Friendly relations with England were further cemented by a commercial treaty made between the two countries in 1294, when Edward I reigned in England, and again in the reign of Edward III. In 1385 King John of Portugal was assisted in his struggle against Castile by the arrival of five hundred English archers under Northberry, Mowbray and Hentzel. In the following year came John of Gaunt, Shakespeare's " old John of Gaunt, time-honoured Lancaster," son of Edward III, on a voyage which was to have momentous consequences.

John of Gaunt had brought with him some two thousand English soldiers to enforce the rather shadowy claim he made to the throne of Castile, but instead he stayed to arrange a couple of matrimonial alliances which were destined to change the map of the world. One daughter, Katherine, he wedded to the Prince Royal of Castile, and the other, Philippa, he bestowed upon King John of Portugal. He made it a condition in each case that the two peninsula peoples were to remain at peace with one another and with England. King John lived loyally up to the treaty of 1387. He was the first foreign sovereign to receive from the English king, Henry IV, in 1400, the recently founded Order of the Garter. John established his throne on a sound basis and had the good fortune to create a dynasty which survived for two hundred years. But John the Great's best title to fame is that his eighth son, born of an English mother, was' the Prince Henry who in after years became known as Henry the Navigator. It is of this illustrious pioneer of history's thalassic era that Camoens wrote in the *Lusiads:*

> " The Genius then
> Of navigation, that in hopeless sloth
> Had slumbered on the vast Atlantic deep
> For idle ages, starting, heard at last
> The Lusitanian Prince, who, heaven-inspir'd
> To love of useful glory, roused mankind,
> And in unbounded commerce mixed the world." [2]

Henry was born at Oporto on March 4, Ash Wednesday, 1394. From boyhood both he and his older brother Pedro were interested in the recovery of the trade which had been wrested from the Mediterranean ports by the activities of the Moor and the Turk, and in the ultimate extension of that trade to India and the Far East. Dom Pedro travelled diligently in various directions. At Venice he received a copy of Marco Polo's *Travels,* and in England he was pressing once again the advantages of commercial coöperation. Henry, however, look'ng further ahead, began to prepare for the age of commercial adventure on the seas by establishing a school for the study of navigation and astronomy. He fixed its site on the rocky promontory of Sagres significantly overlooking the Atlantic. Here, with the expenditure of the large rev-

enues which came to him as Grand Master of the
Order of Christ, and with an ascetic devotion almost
unmatched in the history of scientific research, Prince
Henry undertook the training of the captains who were
presently to defy the menace of the Moor and the
perils of the uncharted seas, and to lift the veil which
hung southward and westward of the northwest coast
of Africa. Soon, throughout much of western Europe,
the desire was expressed to have a share in the wealth
which it was anticipated must come with a new era of
maritime adventure and discovery.

Prince Henry did not live to see the full realization
of his grandiose vision. After expending his entire
fortune on the enterprise at Sagres, he died, November 14, 1460, and now rests beside his beautiful English mother at Batalha, with the insignia of the Order
of the Garter above the tomb, on which is inscribed
the motto, *Talent de bien faire.* But the work he had
initiated went on, and soon there were daring captains,
trained in the Sagres school and inspired by the resolution of King John II, who were ready at the word
to risk death by pushing out into unknown seas. Not
to mention earlier navigators, we think of Bartolomeo
Diaz, the valiant member of a no less valiant family,
who sailed south and ever south till, without realizing
it at the time, he had rounded the southernmost point
of the African continent. On a small island in Algoa
Bay, the first land beyond the Cape touched by the
feet of a European, Diaz set up a pillar surmounted
by a cross to commemorate his voyage. The name of
Santa Cruz bestowed upon this island survives to mark
the deed. Turned back by the grumbling of his crew,
Diaz reported to his sovereign the discovery of Cabo

Tormentoso, the Cape of Storms, but the prescient monarch cried, " No. It must be the Cape of Good Hope," since now the long coveted passage by sea to India lay open to mankind. The extent of Diaz' achievement may be better understood, when we realize that the great sailor was away from Portugal more than sixteen months and that during this time three hundred and fifty leagues of coast-line were brought to the knowledge of Europe.

A little later we have the heroic story of Vasco da Gama, the first circumnavigator of all Africa, since the half-legendary days of Pharaoh Necho and his Phœnician sailors more than six centuries before the Christian era. Nothing, however, in the story told by Herodotus may detract from the glory of Da Gama's accomplishment. Starting from the mouth of the Tagus in July 1497, the Portuguese ships, three in number, and none of more than three hundred tons' burden, weathered alike the treachery of the seas and that of the natives at the points they touched. Nearly a year later they reached the town of Calicut on the Malabar coast of India, a country rich in pepper and other condiments so dear to the appetites of the European, and seemingly only awaiting the arrival of the trader.

The stirring epic of Vasco da Gama's exploit has been worthily described in the immortal work of the Portuguese poet, Camoens. The *Lusiads* may fitly be called the epic of East and West, and the poet deserves his fame as the historian of a great achievement as well as the chief ornament of Portuguese literature. Born in 1524–5, the poet was twice exiled from his native land, once on account of an unfortunate love

affair, and again for some political offence. For a third
offence he was banished to the overseas dominions in
India and left his country with the bitter words,
" *Ingrata patria, non possedebis mea ossa,*" " O un-
grateful fatherland, thou shalt never hold my bones."
After three years in Goa, Camoens was ordered to
Macao, where he wrote the first six cantos of the great
Portuguese epic. On his return he suffered shipwreck
and only preserved his precious manuscript by holding
it aloft above the waves. The finished work was
printed in 1572, but so meagre were the rewards of
authorship that the poet could keep himself alive only
by the begging expeditions of his Javanese servant.
There is much irony in the fact that so little did Europe
appreciate what was due to the genius of the bard that
not till 1867 was a statue of Camoens erected in the
capital of his native land. Yet it was largely through
his poetry that we are able to envisage the relations of
East and West as these must have appeared to the
navigators of the sixteenth century. As in the classical
age of Greece and Rome, we have a world of clenched
antagonisms, each side under the championship of rival
divinities. The East was represented as under the ægis
of the Indian Bacchus, while the West enjoyed the
favour of the Cyprian goddess. Venus, who of old had
risen above the Mediterranean waves to aid her human
offspring now engaged in the building of a greater Troy
and sending new colonies to the Lusitanian shores,
comes once again to the aid of her descendants. The
epic struggle described is but an extension of that de-
picted long before by Vergil.

The Portuguese were fortunate in the time and place
of their arrival on the shores of India. The kings of

the Malabar coast had little or no share in the great
movements, religious and political, which had been
fermenting in the northwest and in the Ganges valley.
They had, within their own territory, an experience of
nearly six centuries of the rapacity and the ruthless-
ness of the Arab pirates. Almost any kind of newcomers who were ready to give aid against these ma-
rauders would be received with open arms. At the
same time, it is to be noticed that the progress of
Portuguese penetration was at the first cautious and
tentative. Early in 1499 Vasco da Gama returned to
Lisbon to receive the hearty plaudits of his countrymen and the rewards of a more material sort including
the title of Dom. The whole land basked in the sunshine of the discovery. Sermons were preached at
Lisbon on the glories of the new dominions, and the
king added to his former titles the high-sounding one
of " Lord of the Conquest, Navigation and Commerce
of Ethiopia, Arabia, Persia and China."

Fresh expeditions continued to be sent from Portugal to India, and the one led by Cabral had the good
fortune to discover Brazil by going west instead of
east. Of course, many ships were lost, and in one of
these perished the great pioneer navigator, Bartolomeo
Diaz. The influence of Portugal continued in India
with a few petty rajahs occupying the narrow strip of
land between the Western Ghats and the sea. Calicut,
the first settlement, is really *Kolicutta,* " Cock-fort,"
so called because the limits of the place were fixed by
the distance to which a cock-crowing could be heard
from the principal temple. Portuguese India, indeed,
was never very large, but the national interests on the
high seas and along the Malabar coast were sufficient

to engage the attention of a number of very able men.
Vasco da Gama went out again in 1502 and carried
through a most barbarous retaliation on the Moors of
Calicut, using refinements of cruelty from which the
imagination recoils. In 1505 the Viceroyalty of the
Indies was conferred upon Dom Francisco de Almeida.
He was followed several years later by Alphonzo de
Albuquerque who, after an undignified squabble, attained the Viceroyalty in November 1509. His appointment, however, initiated a vigorous policy and in
1510 brought about the capture of Goa, the predestined capital of the Portuguese possessions in the
Orient. In the decadent and somnolent town of to-
day it is hard to conjure up a vision of the Goa of the
sixteenth century, " peopled with 225,000 people of all
nations, and packed with 20,000 houses built of stone,
white painted and terraced, with strings of villas running down the river to the west outside the walls of
the city. Merchants from every country east and west,
ambassadors from every eastern potentate, missionaries, friars, slaves, soldiers and fidalgos crowded its
streets. Each trade had its own separate quarters,
jewellers, joiners, druggists, goldsmiths, dealers in
fruits and vegetables, in cloth and silk, who displayed
their wares, the annual cargo from more than a
thousand ships. Goa was not only the metropolis of
eastern trade, it also boasted of being the Rome of
the East, the centre of all eastern missions, and num-
bered more than a hundred churches, convents, schools
and colleges." [3]

This greatness did not arrive all at once nor to any
very large extent during the time of Albuquerque, who
held the Viceroyalty only from 1509 to 1515. He was

a great but choleric official, whose captains in making their complaints preferred to do it by correspondence. " Sir," they said, " we do this in writing because by word of mouth we dare not, as you always answer us so passionately." He served Portugal, nevertheless, through years of " magnificent projects and of heroic accomplishments," and did much towards transforming the Indian seas from being the lair of Moslem pirates to something like a Christian highway. Yet he was superseded at last and summed up his experience as follows: " In bad repute with men because of the king, and in bad repute with the king because of men, it were well that I were gone." In spite of his misfortunes, he died, in December 1519, not unregretted and " giving many thanks unto the Lord."

Meanwhile, Portuguese rule, whose eastward course had been determined by the Bull of Pope Alexander VI in 1493, even as the course of Spanish conquest had been determined westward, made advance beyond the limits of the Indian peninsula. In 1511 Portuguese sovereignty was extended to Malacca, a town on the west coast of the Malay peninsula. The place had probably been visited earlier by the European sailors, but the attempt made to capture it by Diego Lopez de Siqueira in 1509 was unsuccessful. Albuquerque himself attacked and conquered it in 1511 and from that time for one hundred and thirty years Malacca remained an appanage of the Portuguese throne, though attacks were several times made upon it by Achinese, Dutch and English. It was finally transferred to Great Britain in 1795.

A little later, Raphael Perestrello, learning that the Malays were appealing to the Chinese Emperor as their suzerain, went on a prospecting voyage still further eastward and won the fame of being the first Portuguese to visit the Middle Kingdom. In the following year a visit thither was made in force, with Canton as the special objective, by a squadron under Ferdinand de Andrade, accompanied by a special envoy. The Arabs, who had begun to see their traffic in Far Eastern waters endangered, as it lately had been in the Indian Ocean, did their best to hinder the success of the embassy, but the worst troubles which fell to the lot of the Portuguese were the result of their own rapacity. This was such as to provoke retaliation from the Chinese, and in 1545 almost the entire foreign colony at Ningpo was wiped out by a bloody massacre. The survivors assembled on the small island of Sancian (of which we shall presently hear a good deal), and in 1557 obtained permission to use a small peninsula named Macao in order to dry out their damaged goods. This permission was so generously interpreted that Macao remains to-day a Portuguese possession, though rent continued to be paid until 1848, and Portuguese sovereignty was only formally acknowledged by China in 1887.

Before we reach the date of the occupation of Sancian, we come for the first time upon that singular and somewhat elusive character who forms the subject of the present sketch. I use the word " elusive " because it is rather difficult to determine the precise degree of credit to be given to the narrative of the adventures of Fernando Mendez Pinto as contained in the *Peregrinaçio*. The title of the book is sufficiently alluring, especially as set forth in the English version put out in 1663 by Henry Cogan, Gentleman: " The Voyages and Adventures of Ferdinand Mendez Pinto. A Portugal. During his Travels for the space of one and twenty years in the Kingdoms of Ethiopia, China, Tartaria, Canchinchina, Siam, Pegu, Japan, and a great part of the East Indies. With a relation and description of most of the Places thereof; their Religion, Law, Riches, Customs and Government in the time of Peace and War. Where he five times suffered shipwreck, was sixteen times sold, and thirteen times made a slave. Written originally by himself in the Portugal Tongue and Dedicated to the Majesty of Philip, King of Spain. Done into English by H. C. Gent. London, 1663."

What title-page ever offered the reader more exciting fare, a menu appetisingly Gargantuan almost beyond belief? Unfortunately, this phrase " almost beyond belief " is but too well justified. What are we to say of the veracity of the *Peregrinaçio* before we venture to describe its contents and the story of its author?

It cannot be denied that the narrative has aroused incredulity in the minds of a large number of discerning persons. For example, Cervantes refers to Pinto as " the prince of liars." The dramatist Congreve, in *Love for Love,* puts into the mouth of one of his characters the words: " Mendez Pinto was but a type of thee, thou liar of the first magnitude." And again, it was a fellow-countryman of the traveller who wrote: " *Fernão, mentes? Mento,* ' Fernando, dost thou lie? I lie.' " It is therefore not surprising that the appellation *Mendax* came to be used as more descriptive of the man than *Mendez.*

Among modern historians, Murdoch has small respect for Pinto, either as a discoverer or a narrator, and he gives his reasons. It must be acknowledged that there is much in Pinto's story which gives evidence against the accuracy of his narrative. His dates are frequently confused, his references to countries and to personages in these countries oftentimes so exceedingly vague as to place them outside the possibility of identification, and a good deal of the description is so obviously absurd as to mislead no one, at least in modern times. Thus, when he speaks of the men with round feet, of the rivers in China which swarm with serpents, or of the thousands of chariots belonging to the king of Manchuria drawn by rhinoceroses, the reader's judgment is readily disposed to render a verdict against the writer. In some cases Pinto saves himself with a *relata refero*, after the manner of Herodotus, but in most instances he professes to be describing what he has himself seen or experienced.[4]

On the other hand, something must be said on Pinto's behalf, at least enough to justify a suspension of judgment. It must be remembered that to stay-at-homes in all ages the traveller has seemed to be drawing a long bow when he gives an account of himself. The very phrase " traveller's tales " has become a synonym for tall talk. The Latin proverb affirms: " *Qui multum peregrinatur raro sanctificatur,*" " He who is a great traveller is rarely a great saint." Even Marco Polo, returning to Venice, found it difficult to convince the Venetians of the genuineness of his experiences and for long after he was denounced as a liar and a boaster. Moreover, there are not wanting those who have lent support to a belief in the general reliability of the *Peregrinaçio*. Xavier makes no extended references to Pinto, but he does refer to the meeting at

Malacca and, after the death of the saint, Pinto was accepted as one of the witnesses, apparently without his veracity being challenged, at the *Procès* preliminary to St. Francis' canonization.

We know also that Pinto was on good terms with the Jesuits at Goa, that he went on his last voyage to Japan with Father Melchior, who has left us a record of the journey, and that letters written by Pinto have survived. Charlevoix, the Jesuit historian, devotes some twenty-two pages to Pinto and his story and does not regard it all as fabulous.

The truth of the matter is that Pinto, writing, for his children, an account of events already twenty-five years in the past, probably without memoranda, and having no suspicion that he was writing for a critical posterity, often relied upon his imagination rather than actual information. He was, moreover, an unskilled author, but half-educated, and when the story was revised, put into chapters, and published by Francisco de Andrade, it may have strayed considerably, without dishonest intention, from the narrow path of historicity. The lapse of years, too, probably made the writer less desirous of accuracy than of seeing the book of his adventures somehow published.

In any case, the *Peregrinaçio* was completed in 1583 through the kindness of the above-mentioned Francisco de Andrade, and first published in folio at Lisbon in 1614. A translation was made into Spanish in 1620, and from that day to this new editions, in many languages, have come from the press. The first English edition was, as already stated, by Henry Cogan in 1663. Apart from the testimony of the Jesuit Fathers in the Far East, the *Peregrinaçio* is about the only source of information with respect to this particular hero of the Portuguese Odyssey. The reader must be prepared to make the necessary deductions.

Fernando Mendez Pinto was born about 1509 in the town of Montemor Ovalho, of poor parents. Many years later he looked back on " the misery and poverty of my father's house," though he observes, a little plaintively, that his later journeys and adventures only led to the increasing of his pains. At the age of eleven or twelve he was taken by an uncle " from the caresses and cockerings " of his mother to Lisbon where he notes that " the furthest thing I can remember " was the funeral, on December 13, 1521, of King Emmanuel of happy memory. His uncle did not keep him long, but placed him in the service of " a very honourable lady," whose bounty seemingly was of too meagre a sort to satisfy the appetite of a hungry, growing boy. At all events something happened—the narrative at this point is not particularly explicit—and the youthful Mendez fled precipitately, at the peril of his life, " with all the speed that possibly I could."

In a small port which the writer names Pedra the runaway found a caravel laden with the horses and furniture of a certain lord who was on the point of sailing for Setuval, where, on account of the prevalence of plague in the capital, King John III was holding his court. With this voyage Pinto commences his epical career of misfortune and adventure. After a stiff resistance the ship was captured by a French pirate, who bound the seventeen survivors and clapped them under hatches, intending to carry them to the Barbary coast. It is plain that at this time it was not necessary to travel as far as the Orient to run the risks of piracy.

On their way, however, the corsair's plans were altered
through the capture of another ship, which turned out
to be so rich a prize that the prisoners were now a
matter of but small concern. So they were set ashore,
naked and destitute, on the French coast, whence they
made their way to Setuval, their first intended destination. Here Pinto entered the service of one
Francisco de Faria, only to find once again the entertainment less attractive than the chances of further adventure by sea. He again ran away and this time
joined a fleet of five vessels which, on March 11, 1537,
sailed for the Indies, that *El Dorado* which was luring
from the beaten paths of life hundreds of the youth of
Europe.

It is not necessary to recount the various vicissitudes
of this voyage, even supposing that the author was
assisted by his memory rather than by his fertile imagination. It is sufficient to say that with his ship-
mates he passed the next winter in Mozambique,
whence they sailed for Diu " in a time full of storm "
and in much fear of the Turk. They dropped anchor
for a while at the island of Socotra, near the entrance
of the Red Sea, where Dom Francisco de Almeida had
built a fortress in 1507. By the torture of captives
taken in the neighbourhood they discovered the whereabouts of the Turks (or rather the Arabs). One of
these prisoners turned out to be a European, a Mallor-
can, who had been converted to Islam and now refused
to recant. So, with Christian kindness, they tied a
stone about his neck and cast him alive into the sea.

Finding themselves now close to the realm of *Pres-
ter John,* that is, Ethiopia, or perhaps what we now
call Somaliland, the Portuguese officials thought it a

good opportunity to deliver a letter from the King of Portugal. They landed and were not a little surprised to find a Portuguese guard on duty at the Prince's palace. The Prince gave them a hearty welcome and sent by them not only rich presents for the Governor of the Indies but also " an Abissin bishop," who unfortunately perished in the subsequent fighting with the Arabs.

At Mocha there was a mutiny on board the ship conveying Master Pinto, and the subject of our sketch was unlucky enough to be one of a number of Portuguese captured by the enemy and exposed for sale in the public market. It was his lot to fall into the hands of a certain Greek renegade, whom, he says, " I shall detest as long as I have a day to live." A better fate, however, awaited him when the Greek sold him to a Jew named Abraham, who took him to Ormuz and presented him to Ferdinand de Luria, captain of the fort, taking as recompense only three shillings and nine pence (as the English translator gives the sum) —a sorry price, one would suppose, for a full-grown Portuguese slave.

Our hero was now able to resume his interrupted voyage. On a ship belonging to one Jorge Fernandez Taborde, he embarked for Goa and arrived at the capital of the Portuguese Indies after seventeen days. Still restless, Pinto next tried a voyage or two on his own account, but had little luck, except that having been again attacked by the Turks, he was fortunate enough to be among those brought back to Goa and welcomed by the Viceroy. Cured of his wounds but not of his *wanderlust,* Pinto next enlisted for the voyage to Malacca, where he found a war being vigorously prosecuted between the belligerent Achinese and the King of Batas. To the latter he went as a kind of ambassador, with what credentials we do not know. But, coasting along the shores of Sumatra, he saw " such a many adders and other crawling creatures, no less prodigious for their length than for the strangeness of their form, that I shall not marvel if they that read this history will not believe my report of them." Many indeed were the wonders encountered on this voyage. " We saw adders that were copped on the crowns of their heads, as big as a man's thigh," " with a head as big as a calf's "; also " a number of baboons, both grey and black, as big as a great mastiff."

Unfortunately for the " ambassador," the King of Batas was badly beaten, and Pinto once again embarked for Malacca, where his previous ill-fortune did not hinder his being appointed as an ambassador from Malacca to the King of Aaru, twenty-five days after his arrival. What he did to justify the appointment we do not know, but on the return journey he was shipwrecked somewhere off the coast of Sumatra. With his customary luck Pinto escaped the death by drowning, which was the fate of the majority of the crew, but he might almost have envied these their speedy end. He tells us, " We sat crouching for the space of three whole days upon this rock, where for our sustenance we had nothing but snails and such filth, as the foam of the sea produceth these."

With three others he presently got away, but two of his companions were eaten by " great lizards," while crossing a river, and the two survivors were soon after captured and sold as slaves. Once again the principle of selection comes into play, for the two wretches were tied to a mast and whipped till one of them fell dead. It is not surprising that although Pinto, the solitary remnant of this miserable crew, was put up for sale three several times, he was in such bad condition that no one ventured an offer. So he was abandoned to fend for himself and for six and thirty days " put a grazing like a cast horse." He also appears to have begged from door to door and in this way recovered his strength sufficiently to fetch presently the equivalent of seventeen shillings and sixpence in English money from a Muhammadan. Pinto's new master was either a generous soul or found no use for his possession, for eventually he was taken to Malacca and there presented to the Captain-General of the port. So it came to pass that the " ambassador " returned home and made a report of his doings, as though nothing particular had happened.

It was perhaps just as well that Pinto was in this way released from his ambassadorial commission, for shortly afterwards the King of Aaru was defeated and slain by the Achinese. The victors treated the corpse with the barbarity customary in these parts. " Having imbowelled and salted him they put him up in a case and so sent him a present to the Tyrant who, after many ceremonies of justice, caused him to be publicly sawed into sundry pieces, and then boiled in a cauldron full of oyl and pitch, with a dreadful publication." Naturally the deceased chieftain's wife was wroth over this and set out to avenge her husband. She summoned the Tyrant to return to her the ravished kingdom and, by a timely defeat of the Achinese fleet, succeeded for a time in recovering her heritage. The

King of Achin was evidently not a good loser, for he
ordered all his soldiers' beards to be shaved off and
forced these discredited warriors to go from henceforth in the garb of women and playing on timbrels.
Nevertheless, a little later, Aaru was again captured
by its truculent foe.

Mendez Pinto now engaged himself to go with Antonio de Faria to the Island of Hainan, but once again
had the misfortune to fall in with the pirates, who
must have been "thick as blackberries" in these
waters. This pirate chief was a very famous bucca-
neer, one "Coia Acem," a terror of the seas. Luck
was, however, on the side of the Portuguese adventurers, for the pirate junk was captured and found to
contain much spoil, such as pepper, nutmegs, mace,
tin, ivory, brass, silk, and so on. A more sinister part
of the cargo consisted of nine wretched children of not
more than seven or eight years of age, who had been
chained together by their hands and feet, and who, on
being delivered, were too weak to stand.

Pinto continued his association with Antonio de
Faria for some time, approaching the Island of Hainan
under a flag of truce, but finding himself unable to
break through the rigorous laws against the entertainment of foreigners. There were more captures of
pirate craft and more discovery of child slaves in irons.
Several "Portugals" were also captured and released.
And all the time the fierce desire burned within the
breast of De Faria and his lieutenant to track down
the ruthless "Coia Acem," who so persistently eluded
them. On one occasion they might have caught him
but for the coming on of a typhoon, "a terrible storm
of wind and rain which by the Chinese is called

Tufan." On another occasion they captured a goodly crew of pirates and were constrained to save sixteen of them, "by the great need we stood in of them for the manning of his Lautias, because he had lost a great many of his people in the former fights." In this capture they obtained great spoil of "sattin, damask, musk, fine pourcelains," and such like, which they were obliged to burn, together with the junk, for lack of a crew to man the vessel.

Apparently Master Mendez passed more than seven months in the employ of Antonio de Faria, all the time on the heels of the elusive "Coia Acem." They decided after a while to winter in Siam, but in the course of the journey thither the four ships suffered "lamentable shipwreck" and 480 of the crew were drowned. Again De Faria and Pinto were among the survivors, but seemed saved from the waves only to perish by starvation. From this fate, however, they were spared, when almost at the last gasp, by what appeared to be the miraculous dropping of a fish at their feet by a kite. Shortly after, again, they were desperate enough, and hungry enough, to scare off a tiger from a newly slain stag. So from hand to mouth they went on till they came upon a junk with its Chinese crew ashore and promptly annexed it. Luck was now with them. They encountered a rather friendly pirate who was willing to enter into a kind of partnership with them, which the ill-mated associates sealed with a vow "sworn on the holy evangelists." Now at last the adventurers came across, defeated and slew their foe, "Coia Acem," who was found to be a Gujerati and the great "Cacio of the King of Bantam." The unlucky wight was tortured, dismembered and cast into the sea, and so " the Shedder and Drinker of the blood of Portugals," as he termed himself, came to the end he had meted out to so many others.

The Portuguese luck did not hold out, for soon after this, De Faria was shipwrecked on " the point of Micuy " and lost his junk with all its accumulation of spoil. Nevertheless, there were more ships in the sea and as opportunity offered he proceeded to take what he wanted. Then he sailed away to Lianpoo (Ningpo), where he was received with so much honour that he and Pinto stayed for some five months to bask in their fame. China seemed to suit the adventurers well, for Pinto records, " China is excellent in that it may vaunt to be the country in the world most abounding in all things that may be desired."

But in May 1542 a fit of restlessness drove them on to " the Island of Calempluy " and thence to Nanking. Of the Yangtse River, called " the River of Serpents," Pinto writes: " We did not think ourselves safe by reason of lizards, whales, fishes and serpents, which in great numbers showed themselves to us." Nor were things better on shore, for " in the mountains were a number of tygers, rhinocerots, lyons, ounces and such like creatures of several kinds, which running and roaring in their wilde manner, made cruel war upon other weaker beasts, as stags, boars, apes, monkeys, baboons, wolves and foxes, wherein we took much delight." In this stage of their experience the Portuguese are introduced to some very primitive people " of so savage and brutish a nature as they feed on nothing commonly but raw flesh and blood." One of these aborigines, if such they were, had red hair hanging down to his shoulders and " his stature was by conjecture above ten feet high." A little later the writer's imagination had somewhat cooled, for " conjecture " now placed the height of this prodigy at about ten or eleven *spans*.

" The Island of Calempluy " was only discovered after eighty-three days' search, a somewhat dilatory piece of exploration, one would suppose. A certain kind of thrift was here noted, since " in some hermitages they collect the silver found among the dead man's bones, money carried as alms to the other world." How the unfortunate ghosts subsequently paid their obol to Charon is not surmised.

On August 5, 1542 (1541?) the wanderers again suffered a " lamentable shipwreck " during the season for typhoons in the Gulf of Nanking. The country was full of " tygers," but they escaped these to fall a prey to certain people at Taypor, who made them prisoners but sent them to the city of Nanking where they gained their sustenance by attending funerals. The feasts provided on these occasions for all comers were at least ample enough to keep them from starving. They suffered ill-treatment in the prison, shared with some four thousand other unfortunates, and they were mercilessly whipped and condemned to lose their thumbs. From this loss—an old precaution to prevent the ex-prisoner from drawing a bow upon his oppressor—they were saved by the intervention of the " proctors for the poor," a very welcome interposition.

Soon after this humane intervention our adventurers were on the way from Nanking to Peking. Apparently they went by way of the Grand Canal, at least by water, and for once we have a fairly lucid description of the journey. This part of China, however, must

have been vastly different from the same region of to-
day, for we read of " great woods of fir, groves, forests,
orange trees, plains full of wheat, rice, beans, pease,
millet, panick, barley, flax, cotton," and " an infinite
number of cattel." There were also mighty castles,
huge walls and fine appearing houses. It was to Pinto's
credit that he was able and minded to record these
things, for the prisoners, he tells us, were bound hand
and foot and occasionally given a hundred lashes just
to keep them in their place. On one occasion, they
encountered a woman with a cross on her arm and
learned that she was Inez de Leyria, daughter of a
" Portuguese ambassador to China," and that she had
been brought up in the Christian faith. Naturally
enough, Mistress Inez was very generous to Pinto and
his companions.

Further on the traveller marvels at the number of
people who, then as now, lived on the rivers. He notes
also the existence of engines for the making of sugar
and presses for wine and oil. He comes upon innumerable raisers of ducks and sees herds of red deer
which had been lamed in their right legs to prevent
their straying. He remarks, as have modern travellers,
on the habit of redeeming, fêng-ing, the lives of birds
and fishes in order to acquire merit. He passes barges
with cages of wild animals which were shown to a
curious public for money. The hungry men were
much impressed by the great abundance of several
sorts of victuals. " I do not think," writes Pinto,
" that there is in all Europe so much as there. is in
China alone."

We are told that Pinto arrived at Peking on October 19, 1541—a date which does not square with the

reference to his arrival at Nanking. It was, of course, an offence punishable with death for a European to be seen in Peking, but the prisoners passed themselves off with no great difficulty—possibly by connivance—as natives of Siam. They were tied together by a long chain and found many illustrations of their possible fate in the pictures of Hell torments, with which the temples they entered were commonly filled.

Like Marco Polo, several centuries before them, they were duly impressed with the splendours of Peking, a much finer city in Pinto's time than in the day of the Venetian. They thought it might truly be termed " the capital of the monarchy of the world." They saw " the houses of the Son of the Sun," where all those who had been hurt in the wars, when engaged in the king's service, dwelt for the rest of their days. These ex-soldiers had even improved upon the claims of our modern veterans, for " they were exempted from any incommodity " and received a certain pay. The travellers went on to view the Inns and Universities of the Imperial City and paid a visit to the Great Wall. About this time the prisoners were set at liberty, after being branded on the wrist of the right hand to make future recognition easy.

How much of all this part of the narrative is true it is impossible to decide, for Pinto again makes a sad muddle of his dates, or else his reviser and translators did it for him. It is stated that the Portuguese stayed in the capital two and a half months and left on Saturday, July 13, 1554, though it was previously mentioned that they arrived on October 19, 1541. Pinto was badly mixed on his dates for just a little later we find him at Quinsay, enduring an eight and a half months'

captivity, and meeting his fellow countryman, Vasco
Calvo, on July 3, 1544. The flight of time, however,
forward or backward, did not trouble him much, since
we find him at Quinsay joining a certain Tartar commander who, with the help of a number of Portuguese,
was engaged in the siege of a castle. These Tartars
elicit the first reference in the narrative to the Japanese, for he says of the Tartar soldiers that they were
" almost as resolute as those of Japan." It seems a
kind of premonition of the journey so soon to be
undertaken.

At this point it is extremely difficult to reconcile
Pinto's story with the known facts of history. To follow his own narrative, the Tartars captured Quinsay,
made an apportionment of the spoil, which led to great
dissatisfaction on the part of the foreign mercenaries,
and then proceeded to camp before Peking. Here they
fared badly and were presently compelled to retreat
with three hundred thousand horses and twenty thousand rhinoceroses. The dead left behind included
450,000 men, 100,000 horses, and 60,000 rhinoceroses
—all of which we are told were eaten in the space of
the next two months and a half.

Apparently by this time Messer Pinto had had
enough of North China, for we next find him leaving
for Cochin China and planning the voyage to Japan.
For this purpose the Portuguese Commander, Jorge
Mendez, " gave us a thousand duckets, which was easie
for him to do." The first stage of the journey was
from Cochin China to Sancian, the island off the south
coast of China, famous in the story of St. Francis
Xavier. Desiring in the meantime to get back to Malacca, Pinto took ship with a well-known Chinese cor-

sair, whom he calls Sami-pocheea, one who apparently had already a ship full of loot which he was willing to dispose of at any port he might chance to reach. But the vessel was badly damaged in a fight and the captain deemed it wise to run under full sail towards the Loochoos or Ryukyu Islands. They "beat up and down with labour enough from one rhomb to another for three and twenty days together," and at length perceived a coast with a great fire burning upon it to which they approached near enough to see junks. By good fortune they had arrived at the little island called Tanegashima, off the southern coast of Kyushu. By ideographs drawn upon the sand some Chinese members of the crew succeeded in describing the case of the newcomers, and everybody agrees that they were all received with the greatest possible courtesy. As the ship contained many desirable commodities, trade was welcomed and soon became brisk, after the payment of the accustomed dues.

It is impossible not to face the question whether Pinto was actually the first of the Portuguese adventurers to reach Japan, but it is not likely to be settled satisfactorily. He probably appropriated the exploit of certain fellow countrymen who reached the islands just before. Murdoch is quite explicit in discrediting Pinto's entire claim and gives a number of reasons, more or less cogent, to justify his conclusion. The Ajuda Library at Lisbon, composed by *religieux* who were in Japan between 1575 and 1634, describes a junco as having been driven ashore at Tanegashima by a typhoon containing three Portuguese, who are said to have taught the natives the use of the arquebus. But this narrative gives the names of the men as

Antonio da Motta, Francisco Zeimotto and Antonio Peixotto, making no mention whatever of Pinto. As about this time quite a number of foreign ships— mostly piratical, with one eye open to the possibilities of profitable trade—seem to have sailed and probably fought together, all of them manned in part by Portuguese adventurers, it is probable that more than one junco with sailors from the Peninsula kingdom reached the Japanese coast about the same date. In the absence of irrefutable disproof we may take the main outline of Pinto's narrative to be history.[5]

In any case he tells us that his two companions were Diego Zeimotto and Christofero Borello, that they found no reluctance on the part of the Japanese to receive them, nor any obstacle to trade. Indeed, the furs, silks, woollen goods, taffetas, and other things they had on board were just what attracted the Japanese. Readiness was expressed to receive more cargoes of a similar sort. Thus was commenced the traffic between Europe and Japan which was to have important consequences in the future.

Their hosts did not recognize the newcomers as Europeans. They indeed asked many questions, and concluded that they could not possibly be Chinese because of their beards and features. Pinto replied that they were of a " country called Malaca, whither many years before " they " were come from another land, named Portugal, which was at the further end of the world." Some of the natives claimed to recognize the strangers and their ships as visitants whose coming had long been predicted. They were " the Cheuchicogis of whom it is written in our books that flying on the top of the waters they shall come to subdue the inhabitants of the earth." Soon thereafter curiosity waned and the Portuguese were left to get on as best they could. They found an interpreter in a woman from the Ryukyu Islands and through her they informed the astonished natives that Portugal was larger and richer than the whole Empire of China—an exaggeration which, under the circumstances, was quite safe. They added that " our king had upon the sea conquered the greatest part of the world," and that this illustrious monarch had two thousand houses full of silver and gold to the very tops.

It is no wonder that the strangers were sumptuously entertained, but the Japanese interest in them was aroused to its highest pitch by the arquebuses they possessed. One day Diego Zeimotto went out shooting with his arquebus and came back with a bag of twenty-six wild ducks. Great was the excitement, and word was sent forth by the admiring Prince of Tanegashima that all honour was to be paid to these mighty ones. Zeimotto, with due gratitude, made a present of the potent weapon to the Prince and promised to teach him how to manufacture the powder. Soon the skilful Japanese seem to have been able to better their instruction, for we are told (without being obliged to believe the tale) that five and a half months later there were six hundred arquebuses in the country of Japanese make. By 1556, it is further affirmed, there were over 300,000 in the capital alone. There was not " so small a hamlet but hath a hundred at the least." But the original source of supply still preserved its fame and the word " Tanegashima " in the Japanese dictionaries still means a kind of gun or a pistol.

Altogether the Portuguese must have had a pleasant

time during their twenty-three days at Tanegashima, hunting and fishing, and being entertained by the *élite* of the land. But, meanwhile, as was inevitable, under the feudal system, word had gone on to the King of Bungo on the adjacent island of Kyushu, of the coming of the foreigners, men, said the report, having " the quality of persons that make profession of honour." It was deemed fitting that one of these strangers should be despatched forthwith to interview the Prince's overlord, and Pinto, by no means new to the ambassadorial game, was selected. He started in a vessel with oars and arrived presently at Quanquexumaa (Kagoshima), " a very sweet place." He was then taken to a fortress of the King of Bungo's called " Osquy," and here had a most cordial reception from the king and his son, a boy of nine or ten. " Thy arrival," declared the king, " in this my country is no less pleasing to me than the rain which falls from heaven is profitable to our fields that are sowed with rice "—a pretty compliment.

At the court of the King of Bungo, Pinto played the courtier to his heart's content, responding to the king's flattery with the declaration that, by comparison with the king, he was " no more than a silly ant." And here come in the two famous stories on which the interest of Pinto's first visit to Japan has been mainly concentrated. The first tells of his curing the king of a disease from which he had been suffering for two years. His majesty, it appears, was of a gouty and hypochondriacal habit, and, since Pinto had been selected as the emissary from Tanegashima " because he was of a more lively humour " than his fellows, it may be taken for granted that the cure was psychological as much as physical. The other story relates how Pinto was brought within an inch of losing his life. The king's second son, aged sixteen or seventeen, was very much taken with the foreigner's arquebus, and exceedingly anxious to try it on his own account. Too impatient to wait for a lesson, he took the weapon when its owner was out of the way, and filled it full of the mysterious powder. The result was what might have been anticipate 1. The gun was blown to pieces and, more serious still, the boy was dangerously wounded in the forehead and in the hand. After the explosion, when the attendants rushed in and found their young master unconscious and weltering in his blood, they jumped to the conclusion that Pinto was the murderer. He would surely have been lynched, but fortunately the victim recovered consciousness and told the truth before it was too late. Then Pinto promised to effect a cure, attending first to the almost severed thumb, which he gave " seven stitches where peradventure if a chirurgeon had dressed him he would have given it fewer." He added four stitches for the wound in the forehead, and, wrapping both wounds in wet tow moistened with white of egg, trusted to Providence to bring the patient back to his former health. Happily the treatment proved effective and the wonderful cures brought Pinto much honour and rich rewards. He was given " many sutes of silks," a scimitar, and the sum of 1,500 ducats, not bad pay for an unskilled leech, though, all things considered, Pinto was lucky to get off without the loss of his head.

Master Mendez stayed fifteen days longer in Japan and then took passage in another Chinese pirate ship for Lianpoo (Ningpo). Before, however, reaching his

destination he suffered yet another shipwreck and
another period of imprisonment. He arrived at last at
Ningpo only to start again for Malacca, " from whence
the captain of the fortress sent me to the Chaubainhaa
at Martabano." We again find ourselves embarked
with Pinto on a series of more or less veracious adventures by flood and field. He gains a very notable
victory in which he recaptures a number of Christian
slaves, who had so long been kept in captivity that
they had become strangers to the Christian faith. " We
ordained," writes Pinto, " a kind of Church amongst
them for the instruction of those that were newly converted." On Michaelmas Eve 1544, on the voyage to
Martaban, another " glorious victory " was won, which
was spoken of for three years after and through which
the fame of the Portuguese was raised to the highest
pitch.

We now pass to another scene and find ourselves in
the midst of a most ferocious war waged by the King
of Burmah against the Queen of Martaban. Burmah
must have been at this time a very attractive place for
adventurers, since we are told that in the capital were
36,000 strangers, belonging to forty-two different
nationalities. It was flattering to Pinto's pride to learn
that the Portuguese were the most numerous of these
foreign mercenaries. The cruelties of the Burmese
monarch against the Queen of Martaban and her subjects were of the most unspeakable character, though
the Portuguese themselves were not exactly scrupulous
in their dealings with a foe. In the sack of the Chaubainhaa's palaces, 140,000 houses and 17,000 temples
were burned, 60,000 statues were destroyed, 3,000
elephants were slain and eaten during the siege, and

6,000 pieces of artillery captured. Sentence of death was executed upon the Chaubainhaa, that is, the King of Martaban, his wife and a hundred and forty-two women of the palace. At least such are the figures given by our chronicler. Pinto himself was among those captured and sentenced to death, but after lying in prison, loaded with chains, for thirty-six days, he was whipped and tortured by having hot lacquer poured over him. After this his life, such as it was, was spared. The victorious sovereign of Burmah proceeded next to the siege of Prom and presently captured it. Here the Queen was seized, stripped, whipped and tortured to death. Her body was then bound to that of her still living consort and both were cast into the river with a stone around their necks. Three hundred gentry were also similarly disposed of, after having been first impaled, like spitted pigs.

One might have supposed that Messer Pinto would under these circumstances have obtained little leisure for the description of other things than battle and massacre. As a matter of fact, he gives us some very interesting information about life in Burmah. Among other items he tells us how people obtained absolution from their misdeeds by weighing themselves against things which were thought to be symbolical of their sin—a truly Dantean conception. Thus, for example, gluttons were weighed against so much honey, sugar, eggs and butter, doubtless paid as a fine. Sensualists were weighed against wool, feathers, apparel, wine and odours; uncharitable persons against copper, tin or silver coin; the slothful against wood, rice, coal or fruit; the proud against cow-dung; and so on. We have also a discourse reported between a Burmese

priest and a Portuguese on the matter of religion,
which, however, does not seem to have ended in any
satisfactory manner.

Pinto's narrative now runs into a veritable jungle of
information concerning the Kingdom of Pegu, whither
he was taken, in the train of the Burmese High Treas-
urer, "whose slaves we Portugals were," on the invasion of that country by the ever truculent King of
Burmah. Much of this information places a considerable strain on the reader's credulity. He describes
people whom he calls Calogens and Funcaos, "tawny
men and great archers, having their feet like unto
oxen," and " at the end of the backbone a lump of
flesh as big as one's two fists." He tells us also about
the Oquens and Magores, who feed on wild beasts
which they catch in hunting, and eat raw, as also on
all kinds of contagious creatures, as lizards, serpents
and adders. He continues: " They hunt these wild
beasts mounted on certain animals as big as horses,
which have three horns in the midst of their foreheads,
with thick, short legs, and on the middle of their back
a row of prickles, wherewith they prick when they are
angry, . . . on the joynts of their shoulders short
wings like to the fins of fishes, wherewith they fly, as
it were, leaping the length of five or six and twenty
paces at a jump. These creatures are called Bonazes."
More veraciously, perhaps, he mentions coming upon
certain people clad in silk cassocks like the people of
Japan, "who carried meat to their mouths with little
sticks after the manner of the Chineses."

After some experiences of this sort Pinto took advantage of a great earthquake, in which all the habita-
tions of the capital of Pegu were destroyed, except

the hermitage which was erected in memory of the
85,000 children massacred by the Burmese king, to
make his escape. So our story brings its hero back
to Goa, the capital of the Portuguese East Indies.
But the itch for further adventure was by now in
Pinto's blood. Shortly after his arrival at the capital
the gad-fly of his fate was driving him " once more to
try my fortune in the kingdoms of China and Japan,
to see if in those countries where I had so many times
lost my coat, I could not find a better than that I had
on."

So he sailed first to Banta, where he comments on the
habit of chewing betel, " because it makes them have
a sweet breath and also purges the humours of the
stomach." He speaks also of the Pangueyran, as the
Emperor over all the kings of that great archipelago,
" which the Chineses, Tartar, Japon and Lequios
(Ryukyu Is.) historians are wont to call ' the Eye-
lids of the World.' " Thence he made his way to
Sunda and so on to China, where, in company with
four other ships, he soon involved himself with adventures too numerous to recount. In the course of
these he made the acquaintance of one Joano Rodriguez, a renegade Christian whom, out of the new-
born zeal he had brought from Goa, Pinto had the
happiness of bringing back to the faith. The repent-
ance was by no means premature, for Rodriguez died
the next year in the odour of sanctity.

Our traveller's exploits at this time are much involved with the prevalence of piracy along the coast
and with the efforts of the trading ships to cope with
it. He had, moreover, some further experience in the
matter of shipwreck. His ship was a total loss, but

the twenty-eight Portuguese survivors calmly annexed the raft on which a number of Chinese had taken refuge. With Christian readiness they slew these unfortunates " in the space of two or three credos." Pinto spent his Christmas Day upon a rock and a few days later was reduced to eating the body of a Caphar (Kafir), though he retained his scruples against making a meal off the dead Portuguese. Only eleven Portuguese survived out of the original thirty-eight, and when these finally succeeded in making a landing, their situation was not greatly improved, since the country was swarming with elephants and tigers which they had to climb trees to escape. As it was, three of them were eaten by " great lizards " when swimming to a barque. Once again the unfortunate wretches were sold into slavery, this time in the Celebes, where, however, they stayed only a month, being resold to the King of Calapa. This monarch, having no particular use for them, sent them on to Sunda, where they were enabled to join a Portuguese ship just about to sail for China, by way of Siam. Arrived in Siam, Pinto, with six score other Portuguese, decided to enlist in the Siamese service against the King of Burmah, who was still on the rampage. This too active and ambitious potentate was anxious, through an invasion of Siam, to make himself, first, " Lord of the White Elephant " of Siam, and then to conquer Peking, " the incomparable pearl of all the world." In the course of two and a half months he is described as raising an army of 800,000 men, including 100,000 foreigners. Of these a thousand are said to have been Portuguese.

Pinto's narrative at this point, with its interminable tales of war and siege, victory and defeat, becomes a

little tedious, and also plainly runs beyond the date
of the traveller's stay in the land. We may safely skip
all that precedes another embarkation for Malacca and
the second sailing for Japan in 1547. Of this visit we
really know very little, except that Pinto sailed in a
ship under the command of Captain George Alvarez,
that in Japan he revisited the Satsuma city of Kagoshima, and that when he left he took with him two or
three Japanese fugitives. One of these was the famous
Anjiro (more properly Yajiro), who was destined to
influence so remarkably the career of St. Francis
Xavier two years later. Yajiro apparently did not
leave his native country from mere love of adventure,
but because he had been guilty, unintentionally, of an
act of homicide, and would have been forced otherwise
to take his own life by *seppuku* in expiation for his
fault. Pinto seems to have persuaded the Satsuma man
that an unbosoming of his fault to the Apostle of the
Indies would be a better method of expiation than
suicide. He did his best, on arrival at Malacca, with
the help of the estimable George Alvarez, to introduce
the fugitive to the saint. The meeting, however, did
not immediately take place, owing to the absence of
Xavier from the port, but a little later the two encountered one another and Yajiro, later baptized as
Paul of the Faith, became the first Christian convert
from Japan.

Pinto's story during the next years is not a little
obscure. He seems to have taken considerable interest
in the plans of Xavier to visit Japan and even to have
assisted the great missionary with advice and financial
aid. According to Charlevoix, Pinto was in Japan for
a third time during Xavier's stay and carried on as a

kind of ambassador from the King of Portugal to the King of Bungo. In brief, he must have been of considerable use to the saint during the closing months of his stay in the Empire and returned with him to Malacca in the September of 1551, bearing letters to the Governor of the East Indies at Goa, with a request that other missionaries be sent. Charlevoix seems to regard Pinto's connection with Xavier as authentic, and, as mentioned earlier, names him as one of the witnesses called to testify at the *Procès*.

It is clear that at this time Pinto had a serious inclination for the religious life and that on his arrival at Goa he entered the *Order of Jesus* as a novice. But it will hardly be suspected that so restless a soul found it possible to proceed far with the discipline prescribed. This discipline which included two years' study of philosophy, two years of theology, a year devoted to the intensive study of Holy Scripture, not to speak of other things, could hardly have been congenial fare for so vagabond an individual. There is no reason to question the sincerity of his impulses, especially as he appears to have devoted what capital he possessed to the work of the Order, but it is hardly surprising that Pinto's connection with the Jesuits represents but a passing phase of his career.

Yet the connection lasted long enough for him to undertake, as a Brother, still another journey to Japan in the company of Father Melchior Nunes Barreto. Ere departing on this his last journey to the Far East, Pinto seems to have discharged his responsibility as ambassador by presenting to the Governor, Francisco Barreto, the letters sent by the King of Bungo, together with the arms, scimitars, and other gifts he had previously received for this purpose. The Governor, according to our chronicler, made a suitable address of thanks, as follows: " I assure you that I prize these arms which you have brought me as much as the Government of India: for I hope that by the means of this present and this letter from the King of Japan (*sic*) I shall render myself agreeable to the King our Sovereign Lord, that I shall be delivered from the fortunes of Lisbon, whence almost all of us who govern this state do go and land for our sins." Pinto in turn expressed himself freely as to the tribulations he had endured for the honour of Portugal and humbly ventured the hope that his services would suffice to keep him from being refused, on his return, the reward he deemed his due.

We have preserved for us in the *Ausgabe der Peregrinaçam* von J. I. de Brito Rebello (Lisbon, 1910) two letters from Pinto, three from Father Melchior, and two from Froez, all relating to the journey which was taken to China and Japan in 1554. With Pinto and Father Melchior was Brother Estevão de Gois, who plays no particular rôle in the story. Schurhammer, in connection with this journey, describes Pinto as " der weltberühmte Abenteurer und Verfasser des ' *Peregrinaçam*,' der kurz zuvor in Goa in die Gesellschaft Jesu eingetreten war, und jetzt als Gesandter Portugals zum König von Bungo führ," " The world famous adventurer and author of the *Peregrinaçio*, who shortly before had been admitted into the Company of Jesus at Goa, and had now gone as the ambassador of Portugal to the King of Bungo."

The termination of this last stay in Japan was marked by another terrific storm, encountered on the way to Malacca, in which Father Melchior and the two Brothers were saved only to run the risk of another capture by pirates. They were saved at the eleventh hour by the timely arrival of a galleon. In all Pinto's narrative we are struck both by the number of those who fell victims to storm and tempest and also by the number of those prepared to run any risk for the sake of adventure or gain. For example, we are told that at this time " there was not a port or road(stead) in all this island of Japan where there were not thirty or forty junks at anchor and in some places more than a hundred. In the course of the year as many as two thousand merchant ships came to Japan from China, with cargoes of merchandize, mostly in the form of silk, which at this time was sold cheaply in Japan. When a typhoon occurred there was naturally terrific loss. In that of December 5 (year uncertain) nearly two thousand junks were lost, including twenty-six Portuguese vessels." Pinto says that in this disaster " 502 of our nation " were drowned, with 1,000 Christians of other nations, and 800,000 ducats' worth of goods. Of the Chinese vessels 1,936 were lost, with 160,000 persons drowned, and two millions' (ducats) worth of goods destroyed. Not above ten or eleven ships escaped. It was in one of these surviving vessels that Pinto left Japan for the last time, to arrive in China fourteen days later, but, as mentioned above, to suffer shipwreck when only a few miles from Malacca.

He had started on the return journey from Japan in November 1556 and, still in the company of Father Melchior, reached Goa on February 17, 1557. By this time he had discovered his lack of vocation for the

Jesuit Order and, at his own request, was soon after
released from the vows he had already taken. Some
say that the release followed an accusation that he
was a *marrano*, that is, of Jewish blood.

Probably Pinto's felt lack of vocation for the religious life was one of the causes for his manifest cool-
ing of desire for further adventures in the Far East.
For not long after the arrival in Goa, we find him
putting to sea for the last time on his way to Portugal.
He reached Lisbon on September 22, 1558, " at such
time as the Kingdom was governed by Madam Kath-
erina, our Queen of happy memory." Pinto, no doubt,
on his return home had considerable expectation of
recognition and reward. If so he soon had occasion
to recall the bitter words of Governor Francisco Barreto. He, however, lost no time in presenting his case
as a pioneer of Empire before the Minister of State,
but that was about as far as he got. The Minister kept
" these miserable papers of mine four years and a
half," and after all this delay Pinto got nothing. He
then retired in dudgeon, leaving, as he said, the recti-
fication of things to Divine Justice. Yet he could not
refrain from harping on the injustice of earthly authority, and in the conclusion of his famous work he
writes: " Behold what the services have been which I
have done for the space of one and twenty years, during which I have been thirteen times a captive, seventeen times sold into slavery," and so on through the
whole lengthy catalogue of woes.

Nevertheless, not to end on too dolorous a note, we
discover, ere the end of Pinto's life, that kings could
be occasionally generous. King Philip II of Spain,
possibly elated by the union of the Crowns of Spain

and Portugal in 1580, was pleased, at no expense to himself, to accept the dedication of the *Peregrinaçio*. Our traveller was grateful for the favour, but still more religiously assured that his cause was vindicated in Heaven. " In regard whereof I render infinite thanks to the King of Heaven, whose pleasure it hath been that His Divine Will should be in this way accomplished, and do not complain of the kings of earth, since my sins have me unworthy of mentioning more."

King Philip's pension for Pinto for " services in the Indies " was awarded in 1583, but it came too late to do the traveller any good. On July 8 of the same year, though the date is by no means certain, Ferdinand Mendez Pinto set out on his last and longest journey. We should have said that on his return from the Indies Pinto had married and settled down to family life. His book written for the delectation of his children came out only after his death. He was not an educated man and his work probably owes something in the way of finish to the aforementioned editor, Francisco de Andrade. Yet it is in general, even in the matter of style, a notable work, simple, natural and clear. It has probably done for Portuguese prose what Camoens, through his *Lusiads,* did for Portuguese poetry. At any rate, both in poetry and prose, the great epic age of Lusitania is worthily recorded, though neither author reaped much in the way of earthly reward. It must suffice that through the verse of Camoens and the prose of Pinto, we are placed on intimate terms with the heroic centuries, when neither European merchant nor missionary had access to the Far East except with the sanction of the King of Portugal. During part of this time, moreover, there was no other flag than that of the Lusitanian kingdom in all the vast expanse of water from the Red Sea and the Cape of Good Hope to the Moluccas and Japan.[5]

It is a pity that the daring and courage which went into the inauguration of Portuguese dominion in the Far East formed the unfortunate and even disgraceful prelude to a period of selfish exploitation which from its very nature was bound to bring that dominion to an end.   Our next study will show how some at least strove to employ the period of opportunity to a nobler end.

NOTES

[1] Gowen, *Asia, a Short History,* Chapter VII.

[2] Camoens, *" The Lusiads,"* Book I. Translation by William Julius Mickle.

[3] Gille, *" To the Tomb of Xavier,"* p. 63.

[4] The account of Antonio Galvano, printed in 1563, runs as follows: " In the year 1542 when Diogo de Freytas was Captain of a ship in the Kingdom of Siam and the town of Dodra, three Portuguese deserted him in a junk which left for China. Their names were Antonio da Mota, Francisco Zeimoto, and Antonio Pexoto. While steering their course to seek harbour in the town of Liampo, which is situated on somewhat more than 30 degrees latitude, they were overtaken by such a violent storm from astern that they drifted from land, and after some days sailing towards the east they saw an island on 32 degrees, which is called Japoes and which seems to be the Sipangas islands, about which the writings have so much to say and also of their wealth. Even these islands (Japoes) possess gold and silver besides other riches."

On the whole subject see E. W. Dahlgren, *A Contribution to the History of the Discovery of Japan,* Transactions of the Japan Society, London, 1913. Dahlgren thinks that Portuguese may have visited Japan as early as 1534, or even 1530. His general conclusion as to the discovery is negative: " The history of the discovery of Japan by Europeans is hidden by a veil which modern research has not succeeded in completely lifting. We do not know with certainty the names of the person or persons who made the discovery, nor the date when it took place."

[5] Material on the story of Mendez Pinto is to be derived first, with all due caution, from the *Peregrinaçio,* editions of which since 1613 have appeared in many languages, with Henry Cogan's edition of 1663 the most accessible in English. Other works which will prove useful are: James A. Williamson, *Maritime Enterprise, 1485–1558,* Oxford, 1913; R. K. Douglas, *Europe and the Far East, 1506–1912,* Cambridge University Press, 1913; T. T. Chang, *Sino-Portuguese Trade from 1514 to 1644;* H. Thomas, *English Translations of Portuguese Books before 1640,* London, 1927; G. Schurhammer, *Fernão Mendez Pinto und seine Peregrinaçam,* Asia Major, 1926; and Freitas, *Fernão Mendez Pinto e o discobrimento do Japão,* Lisbon, 1907.

II

SAINT FRANCIS XAVIER

A ROMAN CATHOLIC friend, priest in charge of the Shrine of St. Francis on the Island of Sancian, near Macao, wrote to me several years ago of his first service in that sacred and historic spot. The account mentioned a number of things that to the outsider would have savoured of the disagreeable, such as the necessity of cleaning out the buffalo dung which had for a long time accumulated in the neglected Chapel prior to Father Cairns' arrival. Though only one Chinese woman, and she blind, furnished the congregation for the first Christmas Mass, the writer ends his letter with the words: " And so ended the happiest Christmas I ever spent."

To labour anywhere along the path blazed by the great Apostle to the Indies must inevitably bring its own special joy. Even to write of one who so strongly stamped his personality and his faith upon the peoples of the Far East has a happiness of its own, though I am fain to ascribe to human credulity and enthusiasm many of those miraculous incidents for which such abundant testimony was offered, when the subject of canonization came up before the ecclesiastical authorities after his death. Yet I in no degree feel that the excision of these things from the story of St. Francis makes it the less wonderful. On the contrary, it has the advantage of making the saint a more human personage than some have represented him. Perhaps it was inevitable that the narratives of Turselline and Orlandino, of Poussines and Bohours, and the translation of the last named by John Dryden, should be full of the miracles which the simplicity and credulity of converts, and the faith of the narrators, felt to be, under the circumstances, natural rather than the reverse.

In this sketch I have in mind the work of Xavier in Japan rather than elsewhere, yet it will be necessary to go back to the beginnings and describe the steps by which he was led to the land which had just been visited by Pinto and other European pioneers.

St. Francis came from an illustrious family which traced its ancestry to the Kings of Navarre. His father was Don Juan de Jasso, a man high in the Council of Jean d'Albret, King of Navarre. His mother was no less highly descended, for Maria de Azpilculta of Xavier was the sole heiress of two distinguished families in the same kingdom. It was because his mother was the last of her line that her famous son took the name of Xavier, the castle at the foot of the Pyrenees, about twenty miles from Pampeluna, where he was born.

Francis was the youngest of a large family and was born on April 7, 1506. The " Natus est die Aprilis 7, anni 1506 " of the record is probably correct, though some early biographers have set back the date to 1497. The little boy, who was from childhood " of a strong habit of body," with complexion lively and vigorous, and as throughout his life of a gay and cheerful temper, was brought up with exact attention to religious matters and the strictest care as to his mental training.

Perhaps it was this care given to him as the youngest son that turned his attention away from those feats of arms, in which his brothers excelled, to the attractions of study.

It was natural therefore that, at the age of eighteen, Francis should be sent to that capital of learning, the University of Paris, to which students were flocking from Spain, Italy, Germany, and from all parts of France. Here, as a member of the College of St. Barbara, the favourite rendezvous of scholars from Spain and Portugal, he remained for several years, becoming proficient in Aristotelian philosophy as well as an attractive figure to the many who appreciated his cheerful habit of mind. There was, indeed, a time, prior to the taking of his Master's degree in 1530, when the youth was in danger of being withdrawn from the University, for his father was in straitened circumstances through the necessity of bringing up so large a family and began to think that he had done enough for the youngest. Fortunately in this matter Don Juan consulted his sister Magdalen, then Abbess of the Convent of St. Clare in Gandia, and this good lady received, as she believed, by divine inspiration, a message which she transmitted to her brother to the effect that Francis was " a chosen vessel " and should be allowed full time for his studies at the University.

It was this longer stay which brought the young Navarrese into intimate association with the famous founder of the Order of Jesus, Ignatius Loyola. He had come to Paris, shortly after his conversion and recovery from the wounds received in the siege of Pampeluna, to complete his training for the great enterprise he was already envisaging. Like Xavier,

Loyola was a native of the Basque country, and the two enthusiasts soon became fast friends. Yet from the first the older man pursued his comrade with the insistent question, " What shall it profit a man if he gain the whole world and lose his own soul? " Possibly at this time, in spite of his zeal for learning, Xavier was in some danger not only from the restless disposition of a gay and sometimes careless youth but also from some disposition to toy with that " heresy of Luther," which was disturbing many other minds at the time. To men like Loyola, Xavier was showing not only signs of being unmindful of his destiny but was even in peril of making shipwreck of his faith.

The change came in an unexpected way, for on a certain occasion when the usual remittance of money failed to reach Xavier from home, it was Loyola who discovered and supplied the necessity. Soon after, the renewed insistency of the Gospel challenge won its response. Xavier resigned himself, in body and mind alike, to the influence of his friend, and so became the first " Companion." He accepted whole-heartedly the discipline of the *Spiritual Exercises*, sometimes making his devotions " with hands and feet tied," to show his absolute consecration to the will of God.

At this time there were seven members of the little body which was predestined to so wonderful a future. To these the Founder revealed his plan, hitherto kept secret in his own breast. It was that the members of the *Order* should journey to the Holy Land and there, by their life, or perchance by their death, bear witness to the faith. Before the tombs of the martyrs at Montmartre, on the Feast of the Assumption, August 15, 1534, the brethren made their vows and inaugurated

the *Order of Jesus,* whose motto was to be henceforth
" Perinde ac cadaver."

In the following year, or perhaps as late as 1536,
Francis Xavier, with eight others, journeyed to Venice
for the purpose of rejoining Loyola and starting thence
for Palestine. It was necessary to formulate their
plans carefully. Long before their own time, Raymond
Lull, the Franciscan, had attempted the same task and
failed. It was necessary now to proceed wisely as
well as with zeal. So the little band stayed in Venice
nine weeks and during this time Xavier, though, as
is reported, he was " wholly ignorant of Italian,"
laboured in a hospital for incurables and in other forms
of Christian work. It may be said here once for all
that it is extremely difficult to accept all that St. Francis' biographers have written about his shortcomings
as a linguist and with regard to his being miraculously
endowed with " the gift of tongues." It is more likely
that Xavier had a considerable facility in picking up
the languages of the countries he visited, and this
facility was aided by hard work, which it is not at all
unmeet to describe as a gift of the Spirit.

With the eight companions Loyola now set out for
Rome and there obtained the approval of Pope Paul
III for his missionary plans. As for Xavier he took
the opportunity to rededicate himself at the tombs of
the Apostles and soon after returned to Venice for his
ordination to the priesthood in the June of 1537. He
had expected to sail with his brethren from this port
for the Holy Land, but just then a war broke out between Venice and the Turks which for the time being
stopped all travel from Europe to Palestine. Thereupon Xavier continued to labour at his hospital and

also spent much time in a solitary place in preparation for the celebration of his first Mass. The Mass was said at Vicenza and while his other companions were temporarily dispersed, to preach in the cities of Italy, Xavier worked with Bobadilla at Bologna till they received a summons to Rome from the Head of the *Order* at the end of 1538. It was in work assigned them at Rome by Pope Paul himself that the two Jesuits continued until 1541.

Meanwhile, an appeal had come to the Pope, and through the Pope to Loyola, from King John III of Portugal, transmitted by his envoy Mascaragnas, for " some lovers of the Cross," who might be despatched to the newly conquered Indies for the purpose of planting and propagating the faith. Loyola saw in this appeal an opportunity presented expressly by Providence and immediately answered that although he could not then spare the ten asked for, he was more than glad to send two. He selected Rodriguez, a Portuguese, and Bobadilla, a Spaniard. The former, though sick at the time, immediately started for Lisbon. Bobadilla, however, was also taken ill and at the last moment Loyola substituted Xavier for him and bade him set out for Lisbon, by land, in the company of the envoy. It was with a kind of exultant joy that Xavier, who had been fretting himself into sickness at the delays interposed to his work as a foreign missionary, immediately sought the Papal blessing and set out for the designated port. He reached Lisbon in the early spring and there found his fellow missionary awaiting him. With Rodriguez he went three or four days later to the Court, where they were kindly entertained by the King and Queen. Even now there were delays, while briefs were being hurried from Rome, one appointing Xavier as Apostolic Nuncio, a second assigning him special authority for the extension and maintenance of the Faith in the Orient, a third recommending him to David, Emperor of Ethiopia, and a fourth commending him to all the princes of the isles of the sea and all the princes of the continents from the Cape of Good Hope to the River Ganges and beyond. It was the wish of King John to supply Xavier and the two companions who were now to journey with him all the things needful for a long voyage and a longer sojourn in the Indies. But the saint refused everything, content with his priestly garb, his breviary and his letters, and well aware of the sufferings he was destined to endure. To all of these he had already steeled his soul, crying out amid his manifold pains: " Yet more, O Lord, yet more."

So, on his birthday, April 7, 1541 (as Bohours gives the date), in the thirty-sixth year of his age, and the seventh of his profession, Father Xavier sailed in the fleet commanded by Don Martin Alphonso de Sosa, for the shores of India. Though invited, while on board ship, to have his meals with the captain, Xavier insisted on living among the sailors. He ministered to them through a frightful scourge of scurvy, instructed them daily in the principles of religion, and even shared occasionally in their games in order that he might keep their language and conduct within decent bounds. It was a voyage of five months to Mozambique and here they were glad to winter, though during much of the time Xavier was prostrate with fever. Early in 1543 they resumed the voyage and Xavier wept tears of joy at the sight of the Portuguese flag

on the African coast at Malinda. At Socotra, near the
entrance of the Red Sea, the missionary laboured devotedly for the conversion of the pagans and on leaving, promised them another priest as speedily as
possible. Then the ship crossed the ocean on the last
stage of its eastward way and reached Goa on May
6, 1542. The town, situated on a small island, was at
this time, as described in our previous chapter, the
capital of the Portuguese Viceroyalty and the see of
a Bishop. This latter was Don Juan de Albuquerque,
and from him Xavier at once obtained a dispensation
to preach.

In this sumptuous but still rather nondescript town,
wherein the Portuguese, who had been practically re-
paganized, jostled representatives of many Indian
creeds, Xavier laboured earnestly for some five
months. The American poet has described him going
up and down the streets with his bell, giving his " loud
summons to the fathers of families that, for the love
of God, they should send their children and their
slaves to catechism." With consummate tact the
missionary showed himself masterly in his power to
deal with all sorts and conditions of men. He even
spoke compassionately with the " concubinarians " and
others who had been openly flouting the law of Christian morals. In the end, we are told, the Goanese
showed themselves quite another sort of people, as
compared with the careless rout St. Francis had found
on his arrival.

But by this time another call had come. On the
coast of Fishery, a little to the south, dwelt a much
neglected people known as the Paravas. They were
pearl divers by profession and had once been Chris-

tians. But their evangelization had stopped with the administration of baptism and they were now in a most miserable case. It was just the kind of situation which would appeal to Father Xavier, and thither he made his way in the October of 1542. For fifteen months he worked among these degraded people and, in spite of the bitter opposition of the Brahmans, accomplished magnificent results. At the end of 1543, he left behind him other workers and translations of religious literature, and returned to Goa. By this time the missionary had gained some conception of the vastness of his task, and with ripened experience and with unabated faith he now wrote back to Portugal, pleading for the awaking of " new workers for the great employ " and in particular recalling his promise to the people of Socotra.

We next find the indefatigable saint in Travancore, where he is said to have founded as many as forty-five Christian communities. So far in the story there is no suggestion of any miraculous gift of tongues, for Xavier is expressly said to have taught by means of signs and with the help of interpreters. One great miracle, however, is here recorded, namely, the meeting and repelling of a pagan horde under one who is called the " Great Monarch." His advance threatened the very existence of the Christian community, but Xavier met the foe with uplifted crucifix and compelled him to halt. When the daring churchman was brought into the King's presence, the latter remarked: " Men call me the Great Monarch, but you are the Great Father."

The next step in the Christianizing of the Indies was to send missionaries to the little island of Manaar, to

the north of Ceylon, and to visit personally the island
of Ceylon itself. At Meliapur Xavier paid his reverence at the reputed tomb of the Apostle Thomas,
" whom he had taken for his patron and his guide in
the course of all his travels." Xavier had come to
Meliapur by land, travelling along the Coromandel
coast. He found here great spiritual solace in his
night visit to the cave, where it was said the Apostle
had met his death through the spear thrust of a Brah-
man. Much legendary material had naturally gathered around the little chapel, which the Portuguese
found in ruins on the top of a hill, and it is most un-
likely that the site is the authentic place of the
Apostle's martyrdom. It was all too easy for the
Portuguese to confuse the name of the Buddhist saint
Bodhi-dharma (dha-ma) with the name of the Apostle.
The consolation, nevertheless, was a genuine one.

By this time Xavier was beginning to feel that his
work in India proper was completed and might well
be left to the recruits whom he had requested from
Father Ignatius. Moreover, he was not a little disgusted with the unchristian conduct of many of the
Portuguese whose lives were a scandal to the pagans.
Or perhaps it was the untiring restlessness of the
pioneer which, like the gad-fly, continually drove him
on to fresh fields of endeavour. At any rate, on September 25, 1545 Xavier arrived at Malacca, after a
voyage in which he had once again displayed his sympathy with the sailors by participating in their card-
games. One unfortunate gambler, on the brink of
suicide from his losses, Xavier is said to have saved
and converted by staking him to a fresh play which
turned out successfully. The moral here is not quite

as obvious as the humanity. In Malacca, which was
now occupied by a motley multitude of Indians, Javanese, Chinese, Arabs, and Persians, Xavier laboured
for four months, with small success. The irrespon-
siveness of the heathen so distressed him that he departed from his customary tolerance to the extent of
invoking the introduction of the *Inquisition* for the
suppression of Judaism and heresy. Fortunately for
the saint's good name, the recommendation was not
complied with, at least not until a decade or so after
Xavier's death. Meanwhile, he assuaged his impatience by visiting other places, including Amboyna and
the Moluccas. Then in 1547 he returned to Malacca
and was overjoyed to welcome three recruits for the
Order. This time he gained both fame and influence
by the announcement of a great victory won by the
Portuguese fleet over the navy of the Achinese, which
had come to besiege Malacca. The victory was proclaimed to the people of the port before the return of
the victorious ships. " My brethren," he said, " Jesus
Christ has vanquished for you. At this moment, while
I am speaking, the soldiers of His blessed Name have
completed their victory, by the entire defeat of the
enemy's navy. You shall receive the news of it on
Friday next, and may shortly expect the return of
your victorious fleet."

The fulfilment of this prediction made a great impression, but much more significant for the future history of Xavier and the Far East was the arrival at
Malacca, on a vessel from China, of the Japanese,
Yajiro, mentioned in the preceding chapter. This man,
destined to be the earliest begotten child of the Christian Church in Japan, was a member of the Satsuma

clan, and born in Kagoshima, in the Island of Kyushu.
He had slain a man, probably without murderous in-
tent, and with another fugitive from justice and a
servant had fled to the shore where Mendez Pinto was
just then preparing to sail for Malacca. Though a
party of horsemen, arriving at that instant, demanded
the return of the fugitives, Pinto received them on
board. It is this circumstance which brought about
the meeting of Yajiro and his companions with Xavier.
The saint was at once attracted to the Satsuma man,
who is described as " about thirty-five years old, rich,
nobly born, and one whose life had been sufficiently
libertine. The Portuguese (that is, Pinto), who two
years before had made the discovery of Japan, had
been acquainted with him at Cangoxima (Kagoshima),
the place of his birth, and understood from his own
mouth that, having been much troubled with the remembrance of the sins of his youth, he had retired himself among the solitary Bonzes, but that neither the
solitude, nor the conversation of those heathen priests,
had been able to restore him the tranquillity of his soul,
and that thereupon he had returned into the world,
more disquieted than ever with his remorse of conscience."

Apparently it was Pinto who recommended Yajiro
to confess his sins and his perplexities to Xavier, even
before the homicide which seems to have compelled
his flight. So he made all haste on his arrival at
Malacca to fulfil the promise he had made to the Portuguese. Unfortunately Xavier was at the time on his
journey to the Moluccas and it was only on his return
that, through the good offices of George Alvarez, the
Japanese were introduced. The missionary was trans-

ported with joy at the sight of men in whom he recognized the first-fruits of a new race for the Church's fold. He began at once the instruction of Yajiro and his companions, but presently concluded it would be better to send them to Goa, " there to be more fully taught the truths and practices of Christianity before their baptism." So with twenty or thirty other young men, mostly from the Moluccas, the three " Japonians " were commended to the Rector of St. Paul's College at Goa, and Xavier prepared to follow them in due season. The new prospects for Christianity in the Far East redoubled his anxiety to obtain recruits, as far as possible from the *Order of Jesus*. " I beg and adjure your Majesty," he writes to King John III of Portugal, " by the love you bear to our Blessed Lord, and by the zeal wherewith you burn for the glory of the Divine Majesty, to send next year some preachers of our *Society* to your faithful subjects of the Indies." Describing the work in the Moluccas, he continues: " I preached there, in the morning to the Portuguese at mass; I went again into the pulpit in the afternoon and instructed their children, their slaves and idolaters newly converted, accommodating my discourse to the measure of their understanding, and expounding to them the principal points of Christian doctrine, one after another. Besides which, one day in the week I assembled in the Church the wives of the Portuguese, and catechised them on the articles of faith, on the sacraments of penance and the eucharist. I preached also every day in the fortresses the principles of religion, to the sons and daughters of the soldiers, to their servants of both sexes; in fine to the natives of the country, who were born Christians: and these in-

structions had so good effect that they totally re-
nounced the superstitions and sorceries which were in
use amongst those stupid and ignorant new converts."
It is impossible to exaggerate the immensity of
Xavier's labours at this time and such accounts as we
have from his own pen, or from the report of others,
are much more convincing of his real claim to greatness than any list of miracles. On January 15, 1544
he wrote as follows: " Often my arms are weary from
baptizing and I cannot speak another word from having repeatedly recited the prayers to the people, one
after another, and given instruction in Christian doctrine to them in their native tongue." One who knew
him well at this time has left us the following description of his work in Travancore, which was referred to
earlier: " Father Xavier goes about with bare feet; his
garments are shabby and torn. He is called ' the great
father ' and all love him well. A rajah has given orders
throughout his kingdom that all are to show obedience
to his brother, ' the great father,' as though it were to
himself; all who wish are free to become Christians.
He also gave him much money, but Xavier distributed
it all to the poor. . . . He has four native-born Indians with him whom he had ordained as priests. Six
other Indians from the College of Goa are on the point
of taking orders. He carries with him two, three, four,
yea six thousand men into the open country, climbs a
tree and there preaches to them."
Xavier arrived at St. Paul's College, Goa, at a most
opportune time, found great favour among the postu-
lants at the seminary, and took special delight in renewed acquaintance with Yajiro, who was " leading a
most regular life " and was anxious for baptism. He

was baptized as Pablo (Paul) de Santa Fe, and on receiving the sacrament he experienced the peace of soul he had been seeking vainly for so long. His two attendants were baptized at the same time, one receiving the name of John and the other that of Anthony. In a letter written to Rome at the end of this year, Xavier expressed the gratitude he felt in almost ecstatic terms. Indeed, he had now two major joys. One was that of having received into the Church these " dear Japonians," in the thought of whom he expressed himself in his devotions as " glad to die." The other was that joy he felt for the increase of the *Order,* concerning which he exclaimed: " *Si oblitus unquam fuero tui, Societas Jesu, oblivione detur dextera mea!* ", " If I forget thee, O Society of Jesus, let me forget the use of my right hand! "

Intercourse with Yajiro at this time served to augment Xavier's desire to carry the faith personally to Japan as soon as possible. His admiration for the three Japanese neophytes served to strengthen his high opinion of the race itself. This opinion the reports of recently returned Portuguese merchants helped to confirm. From George Alvarez he learned that " the Empire of Japan was one of the most populous in the world; that the Japanese were naturally curious and covetous of knowledge, and withal docible, and of great capacity; that being generally ingenious and very rational, if they were instructed in the morals of Christianity, they would easily submit to them; and that if the preachers of the Gospel lived according to gospel rules, the whole nation would subject itself to the yoke of Jesus Christ, not perhaps so readily at first, but in process of time and after clearing of their doubts."

Nothing more was necessary to convince Xavier that the finger of Providence was beckoning him in this direction. All his friends united in seeking to hold him back from his purpose. They spoke of the length of the way—thirteen hundred leagues of sea, much of it uncharted. They declaimed about the pirates, and about certain " winds called Typhons " that were wont to catch vessels unaware and suck them down to destruction. But none of these things moved the Apostle of the Indies:

> " He heard a voice they could not hear,
> Which would not let him stay;
> He saw a hand they could not see,
> Which beckoned him away."

So he hurried up a long letter to Father Ignatius, filled with new appointments the positions of Superior-General and Rector of the College at Goa, made suitable disposition of other missionaries to go to Socotra, Ormuz and elsewhere, and to these last wrote detailed and elaborate instructions as to their course of conduct and methods of evangelization. Among other things he wrote: " You shall walk the streets every night and recommend the souls of the dead to the prayers of the living. . . . You shall also desire their prayers to God for such as are in mortal sin, that they may obtain the grace of coming out of so deplorable a condition." " On Sundays and saints' days you shall preach at two o'clock in the afternoon, at the Church of the Misericordia, or in the principal Church of the town; sending first your companion about the streets, with his bell in his hand, to invite the people to the sermon." And again: " You shall set apart one day of the week to reconcile differences and regulate the interests of such as are at variance, and are preparing to go to law. Hear them one after the other and propose terms of accommodation to them."

It is clear that, in undertaking a new work, Xavier was not minded to relax his oversight of those responsibilities which he had earlier incurred. So at last, eight days after he had sent his last appointee to Ormuz in April 1549, St. Francis embarked in a vessel for Cochin, where he expected to find a ship which would carry him to Malacca, and so towards Japan. He took with him the three Japanese, Paul, John and Anthony, and the two Portuguese fathers, Cozimo de Torres and John Fernandez. Cochin was reached on April 25 and Malacca at the end of May. In the latter place the whole town came out to meet Father Francis, welcoming him and his companions with the most unfeigned joy. Many were moved to the profession of religion and one, Juan Brava, was received into the *Order*. It was encouraging, too, to get news from Japan, with a letter from " one of the kings of that island," expressly asking for preachers to be sent to him. Truth to tell, the anxiety of this " king " to receive the Portuguese missionaries seems to have been founded mostly on superstition, since shortly before a violent earthquake had apparently been checked by the setting up of crosses by one of the Portuguese merchants. The story may have been the first intimation to the missionary of the physical menace which hangs perpetually, like the sword of Damocles, over that otherwise favoured land.

In Malacca there were many ships which had Japan for an ultimate destination, but as Xavier desired to go to his new field of labour as directly as possible, these were passed by in favour of a Chinese junk whose master promised the Governor to convey the party to their goal without delay. Unfortunately the junk turned out to be a pirate ship and it was in the " Robbers' ship," as Xavier calls the vessel, that they embarked. As things turned out, they passed through all kinds of perils and, in spite of the use of every kind of heathenish incantation, were brought to the very verge of shipwreck. The captain, moreover, so far from observing his promise to the Governor, turned aside to visit every island it was possible for him to reach, and ultimately announced that it was his intention to land his passengers at Canton. To Xavier it seemed, indeed, that by reason of the captain's obstinate resort to idolatrous rites, the devil himself had become master of his destiny. Nevertheless, Providence had not deserted him, for presently a contrary wind arose of such force that the vessel, in spite of the captain, was driven in the direction exactly opposite to that planned. So it came to pass that on August 15, 1549 the ship made port at the actual birthplace of Yajiro, Kagoshima, the Satsuma capital, the place most favourable for the commencement of the evangelistic campaign.

It may be imagined with what gratitude the fathers found themselves in the island of Kyushu, under their feet the very soil of the land to which they believed the good providence of God had been guiding them. The political situation in Japan, in the middle of the sixteenth century, has already been described in connection with the story of Mendez Pinto. It will be recalled that the prestige of the Ashikaga Shoguns had sunk to a very low ebb. Personal and artistic extravagance, together with a disposition to deal irresolutely with China's claim to a kind of suzerainty, under pressure of the need for financial assistance, had provoked both in the Court and among the people a growing desire to rid the land of these ambitious militarists. Though the predestined instrument of this riddance, Oda Nobunaga, was but a boy of fifteen when Xavier arrived at Kagoshima, intervention to restrain the tyranny of the Shoguns was daily becoming more and more of a possibility, and ere the end of our story we shall have to chronicle that intervention's coming and success.

There is something to be said also of the religious situation, since in this region of Japanese life we are able to detect certain aids to the success of the Jesuits, which Xavier and his companions could hardly avoid regarding as providential. One of these was the growing truculence of the Buddhist priesthood. From very early times the bonzes, contrary to the experience of men in most other Buddhist lands, had made themselves notorious for their turbulence and for their disposition to overbear the will of the rulers by political interference. From the heights of Hiyeizan, overlooking Kyoto, the militant monkhoods of the Tendai sect had been wont to swarm down into the capital and enforce their demands by show of force. It is an oft-quoted saying of one of the Emperors that there were three things he found himself unable to control: the rolling waters of the Kamo River, the fall of the dice, and the turbulence of the monks of Hiyeizan. Ultimately this turbulence, in the days of Nobunaga, brought upon the bonzes a hideous massacre, but even

a short time before Xavier's arrival there were religious commotions of a menacing character. In the
latter part of the fifteenth century, the Hiyeizan monks
had made an attack on the temple of the Shinshu, the
great Hongwanji, applying the torch ruthlessly to the
splendid buildings, and compelling the abbot to flee for
his life. A little later there was a furious war in which
a sub-sect, known as the Takata, ravaged the lands of
three provinces and attempted to take possession of
Echizen. This is known as the Ikko-ikki revolt.
"A few years later," says Brinkley, "the Shin be-
lievers in Echizen joined the revolters and marched
through the province, looting and burning wherever
they passed. No measure of secular warfare had been
more ruthless than were the ways of these monks. The
high constable, Asakura Norikage, now took the field,
and after fierce fighting, drove back the fanatics, destroyed their temples, and expelled their priests." [1]
Again, in 1529, came what is known as Dai-ikki, "the
Great Revolt," in which the Lord Abbot of the new
Hongwanji of Kyoto assumed the title of "Son of
Heaven" and bestowed the title of Shogun upon his
steward. Still later, almost on the eve of the coming
of the Portuguese, we have the Hokke-ikki, or revolt
of the Nichiren Buddhists, to which a reply was made
by the monks of Enryaku-ji, when they poured into
the capital, destroyed with fire the twenty-one temples
of the Nichiren sect, and put to the sword three
thousand of their priests. These examples are sufficient to account for the rising tide of indignation
against the bonzes and the readiness of many of the
daimyos to favour a counter-influence in the preaching
of the friars.

There was further the desire, especially on the part of the southern daimyos, to profit by the opportunity of commercial relations with the foreigners on the most favourable terms. This is not to cast any aspersion on the general sincerity of the converts gained by the preaching of the Jesuits, for that sincerity is abundantly witnessed by the fortitude with which so many of them in later years faced the risks and torments of martyrdom. But it was perfectly natural that where commercial advantage made a close association with the Portuguese important, the possibilities of conversion were immensely enhanced. We may add here that the association of the Japanese with the Portuguese revealed affinities of character and disposition, to which frequent allusion has been made by historians. It was inevitable that two races, equally famous for daring on the seas, should be drawn towards one another.

No account, however, of the circumstances predisposing the Japanese of the time to an acceptance of Christianity may neglect reference to the singular charm as well as the commanding Christian character of the great missionary. It is hardly necessary to discuss the " miracles " of St. Francis, since his personality was itself a miracle. Always without fear and at the same time treating even the worst of his opponents with a disarming courtesy, the saint won men's confidence as readily as he triumphed over his adversaries' efforts to discredit him.

Let us come now to some more detailed account of Xavier's labours in Japan. His description of the country and its religions we may pass by with the briefest reference. It is sufficient to pay tribute to its sub-

stantial accuracy. When he speaks of divine worship
paid to beasts, he may have been thinking of the rites
performed at the so-called "fox temples," such as we
may see to-day all over Japan. The "mysterious deity
whom they call Amida," who "has built a paradise of
such distance from the earth that the souls cannot
reach it under a voyage of three years," is the Buddha
of that name, reverenced especially by the Jodo and
Shin sects. That St. Francis learned something of
Gautama, the Indian Buddha, appears from references
to "Xaca," that is, Shaka (Çakya Muni), "who seems
to be a counterfeit of the true Messiah, set up by the
devil himself, or by his ministers." It was quite natural that Xavier, noting the many similarities between
Buddhism and Christianity, should have jumped to the
conclusion that the former was a diabolical parody of
the latter. Xavier's biographers make frequent reference to this supposed fact that "the spirit of lies has
established in Japan a kind of hierarchy, not unlike
that of the Catholic Church." But they note also the
austerity of the Buddhist bonzes, though finding it a
great temptation to impute this to impiety and hypocrisy.

The unexpected arrival of the little missionary band
at Kagoshima made it both logical and convenient to
begin work with the Satsuma clan. Yajiro paid a visit
to the daimyo and was received with joy as one raised
from the dead. The chief's questions gave a fine opening for the preaching of the faith. Pictures of the
Virgin and Child had their effect on the ladies of the
Court. One of the princesses was so much struck with
the pictures that she forthwith requested that the principles of the faith be put into writing for her more

careful study. Even outside the Court there was
abundant interest shown in the new teaching, and
Xavier's acquaintance with the Japanese language,
strengthened by his association with the three converts,
now appears to have been sufficient to allow expression, if not " with ease and readiness," yet with some
effectiveness. At any rate, he and his companions no
longer stood, as on their first arrival, " like statues,
mute and motionless." He made friends readily and
wrote at this time of the Japanese, " I really think that
among barbarous nations there can be none that has
more natural goodness than Japan."

Though the work of evangelization had begun with
the family of the daimyo, the first baptism was that
of " a man of mean condition, destitute of the goods
of fortune." But before the end of the year others of
higher degree accepted the faith and success brought
in its train persecution. This originated with the
bonzes, who saw in St. Francis " a devil who spoke to
them in the likeness of a man." The chief opponent
was a Buddhist priest he calls *Ningh-sit,* which name
he interprets as " Heart of Truth." This man was
eighty years old and expressed great amazement that
Xavier should have come so far to preach his doc-
trines. Though the saint did not succeed in assuaging
the fury of his adversaries, he won their respect by
giving satisfactory replies to the most diverse questions. They asked, for example, as to " the immor-
tality of the soul, the motions of the heavens, the
eclipses of the sun and moon, the colours of the rain-
bow, sin and grace, heaven and hell "—a truly comprehensive category.

Partly because of the fury of this persecution and

partly on account of the plans of the Portuguese merchants to make their headquarters at Firando (Hirado) rather than at Kagoshima—a circumstance which infuriated the Satsuma daimyo—the missionaries now determined to move likewise. There were now copies available of the Christian catechism and other instructions and expositions designed for circulation, so that it was an advantage rather than otherwise for the fathers to break fresh ground. They left Kagoshima at the beginning of September 1550, Xavier being accompanied by Father Torres and Father Fernandez. The latter, as was his wont, carried upon his back the utensils necessary for the performance of Mass. Yajiro was left behind to strengthen his brethren in the home district.

Xavier's visit to Firando was partly through the need of giving Christian ministration to the Portuguese sailors and merchantmen, who were now here in considerable numbers. The missionaries were received with almost royal welcome, with the discharge of artillery, the sounding of trumpets, and the display of ensigns and streamers. " All the ships gave shouts of joy when they beheld the man of God." Moreover, the work begun was of so successful a character that " in less than twenty days (Xavier) baptized more infidels than he had done in a whole year at Cangoxima (Kagoshima)." The ease with which he found the work of evangelization progress in this place even suggested that Father Torres might well be left to carry on by himself, while Xavier fulfilled his long-cherished dream of visiting the Imperial city of Kyoto, and there boldly attempt the conversion of the Emperor.

With this great end in view, about the end of October, the saint took with him Father Fernandez and two Japanese Christians and started from Firando for the capital by sea. He reasoned that if the favour of Matsuura, daimyo of a comparatively small fief like Firando, could have such miraculous influence, what must be the effect upon the Empire if he could succeed in winning the good graces of the Emperor? He did not, however, realize the extent to which the welcome of the Portuguese at the port had affected the good opinion of the daimyo.

On the way to the capital St. Francis stopped at the town of Yamaguchi, chief city of the province of Nagato, and one of the richest towns in all Japan. The wealth of the place was due to its proximity to the silver mines and to the natural fertility of the soil. It was, moreover, notorious for its vices, a circumstance which gave Xavier so much concern that he felt bound to stay a while for the proclamation of the Gospel. " He appeared in public, on a sudden, burning with an inward fire, which mounted up into his face, and boldly declared to the people the eternal truths of faith." In another part of the town Father Fernandez preached with like fervour, but the stiff-necked inhabitants of Yamaguchi concluded that the missionaries were mere mountebanks and the faith they proclaimed a fable. However, the notoriety gained had the one advantage of publicity. Among those interested was " the King of Yamaguchi," but although Xavier was heard with attention, his message had small success. It seemed best, after a month of unproductive labour, for the missionaries to resume their way to Kyoto.

This journey is described by one of the saint's biographers as follows:

" They departed towards the end of December, in a season when the rains were continually falling, during a winter which is dreadful in these parts, where the winds are as dangerous by land as tempests are at sea. The colds are pinching, and the snow drives in such abundance that neither in the towns nor hamlets dare people adventure to stir abroad, nor have any communication with each other but by covered walks and galleries. It is yet far worse in the country, where nothing is to be seen but hideous forests, sharp-pointed and ragged mountains, raging torrents across the valleys, which sometimes overflow the plains. Sometimes it is so covered over with ice that the travellers fall at every step; without mentioning those prodigious icicles hanging overhead from the high trees, and threatening the passengers at every moment with their fall." For travellers well equipped and warmly clothed there are much worse winter climates than that of the neighbourhood of Kyoto, but we must remember that Xavier and his companions went most of the way on foot, barefooted, bearing on their backs the necessities of their life and mission, and without other provision than the roasted grains of rice which Brother Bernard carried in his wallet. Moreover, the journey which in good weather would normally have occupied but fifteen days for these travellers was lengthened to two months of painful tramping. During much of this time, moreover, Father Xavier was ill with fever as well as with fatigue. Nevertheless, none of their trials and tribulations abated their zeal in preaching, as they passed through the villages on their route, though for the most part the people listened only to mock and the little children cried after

the missionaries the word "*Dios*" (God), which was
the term they caught most often from the lips of the
evangelists. Xavier explains that he always insisted,
on using the Portuguese word because he was by no
means certain that the Japanese word "*Kami*" re-
flected the essence and perfection of the Divine
Majesty he sought to proclaim. He feared also lest
the heathen should confound the God he worshipped
with the numerous false gods represented in the idols
he noted in the temples.

Xavier's little company reached Kyoto in February
1551, visibly moved at beholding, after all their toils,
the famed capital of the Empire, "the Jerusalem of
Japan." But, alas, it was an inopportune time for
such a visit. "On every side ruins were to be beheld,
and the present condition of affairs threatened it with
a total destruction. All the neighbouring princes were
combined together against the Cubosama, and nothing
was to be heard but the noise of arms." Indeed, everything was hostile to the fulfilment of Xavier's dream
of converting the Emperor. There were no means even
for getting access to the Imperial presence. High officials demanded bribes to the amount of "six hundred
French crowns," a sum it was ludicrous to suppose the
missionaries had to give, even had they willed to do
so. As the town, too, was all in confusion and everybody taken up with the thought of war, Xavier's
preaching in the public places fell on deaf ears. The
most earnest efforts, carried on unflaggingly for a fort-
night, seemed to promise nothing but failure in this
Athens of the Empire, and Xavier came to the reluctant conclusion that it was better to return to Yamaguchi, trusting that the sufferings he had endured on

the way to, and in, Kyoto, might somehow be accepted by his Master as service, and yield fruit in ways beyond his present capacity to understand.

There is something not a little pathetic in the story given us by Father Fernandez that Xavier, when on board ship for the return journey to Yamaguchi, could not, as long as the capital was visible, take his eyes from the " stately town " from which he had expected so much and received so little. Standing on the deck he chanted the words of the 114th Psalm: " In exitu Israel de Egypto, domus Jacob de populo barbaro." The missionary was evidently inclined to blame himself as well as the heathen for his failure, since we find him from henceforth inclined to pay a little more attention to his clothes, having become convinced that his ragged habit had in Kyoto rather shocked his hearers than impressed them with his humility. So with the alms which the Portuguese merchants had pressed upon him he now bought himself a new robe, " being verily persuaded that an apostolic man ought to make himself all to all, and that to gain over worldly men it was sometimes necessary to conform himself a little to their weakness." In conformity with this same principle, Xavier even sent to Hirado for a little striking clock, " an instrument of very harmonious music," and some other trifles, in order that he might follow the custom of obtaining audience with the " king of Yamaguchi " by offering presents. Whether due to this concession or to the fact that Xavier together with the presents brought the daimyo letters from the Governor and Bishop of the Indies, the second sojourn at Yamaguchi was vastly more successful than the first. The refusal of Xavier to accept any return for his presents induced the reflection that this European bonze was very different from the ordinary run. An edict was presently posted in the public places, proclaiming toleration for the preaching of Christianity and forbidding all molestation of the missionaries while in the discharge of their mission.

The saint now preached with fresh force and courage, a circumstance which may have given rise to the belief that at this time he had restored to him " the gift of tongues." It was this gift, men said, that enabled him to appeal to the Chinese merchants of the port as well as to the Japanese. The people who had once been so hostile and even truculent now gave him much joy because of their willingness to hear his words. About this time he wrote home to Portugal: " Though my hairs are already become all hoary, I am more vigorous and robust than I ever was; for the pains which are taken to cultivate a reasonable nation, which loves the truth and covets to be saved, afford me matter of great joy. I have not in the course of all my life received a greater satisfaction than at Yamaguchi, where multitudes of people came to hear me by the king's permission. I saw the pride of the bonzes overthrown and the most inflamed enemies of the Christian name subjected to the humility of the gospel. I saw the transports of joy in those new Christians when, after having vanquished the bonzes in dispute, they returned in triumph. I was not less satisfied to see their diligence in labouring to convince the Gentiles and vying with each other in that undertaking; with the delight they took in the relation of their conquests, and by what arguments and means they brought them over, and how they rooted out the heathen superstitions; all these particulars gave me such abundant joy that I lost the sense of my own afflictions."

Naturally this joy was not without some admixture of bitterness, for there were still those, as the quotation makes evident, who did their best to oppose, and a few who met the missionaries with insult. Nevertheless, the conversions were so numerous, as at once to account for the hostility of the bigots and to confirm the joy of the apostle. Some of these conversions were of men notable for their rank and learning. One who is described as " much esteemed for the subtlety of his understanding and educated in the most famous universities of Japan," was baptized by the name of Lawrence, and became from the first a great support to the Christian cause. In due time this Lawrence was received by Xavier into the *Order of Jesus* and exercised the ministry of preaching with so much power and such great success that he converted " an innumerable multitude of noble and valiant men who were afterwards the pillars of the Japanese Church."

The favour of princes, however, is notoriously uncertain and ere long the daimyo's enthusiasm manifested a decided chill. He did not revoke his edict of tolerance but, in spite of it, began to treat the Christians with so much severity that the heathen priests regained the courage to assert themselves more virulently and began to belabour the missionaries with invective. They circulated the rumour that Xavier was a mere vagabond who, not knowing how to maintain himself in India, had come to Japan to live on charity. They declared furthermore that he was a notorious magician who, through the power of his charms, had forced the devil to obey him, and had thereby seduced the people.

We cannot suppose that this fresh outburst of opposition had any really deterring effect on Xavier's enthusiasm for his mission. He had around him a loyal band of some thousands of Christians and he believed these to be ready at any time to seal their faith with their blood. But for some time the conviction had been strengthening itself within him that it was from China—the motherland of Japanese culture—that his campaign of evangelization should have begun. He had conversed much with the Chinese merchants at Yamaguchi and had become convinced that a nation so polite and intelligent would readily be persuaded to accept Christianity, and that once this task was accomplished the Japanese would follow of their own accord. He remembered also the statement of many of the unbelieving Japanese to the effect that they would not alter their religion till the Chinese had led the way. Let him carry, said they, his gospel to that vast and flourishing empire, and when he had opened its brazen gates to the Gospel of Christ then they also would think of becoming Christians.

Xavier's increasing determination to leave Japan in order to engage in a mission of still wider importance was further fortified by the news brought by a ship from the Indies, which had just come in from Bungo. This vessel, under the command of Edward da Gama, was said to be soon thereafter planning a voyage to China after the return voyage to the Indies. Its stay of a month or so in Japanese waters gave St. Francis just the opportunity he desired. So it came to pass that in the middle of September 1551, together with

Brothers Matthew, Bernard and Lawrence (who was surnamed the *Squint-eyed*), and two Japanese lords who had received baptism, Xavier bade farewell to Yamaguchi and sailed for Bungo. On arrival there the little party received a great ovation, with volleys from the cannon of the Portuguese and flags streaming from all the ships. The natives were amazed beyond expression at such signal honours bestowed upon men in appearance so poverty-stricken and mean. Even the " king " of Bungo, a daimyo named Otomo, was impressed and requested that the foreign bonze should present himself at court. Of this invitation the Portuguese determined to make the most, whether out of regard for Xavier or with a due appreciation of future favours to be gained from the Japanese officials we may not say. Father Xavier was persuaded to comply, in spite of the aversion he had for the pageantry which had been planned, that he maintained was " so unsuitable to the condition of a religious man."

In any case, the procession to the court was carefully arranged. There were thirty Portuguese in the van, all richly habited, with chains of gold adorned with jewels. Servants and slaves, suitably attired, attended their masters. Then came Father Xavier, in a new cassock of black camelet, over which was worn a surplice and a stole of green velvet, garnished with gold brocade. The boats by which the foreigners passed from the ship to the shore were hung with silken banners, while the musicians " made a most harmonious concert " with trumpets, flutes and hautboys. When this imposing procession reached the palace, accompanied by a great crowd of wondering people, there was a still more lavish display. Edward da Gama went first, cane in hand, as major-domo. Then followed several Portuguese, one with a book on a cushion of white satin, one with a gold-headed cane, one with Father Francis' slippers, one with a picture of the Virgin, and another carrying a magnificent parasol. Behind these came Xavier himself, before whom all opened a way as they reached the palace gates. Within the daimyo received his guests with equal ceremony and at once engaged the father in a conversation which lasted until dinner time. The king requested the saint to share his meal, an honour accepted very reluctantly for the sake of continuing the discussion. The interview made a great impression on the court and naturally a still greater impression upon the populace. So much success, indeed, attended the preaching of the missionaries that Xavier was kept whole days baptizing. He might have gathered a still richer harvest but for his conviction that much teaching was necessary for the converts in order " to fortify them well against the tricks " of the adversaries. Otomo himself apparently might have been baptized at this time, if Xavier had been disposed to hasten the process of conversion. As it was, the daimyo sent a letter to his younger brother, who had just succeeded to the daimyate of Yamaguchi, asking that special protection be extended to Fathers Fernandez and Torres.

It may be imagined that the enemies of the faith were by no means slow to muster the forces of opposition, especially as the calumnies which had been circulated in Yamaguchi were already beginning to filter into the communities of Bungo. It was said, among other things, that Xavier was accustomed to cut the throats of little children by night, to suck their blood and eat their flesh; that the devil had declared by the mouth of an idol that Xavier was his disciple; that the missionaries were wont to dig up the bodies of the buried in order to obtain means for their enchantments; and the like. Though St. Francis had now been some forty days in Bungo and the Portuguese ship was in readiness to sail, it was felt by the missionaries that for him to leave just now would have too much the appearance of running away. So Xavier pleaded for a little longer delay and in the meantime repeated his final farewells. He engaged, moreover, in a number of disputations wherein he was always victorious, though the unlearned were naturally unable to follow his arguments. There is a certain *naïveté* in the saying of one of the Portuguese merchants, in describing one of these debates, that he " durst not undertake to write the solutions of them, if we will believe himself, because they surpassed the understanding of a merchant."

Farewells and disputations alike, however, came at last to an end and on November 20, 1551, after a morning spent in taking leave of the prince who had been throughout so gracious a patron, Xavier went on board the waiting vessel and soon thereafter beheld with regret the fading from sight of the hospitable coasts of Japan. He had been in the country but two years and four months, yet the impress of his character and his work was to remain stamped forever on the history of the land. A little later we shall see something of what that influence was. Xavier had conceived a great affection for the people of Japan; and several months later he wrote to Ignatius Loyola, " This is the only country yet discovered in these regions where there is hope of Christianity permanently taking root."

On the same vessel with Xavier were the two Japanese brothers, Matthew and Bernard, and one who went as an ambassador from the daimyo of Bungo for the double purpose of cementing friendship with the Viceroy at Goa and of obtaining from him a preacher who might remain permanently in Japan to complete the work inaugurated by the Apostle to the Indies. The journey to the Chinese coast was anything but a pleasant one. So stormy was the weather that the ultimate preservation of the ship was believed to be due solely to the prayers of the saint. He, too, was desperately ill and in his sickness owed something to the kindness of the man described in our last study on " Mendez Pinto." Pinto is described simply as a Portuguese merchant who, moved with compassion for Father Xavier, desired him to repose himself in his own cabin, instead of sleeping on deck, as had been his wont. The saint, who knew how to receive a courtesy as well as to confer a favour, accepted and also allowed the merchant to station a Chinese servant before the cabin door, that no one should interrupt his rest.

After thirteen days of sailing, Captain Edward da Gama brought his ship to the little island of Sancian, where a few months later Xavier was to die. It was here necessary to change vessels, and the little party then embarked in a small ship called the *Santa Cruz*, under Captain James de Pereira. Between this man and Xavier there developed a great intimacy. The Father told him with enthusiasm of the work which had been accomplished in Satsuma, Yamaguchi and

Bungo, and dwelt upon the sanguine hope he now entertained of bringing about the conversion of the entire archipelago, provided that first of all the Chinese were brought to a knowledge of Christ. So he went on to tell of his resolution to visit China, after he had paid the necessary visit to Goa and attended to the business of the *Order*. For this reason he informed Pereira he had brought with him a translation of the *Catechism* he had caused to be made in Chinese from the Japanese. Although he learned with dismay that all entrance of foreigners into China had been forbidden under penalty of death, he yet expressed the belief that if only a solemn embassy were sent there from the King of Portugal, it would be easy to obtain entrance for the missionaries. To Xavier's great delight, Pereira, " who under the habit of a merchant had the heart of an emperor and the zeal of an apostle," made offer of his ship for the use of such an embassy, and Xavier immediately engaged on his own part to obtain the embassy for his friend. Alas, in this plan, adopted with so much hopeful anticipation, the saint was doomed to the bitterest of disappointments.

It was an earlier disappointment for Xavier to discover that yet another change of ship was necessary, ere he could reach Goa. He had first to go to Malacca, where it was expected that Captain James Pereira's brother, Antonio, might be found, and in whose vessel the travellers might conveniently proceed. This plan was carried out, though a typhoon almost brought the voyage to a premature and fatal ending. They stayed in Singapore a few days, there learned that their surmise as to the whereabouts of Antonio Pereira was correct, and so arrived at length at Malacca, to be received most hospitably by the Jesuit Superior, Father Francis Perez. Indeed, the whole city welcomed Xavier with " all the tenderness of affection and all the reverence imaginable." Then the saint said a reluctant farewell to James Pereira, with whom he renewed his resolution concerning China. He then bade adieu to the good Christians of Malacca, entered with his " Japonians " into the vessel of Antonio Pereira, and set forth for Cochin and Goa.

On the voyage they passed through a variety of perils, but " the saint's vessel," as the *Santa Cruz* came to be called, escaped them all and arrived at Cochin on January 24, 1552. Here Xavier made the opportunity to write letters to the King of Portugal and the General of his *Order,* giving particulars of the work accomplished and his plans for the future. Then he re-embarked, had the good fortune to have a speedy voyage, and reached Goa safely about the beginning of February.

It must have been with much emotion that the saint found himself once again at the headquarters of his mission. There was a great deal to hear about and very much to do, apart from the voluntary resumption of his visits to the hospitals of the city. He learned with joy of the prosperity of the work in Ormuz, Cochin, the coast of the Fisheries, Bazain, Meliapore and the Moluccas. He noted gratefully also the improvement of manners and morals in Goa, where " the soldiers lived almost like men in orders," so that their piety edified the people.

Amid so many occasions for satisfaction, however, one thing troubled him. This was the ill conduct of Antonio Gomez, whom he himself had constituted Rector of the College of St. Paul. A man of great gifts, Gomez was, nevertheless, " wonderfully self-opinioned," and had taken advantage of Xavier's absence to usurp almost the whole power in the College. The consequences had been deplorable, and Father Francis felt bound to take instant and drastic steps to restore discipline. He, who had been so tender with sinners and so patient with opposition from the heathen, now showed that he could be very stern. He judged that such a man, who was neither humble nor obedient, was unworthy of membership in the *Society of Jesus*. The least he felt he could mete out by way of punishment was to send Gomez to the fortress of Diu, there to receive his dismission, rather than strip from him his habit before all his associates at Goa. Antonio Gomez was thereupon forced to embark for Diu, but the vessel on which he sailed was wrecked, and the deposed Rector drowned. The tragedy was naturally regarded as a judgment from God and a confirmation of Xavier's authority.

While Father Francis was still on the way from Japan there had arrived at Goa two letters patent, written by the General of the *Order,* one bearing the date of October 10, 1549 and the other that of December 23 of the same year. In the former of these Xavier was constituted Provincial of the Indies and all the Kingdoms of the East. In the second he was endowed with all the privileges granted by the Popes to the head of the *Order* and to those members of it whom the General might regard as worthy of the responsibility. Armed with this authority, the new Provincial at once set out to make provision for the despatch of fit members of the *Order* to the various missions he had founded. When this was done he returned with unabated zest to the fulfilling of the plan for securing an embassy to China from the King of Portugal. The Viceroy, Don Alphonzo de Norogna, showed himself enthusiastic for the idea as soon as it was laid before him. Moreover, he willingly granted Xavier's plea that James Pereira should be the man chosen as ambassador. The Viceroy went further and proceeded to provide very handsome presents for the Emperor of China, which Pereira was requested to convey. The Bishop of Goa was no less favourable to the project and provided an epistle of greeting, beautifully inscribed in letters of gold, and bordered with curious paintings. Next came the task of selecting the missionaries who were to accompany Xavier as attendants on the ambassador. Here there was an embarrassment of riches, since of some thirty fathers, every one was clamorous for permission to undertake the adventurous and dangerous journey. After discussion, it was generally recognized that the fittest of all was Gaspar Barzaeus, but Xavier was very reluctantly compelled to leave him in charge of matters at Goa as Vice-Provincial and Rector of the College. Barzaeus bowed, as in duty bound, to the decision of his Provincial, though all felt that in so doing he was making the noblest of sacrifices. Ultimately five men were chosen as Xavier's companions, together with a secular Chinese who, since his baptism, had been known as Antonio de Sainte Foy. About the same time, in obedience to instructions from Rome, a member of the *Order*, Andrew Fernandez, was selected for return to Europe to report on the general success of work in the Far East.

Now at last all was in readiness for the projected voyage. The ship was ready and the last instructions had been given to the Christian community of Goa. One who was present has left us an account of the affecting farewell: " The Father, Master Francis, embracing his brethren before his departure for China, and weeping over them, recommended constancy in their vocation to them; together with unfeigned humility, which was to have for its foundation a true knowledge of themselves and particularly a most prompt obedience. He extended his exhortation on this last point and enjoined them obedience as a virtue most pleasing to Almighty God, much commended by the Holy Spirit, and absolutely necessary to the sons of the Society."

The missionary band left Goa on Holy Thursday, April 14, 1552, and enjoyed calm seas till they arrived in the neighbourhood of the Nicobar Islands, to the north of Sumatra. Then arose a furious tempest which threatened for a time to make an end of the ship and its mission. They arrived, however, in safety at Malacca, only to find the city in the grip of a terrible and contagious epidemic. It was a situation such as never failed to appeal to the selfless heroism of Xavier. He literally ran from street to street to gather up the sick and dying, who lay languishing on the ground for want of succour. When the hospitals were filled to overflowing, he had cabins built along the shore. He begged food and medicines from people of the wealthier and devouter sort. Yet, though he and his companions kept up their ministrations night and day, they continued in health after a manner naturally deemed miraculous. Nevertheless, after all this self-denying

labour, Xavier was ill repaid, for the Governor of
Malacca, Don Alvarez de Ataide, a son of the great
Vasco da Gama, remembered a grudge against Pereira
which dated back to the latter's refusal to lend the
sum of 10,000 crowns. This refusal he was now able
to avenge, so he opposed obstinately the choice of
Xavier and denied Pereira the right to proceed to Peking as ambassador. The *Santa Cruz,* moreover, was
seized and deprived of its rudder, lest it should make
its escape from Alvarez' jurisdiction. All remonstrance
was in vain, even when the royal orders were quoted
to the effect that the sailing of the Portuguese ships
was positively not to be hindered. Xavier himself in-
tervened with an offer to raise 30,000 crowns to satisfy
the avarice of the Governor. But Don Alvarez was
by this time anxious to gratify more than a love of
lucre and declared " that he was too old to be coun-
selled; that as long as he continued Governor of Malacca and captain of the seas, James Pereira should not
go to China, either as ambassador or merchant; and
if Father Xavier was intoxicated with the zeal of converting heathens, he might go to Brazil, or to the Kingdom of Monomotopa." The Provincial, having ex-
hausted the means of settling the matter amicably, now
felt called upon to exercise his authority as Papal
Nuncio by pronouncing a sentence of excommunica-
tion against the Governor.

It was a sad blow to a grand and promising plan,
all the more so that Xavier resented less the railing
language of Alvarez describing the saint as " an ambitious hypocrite and a friend of publicans and sinners," than the thwarting of an enterprise of such
manifest importance for the Church. Xavier wrote to

Pereira, who now lay hidden in Malacca, to the following effect: " Since the greatness of my sins has been the reason why God Almighty would not make use of us two for the enterprise of China, it is upon myself that I ought in conscience to lay the fault. They are my offences which have ruined your fortunes and have caused you to lose all your expenses for the embassy of China."

Xavier did all he could to remedy the situation, writing letters to the King of Portugal, without, however, a word against Don Alvarez. It was plain that his own scheme for reaching China was not to be fulfilled. Yet he did not despair of being able to preach the Gospel to the Chinese. He thought, if he could only get to some island in the neighbourhood of Canton, he might be able to slip over from thence to the continent, without being noticed, and if he were seized and put in prison he might at least preach to his fellow prisoners. Perhaps this was God's way of bringing the good news to the towns and cities of the Middle Kingdom. He even dreamed of the possibility that the Emperor himself, if merely out of curiosity, might be moved to give audience to the man who had dared all to publish the Christian faith.

It was from such considerations that Father Xavier made up his mind at last to join the *Santa Cruz,* which was on the point of leaving Malacca for Sancian, leaving behind Pereira and the presents intended for the Emperor, and taking with him only an Indian servant and the Chinese Brother, Antonio de Sainte Foy. The hours before sailing he spent in the Church of Our Lady of the Mount, recommending his voyage to the protection of the Blessed Virgin. While refusing to pay a farewell visit to the Governor, he nevertheless prayed earnestly for the salvation of his enemy's soul. Then, beating his shoes one against the other, he declared he would not carry away with him the dust of the place which had so thwarted his designs, and boarded the *Santa Cruz*, in which five hundred persons, including passengers and servants, were crowded. The voyage began inauspiciously with fourteen days of becalming during which time the water failed and many persons died of thirst. Then they had seven days of more favourable weather which brought them near the coast of Formosa, but so full of sick people was the vessel that it could not make the shore. In this crisis, so the story goes, the saint provided fresh water miraculously when all had given themselves over for death. A shallop sent out from the ship returned in three days' time with provisions from the coast and, twenty-three days after leaving Malacca, the travel-weary band of survivors attained the desired haven of Sancian.

Sancian, or Shang-ch'uan, sometimes known as St. John's Island, is about thirty miles southwest of Macao. About the time of Xavier's arrival it was the rendezvous of a good many Portuguese ships, and the trading season had just commenced. The Chinese had given the Portuguese permission to carry on their commerce, provided that the fundamental law prohibiting foreigners from setting foot on the mainland was not violated. The saint was much disappointed when he found himself face to face with this obstacle, though he had been previously notified of the existence of the law. Nevertheless, he could not abandon the resolution which he believed he had made under divine guidance. " I am elected," he said, " for this great enterprise by the special grace of heaven. If I should demur on the execution or be terrified with the hardships, and want courage to attempt their difficulties, would it not be incomparably worse than all the evils with which you threaten me? " At last, seeing that the Portuguese merchants steadfastly refused to endanger their favour with the Chinese officials, Xavier consented to defer an effort to depart till the end of the trading season, when most of the vessels would have departed. So he erected a temporary chapel, called the children together for catechism, and did his best for the instruction of the natives generally. In this work he enjoyed considerable success and certain prophecies he made, which were a little later fulfilled to the letter, together with a number of miracles which report attributed to him, gave him an extended influence with the community. Yet the determination was by no means weakened to cross to the mainland, and after the departure of all the ships except the *Santa Cruz,* Xavier was delighted to get a little encouragement from some Chinese who informed him that the Emperor would certainly not object to the presence in China of a learned man such as himself. One Chinese captain, on the condition that he was liberally paid, in *pardos* of pepper, and under pledge of the strictest secrecy, agreed to ferry the saint across to the mainland, there to leave him to his chances. The captain, however, subsequently repented of his promise; at least he did not turn up at the appointed time and place. So Xavier, still on board the *Santa Cruz,* ill with fever and with his sickness aggravated by the motion of the ship, pleaded to be set ashore. In a miserable hut, attended only by his Chinese servant, Antonio (who, through forgetfulness of his own language and ignorance of the " Mandarin," proved to be but a sorry interpreter), Father Francis was now just able to write the final letters to Rome, Portugal, and other places where the *Order* had been established, and to await God's will. His heart was still filled with desire for the good of the *Order* and, writing to Father Barzaeus at Goa, he urged that great care should be taken in admitting men into the Society. " For I fear," said he, " that many of them who have been admitted were better out of our walls than within them."

The saint was now, through the departure of the Portuguese, reduced to great extremities through the lack of provisions. It seems strange that those to whom he had so unselfishly ministered should have left him to such a plight. Possibly the excommunicated Governor had seen to it that his orders to the detriment of Father Francis were obeyed. In any case there falls over the last days of Xavier the shadow of the end. Like Moses he was to reach the very borders of his promised land and then pass to his rest. After being landed from the *Santa Cruz* he was left upon the sands, exposed to the north winds, which in the month of November could be very piercing. In all probability it was this exposure which brought on the fever which on November 20 seized him in its fiery grip. One man, more compassionate than the rest, assisted his servant to bear him into the shelter of a tiny cabin. There he lay, with his eyes fixed on heaven or on his crucifix, till about the 28th of the month. Then the fever mounted into his head and it was plain the end was not far off. For a day or two he talked, half in delirium, of little but God and the journey to China. Then speech left him altogether for three days. It was in the night, probably of the 2nd of December, that Father Francis suddenly recovered his clearness of mind and his power of speech. With his eyes " all bathed in tears, and fixed with great tenderness of soul upon his crucifix, he pronounced these words, ' In Te, Domine, speravi, non confundar in æternum '; and at the same instant, transported with celestial joy, which appeared upon his countenance, he sweetly gave up the ghost, towards two o'clock in the afternoon, and in the year of God 1552." " It was," says Latourette, " a dramatic and worthy close of a great career, this death of the Apostle to the Indies near the portal of the unopened Empire of the Far East."

It has been suggested that at this gateway to the Middle Kingdom, which Xavier had so strenuously laboured to unbar, the body of the saint might well have been suffered to repose. It was indeed here laid temporarily at rest, close to the cabin in which the saint had died, on the following Sunday at noon. At this first funeral there was, of necessity, but little in the way of ceremony. Besides Antonio de Sainte Foy and Francis d'Aghiar, but two mourners were present. It was a cold day and over the few faithful who remained there hung the cloud of the Governor's displeasure. So the little company stripped Father Francis of his tattered cassock, dividing this poor relic of his devotion among them. Then they arrayed the body in the sacerdotal robes and placed it in a large Chinese chest, with unslaked lime, in order that the bones might eventually be carried back to Goa. "At the point of the haven there was a little spot of rising ground and at the foot of this hillock a small piece of meadow where the Portuguese had set up a cross. Near that cross they interred the saint: they cast up two heaps of stones, the one at his head, the other at his feet, as a mark of the place where he was buried."

Towards the end of February 1553 an opportunity occurred to take the remains from their resting place in Sancian to Malacca. Many who had so far yielded to the spite of the Governor in paying dishonour to the saint now came forward to plead with streaming eyes for the transference thither of the body. They declared openly "that Alvarez de Atayda had been the death of Father Francis, both by his persecutions at Malacca and by the cruelties of his servants at Sancian." So the men who sailed away at last with the coffin felt themselves happy in bearing with them to the Indies so rich a treasure.

They arrived at Malacca on March 22. All the clergy of the place, with James Pereira, came down to the shore to receive the coffin. Followed by a great crowd which included Muhammadans and pagans as well as Christians, it was carried to the Church of Our Lady of the Mount. Only stubborn Governor Alvarez refrained from sharing in the last honours paid to Father Francis. Yet the Governor's power was still ample enough to force the burial to be outside the walls of the Church. Hither the multitudes came in such numbers that the body, removed from its coffin, was crushed under the feet of the crowd.

Meanwhile, a coffin of precious wood had been procured by Pereira, and the sadly bruised and mishandled corpse was at length wrapped in cloth of gold, with a pillow of brocade, to await the opportunity for further transportation to Goa. This opportunity came with the arrival of a ship from Japan, belonging to Lopez de Norogna. To this vessel the coffin was borne, while the superstitious who were desirous of returning to Goa made haste to travel by the same ship, believing that so precious a cargo must needs ensure a prosperous voyage.

The faith of these passengers, however, was badly tried, for the vessel, old and weather-worn, was battered about hither and thither by an unsual number of storms before it reached Goa. Here at length they arrived and found the Viceroy himself awaiting the coming of the body of Xavier. At the landing-place a choir of young men sang the *Benedictus Dominus Deus Israel,* and when the procession formed ninety white-robed children, wearing chaplets of flowers, and with olive branches in their hands, led the way. Behind them followed the Brotherhood of Mercy, bearing a magnificent standard. Then came the clergy preceding the coffin, which was borne by the Fathers of the Society. Bringing up the rear came the Viceroy and his court with a great company of the inhabitants of Goa. Flowers were rained down upon the coffin from the windows of the houses and so, with many turns and windings, the procession made its way to the College of St. Paul. Here for three days the saint's body lay in state, in the great Chapel of the College. It is not necessary to speak of the miracles said to have been wrought at this time and during the days that followed. The shrine of St. Francis still witnesses to the reverence which all sorts and conditions of men feel to be the due of the Apostle, who is believed to have brought about the conversion in the Indies of no less than five hundred thousand souls.

The influence of Xavier, moreover, did not cease with his death. In each one of the lands where he had laboured the work inaugurated by him continued. Never was the word more completely exemplified, " He, being dead, yet speaketh." It was the fame of this continually expanding influence which caused Pope Paul V, " after a juridical examen of the virtues and miracles " of Father Xavier, to declare his beatification by a Bull issued October 25, 1619. Two years later, the succeeding Pope, Gregory XV, canonized him, with all the form and procedure observed on such occasions, on March 12, 1622. The Bull of canonization was formally issued by the next Pope, Urban VIII.

How are we, without too much concession to the natural credulity of his age, to frame our estimate of the Apostle to the Indies? There certainly seems no need to draw on the reports of miracles, for which evidence was so laboriously compiled for presentation to the authorities at the time of the beatification and canonization. Many of the marvellous stories told at the time and later are but the reflection of the impression made upon the multitude to whom St. Francis ministered. No doubt genuine cases of healing occurred as, under similar circumstances, in modern times. The power of suggestion, directed towards wills which have long been in a state of suspended activity, is in itself enough to account for some of these. It is to be noted, moreover, that the saint himself did not claim the power to work miracles. With regard to one case of supposed raising from the dead, he wrote: " Alas, poor sinner that I am! They set before me a child whom they reported to be dead and who perhaps was not. I commanded him in the name of God to arise; he arose indeed, and there was the miracle."

It is easy to discover through the mists of legend with which the story has been surrounded a true man, human in the best sense of the word. The description given of him about the time of his death affords us without doubt a fairly accurate picture. " He was," says Father Bohours, " six and forty years of age and had passed ten and a half of them in the Indies. His stature was somewhat above the middle size; his constitution strong; his air had a mixture of pleasingness and majesty; he was fresh coloured, had a large forehead, a well proportioned nose; his eyes were blue but piercing and lively; his hair and beard of a dark chestnut; his continual labours had made him gray betimes; and in the last year of his life he was grizzled almost to whiteness."

We may well conceive of the oncoming of these premature signs of age when we reflect upon the prodigious labours he undertook and the suffering he endured. Probably no figure in the entire history of Christian missions has come so near as did St. Francis Xavier to paralleling that amazing catalogue of experiences, given us by the great Apostle to the Gentiles, under pressure of his critics: " Thrice was I beaten with rods, once was I stoned, thrice I suffered shipwreck, a night and a day have I been in the deep; In journeyings often, in perils of rivers, in perils of robbers, in perils by mine own countrymen, in perils by the heathen, in perils in the city, in perils in the wilderness, in perils in the sea, in perils among false brethren; in weariness and painfulness, in watchings often, in hunger and thirst, in fastings often, in cold and nakedness; Besides those things which are without, that which cometh upon me daily, the care of all the Churches." [2]   There is scarcely an item in this marvellous record, which may not be duplicated in the career of Xavier.

In these long journeyings from land to land, moreover, there is no observable restlessness, such as sometimes makes it easy for a man to begin a task he may never be called upon to finish.   Xavier never left a place where he had begun the work of evangelization, without leaving things in a condition where fresh workers would find a foundation on which to build.   He was, indeed, a founder of churches quite as much as he was missionary and evangelist.   Nor did he see any limit to the work which, under God, he felt to be possible.   Like Alexander, he sighed for new worlds to conquer, and in the very year of his death, he wrote that when once China had been won for the Church, he would return to Europe to recover the north from the heresy of Luther.

Nevertheless, the apostolic greatness of St. Francis is not to be measured merely by the unflagging zeal with which he prosecuted his mission.   Indeed, his zeal, as was natural to the age in which he lived, occasionally betrayed him into acts and attitudes which were harsh and in spirit unchristian.   Xavier had many of the limitations of the sixteenth century theologian, Roman Catholic or Protestant.   Apparently he never made any serious effort to understand the religions of the people to whom he preached.   Whether the teachings and practices of the heathen resembled those of his own faith or whether they were in flagrant contradiction to the same, they were equally the work of Satan and to be overthrown without compromise or sympathy.

Nevertheless, in many things Xavier was better than his own conception of the Christian creed. There was, as we find to be the case with other Spanish mystics, such as St. Teresa, a vein of commonsense which made him practical where others might have been fanatical, and which, at any rate in dealing with the vices of his fellow countrymen, sometimes made him singularly considerate and tolerant.

In the furtherance of his work, too, Xavier was inspired by a real delight in the service of God and man. This made it difficult for him to think of his work as labour or of his sufferings as hardships. How naturally, for example, he writes in 1549: " I am at length arrived in Japan, where there is extreme scarcity of all things, which I place among the greatest benefits of Providence . . . it would be impossible to pamper up my body with delicious fare." This naturalness in the allusions to his experiences is often noted by Xavier's biographers. Nugnez, for instance, says: " The Father, Master Francis, in labouring for the salvation of the Saracens and Idolaters, seemed to act not by any infused or acquired virtue, but by a natural motion; for he could neither live nor take the least pleasure but in evangelical employments; in them he found even his repose; and to him it was no labour to conduct others to the love and knowledge of God."

This joy in service sprang from the love of man as well as from the love of God. Or rather it arose from

the love of God, as directed towards concern for the
souls of men. All sorts and conditions of men were
his constant care. If he tried in certain cases to gain
first those who were high in rank, it was because he
believed that through their influence the poor might
be the better approached. In fact, no one was so poor
as not to be partaker of his charity. To be sick or a
prisoner or in any need was to have the readiest pass-
port to his favour. So on shipboard he lived among
the sailors and took part, without condescension, in
their amusements. And, on land, the hospital for incurables rather than the dwelling of the rich was the
irresistible magnet to his feet. To the Portuguese merchants in the Far East Xavier was the ever ready
friend, while insistent in pressing home the message he
had so often heard from Father Ignatius, " What shall
it profit a man, if he gain the whole world and lose
his own soul? "

It is no wonder then that Father Francis was loved
wherever he laboured, for himself as well as for the
work he wrought. It is said that the men of Satsuma,
from whose territory he had been practically expelled,
kept religiously a stone on which he preached and displayed it as a precious relic. It is a remarkable thing,
too, to find that, in spite of constant journeyings and
unintermitting labours, St. Francis always managed to
keep open spaces in his life for other things. This is
illustrated by the saint's devotion to music. He was
forever composing hymns which by their charm might
banish the ribald songs and ballads, which the " new
Christians," before their baptism, had been accustomed to sing. Some of these hymns, we are told,
came to be sung day and night in the open fields as

well as in the houses of the faithful. One of these, at
least attributed to St. Francis, has been dear to millions of Christian worshippers. It is the hymn which
begins and ends with these verses:

" My God, I love Thee, not because
       I hope for heaven thereby,
Nor yet because, if I love not,
       I must forever die.

" So would I love Thee, dearest Lord,
       And in Thy praise will sing;
Solely because Thou art my God,
       And my eternal King."

Above all, in every stage of this extraordinarily active life, Xavier was a man of prayer. The busier he
was, the more he felt the need of resort to prayer, and
the hours he spent before his crucifix were hours often
of trancelike ecstasy, like those which St. Paul described in the words, " Whether in the body or out of
the body I cannot tell."

In conclusion, we cannot avoid noting that genuine
humility, such as never for a moment afforded opening
for the spirit of self or ambition. Father Francis was
from the first under obedience to Father Ignatius,
though at the time of his death it became known that
he might easily, had he returned to Europe, have been
appointed to succeed Loyola as General of the *Order*.

Defects, of course, he had, or he would not have
been human. As already recorded, he apparently
made no attempt at any time to understand the religious beliefs and practices of the heathen. It is to
be feared also that, where Christians were in control,

Xavier was not averse to the employment of force as well as of persuasion for the conversion of unbelievers. But these were elements in the general attitude of the age, confined to no one type of Christianity.

Alas, not so many years after the death of the saint, the religion he had introduced into the Far East, in Japan, came under the ban of the authorities. One of the fiercest and most thoroughgoing persecutions in all religious history broke out at the beginning of the seventeenth century and was relentlessly carried on by the Tokugawa Shoguns. Mr. Gubbins writes of this persecution: " We read of Christians being executed in a barbarous manner, in sight of each other, of their being hurled from the tops of precipices, of their being buried alive, of their being torn asunder by oxen, of their being tied up in rice-bags, which were heaped up together, and of the pile thus formed being set on fire. Others were tortured before death by the insertion of sharp spikes under the nails of their hands and feet, while some poor wretches, by a refinement of horrid cruelty, were shut up in cages and there left to starve with food before their eyes." [3]

It would be vain to claim that recantations were not frequently extorted as the result of this procedure, especially, as has been shown by the investigations of Professor Anesaki, when those suspected of " the evil religion " were confined apart and left to suffer far from the presence and encouragement of their fellow Christians. Moreover, the systematic pressure exerted by the " Kirishitan bugyo," or *Christian Inquisition*, through the compulsory " trampling on the Cross," and through the bribes offered on the notice-boards (Kosatsu), had its effect. Those who had become Christians, from motives less than the highest, were speedily weeded out, but many others remained ready to go to the cross as a witness to their faith. The Dutch trader, Caron, reports that " the number of Christians was not perceptibly lessened by their cruel punishments, they became tired of putting them to death and attempts were then made to make the Christians abandon their faith by the infliction of the most dreadful torments which the most diabolical invention could suggest. The Japanese Christians, however, endured these persecutions with steadiness and courage; very few in comparison with those who remained steadfast in the faith were the number of those who fainted under the trials and abjured their religion." [4]

It should be said, in fairness to the Japanese authorities, that at this very time there were in Europe persecutions of Christians by Christians, hardly less severe than those which were ordered by Hidetada and Iyemitsu. Moreover, the Japanese regarded the persecution as a patriotic effort to protect their land from the insidious wiles of foreigners, who sent their missionaries first in order to obtain a foothold for the soldiers who were to follow. The opposition, too, of the Dutch to the Portuguese and Spanish stooped occasionally even to forgery, in order to convince the Japanese of what they claimed to be the true meaning of the zeal of the friars. The whole hideous story reflects upon the humanity of the West as well as on that of the East.

Yet, after all, St. Francis had his day of vindication. On March 17, 1865, a day still observed by the Roman Catholics of Japan as the *Feast of the Discovery of the Christians*, a considerable number of men and women,

eventually reaching a total of 2,500, marked the passing of the *Edict of Toleration* by coming forth with
a profession of the religion they had secretly maintained from generation to generation. Japanese
Roman Catholicism is still at its strongest in the
neighbourhoods evangelized by Xavier and his immediate successors. What better tribute could we pay
to the reality of the work inaugurated by the great
Apostle to the Indies? [5]

NOTES

[1] Captain F. Brinkley, *History of the Japanese People*, p. 464.

[2] 2 Corinthians 11: 25–28.

[3] See J. H. Gubbins in *Transactions of the Asiatic Society of Japan*, Vol. VI, Part 1, p. 35; cf. J. H. Longford, *The Story of Old Japan*, p. 264 ff.

[4] *The Crucifixion of the Twenty-six*, T. A. S. J. February, 1916.

[5] There is a vast amount of material from which one may gain a good idea of the life and labours of Saint Francis Xavier. The *Letters* are primary, and these are given conveniently for the general reader in *The Life and Letters of Saint Francis Xavier*, by H. Coleridge, 1872. The older biographies, such as that by Torsellino, need to be read with caution; but that of Father Bohours, translated by John Dryden (Vol. XVI in Dryden's Collected Works) is still useful. Other works to be recommended are Otis Carey's *History of Christianity in Japan*, 2 vols., 1909, and *The Life of Saint Francis Xavier*, by E. A. Stuart. Smaller works, which will be read with interest, include *St. Francis Xavier*, by Margaret Yeo, 1932; *To Xavier's Tomb*, by Father Gille; and Father Reville's *Saint Francis Xavier*, 1927. I wish also to acknowledge the help of Father Robert Cairns, of the Catholic Mission, Sancian.

III

WILL ADAMS, THE PILOT

ON the afternoon of January 24, 1934, in the company of a former student, I made my way to the little shrine in the neighbourhood of the Mitsukoshi Department Store, Tokyo, before which stands the monument marking the erstwhile residence of Anjin Sama, or "Mr. Pilot," the Elizabethan sailor, whose fame it is to have been the first Englishman in Japan. Until a few years ago there was an annual celebration in Anjin Cho, "Pilot Street," on June 15; that observance has ceased. But though the story is forgotten by most people in England and by all except a few in Japan, it is still well worth recalling Will Adams to the minds of men, especially in these days when, on both sides of the Pacific, so many obstacles are offered to the mutual good understanding of East and West.

The Kentish pilot, who in the first years of the seventeenth century found a career and a grave in the heart of feudal Japan, was born towards the end of the sixth decade of the sixteenth century in the little town of Gillingham, about two miles from Chatham, where (as Adams proudly declared many years later) "the king's ships do lye." The twelve years of Will's life at Gillingham left no enduring memory, but in the spring of 1934 the association of Anjin Miura was tardily recognized by the erection of a memorial clock tower, for which the funds were provided by the City of London.[1]

The youthful Will turned his back upon his birthplace to become the apprentice of one Nicolas Diggins [2] and it is not an extravagant fancy to imagine him, pack on back and staff in hand, taking his last look at the Church of St. Mary Magdalene, where he had been baptized, and the school in which he had received a good deal of enforced and possibly profitless instruction, to trudge his way towards the great city of London, as two centuries before Dick Whittington had journeyed to stake his " cat " in one of the ventures on the Barbary coast.

London was at this time a city of 300,000 inhabitants, still kept intact with gates which were locked and guarded during the night. But young Will found a way to his Limehouse lodging and soon wore off the sharp edge of homesickness with the sights and sounds of the docks now represented by those glamourous names, St. Katherine's, London, and West Indies, East India Docks. If the boy had no sea fever when he arrived, he was bound in such a vicinity to catch the infection.

We can only guess at the young shipwright's experience during these twelve years in London. It is no extravagant fancy to suppose that somewhere about this time he may have crossed the path of that other Will, who from a different direction had come up to London and had started a career by holding horses at the door of a theatre. There were only two theatres in London at this time: *The Theatre,* between Finsbury Field and the public road which led from Bishopsgate to Shoreditch Church, and *The Curtain,* still nearer to

Will Adams' lodging. It would be natural for a young man strolling from Limehouse and Stepney, to find himself in the neighbourhood of Finsbury and Shoreditch, and first out of curiosity, to get his initiation into the manifold fascination of English drama.

One day, however, in the case of Will Adams, the desire to " see the wonders of the world abroad " burst the bonds of restraint. It was not that he was over-tired with the demands of Master Diggins, though the worthy Nicolas was not one to allow his apprentices to " wear out their youth in shapeless idleness." Will Adams could no longer remain in the ranks of " home keeping youth "; he must play his own part in the epic struggle he felt by intuition to be shaping itself on the horizon of history. So he abandoned Lime-house for a position as " Master Pilot " in Her Majesty's Ships and, so far from getting his stomach full of fighting in the Armada,[3] proceeded thereafter to offer his services to the Worshipful Company of Barbary Merchants, which had been organized under *Letters Patent* granted by Queen Elizabeth in 1585. This Company claimed, grandiloquently enough, " the whole freedom and liberty in the said traffic or trade, unto or from the said country of Barbary, or to or from any part thereof, for the buying and selling of all manner of wares and merchandize whatsoever, that now or customably heretofore have been brought or transported, from or to the said country of Barbary, or from or to any of the cities, towns, places, ports, roads, havens, harbours or creeks of the said country of Barbary, any law, statute, grant, matter, customs, or privileges to the contrary in any wise notwithstanding."

All this was sufficiently ambitious and explicit, with promise, especially in the concluding phrases, of infinite adventure; but unfortunately information is lacking as to any individual part played by our hero in the brave doings of the Barbary Company. So two or three years before the close of the sixteenth century, we find Will Adams at a loose end, though content enough with life ashore for a time, since during this period he undertook the adventure of matrimony. Alas, poor lady, though Mistress Adams [4] bore her husband a son and a daughter, and so passed on the sailor's roving blood to succeeding generations, she was not destined to have much of her husband's company. During all the years of Adams' exile, from 1598 to 1620, the year of his death, we only know of one letter actually received by Mrs. Adams from the wanderer, and the only benefit the deserted wife apparently derived from her marriage, beyond the gift of her children, was a loan of twenty pounds made her by the London East India Company, or friends connected with the same, and a share in her dead husband's estate which she lived but a short while to enjoy.[5]

Notwithstanding any alleviation of the seaman's restlessness brought about by the responsibilities of marriage, we find Will in 1597 looking for a job abroad in the service of the Dutch, in which direction at this particular juncture certain superior opportunities were to be had.

On the subject of the exploitation of the " Indish trade " by the Dutch a few words may here be said. Had Adams waited two years longer he might have had the chance to serve in the Far East with his own countrymen. But in 1598 the organization of the Lon-

don East India Company was still below the horizon.
Even the Dutch East India Company did not receive
its charter from the Netherlands States-general till
nearly two years later. But the Dutch merchants and
shipmasters had already for several years been enjoying a lucrative business in the trade as carried on by
the Portuguese. This they secured by acting in the
capacity of carriers of the commodities of the Orient,
from the port of Lisbon to the ports of northern
Europe. In this way they supplied " the fasting table
of Catholic humanity with the delicacy of pickled
herring." With this position of middlemen the Dutch
were content till after the union of Spain and Portugal
under one crown in 1580. Thenceforth the selfish and
shortsighted policy of Spain brought about the closing
of the port of Lisbon to the Dutch, and the exasper-
ated Hollanders immediately began to plan commercial
ventures of their own.[6] The initial efforts, in order to
avoid a clash with the naval armaments of the Peninsula kingdoms, were by way of the northeast and
northwest passages. These naturally proved futile.
But by this time a Dutchman had returned from the
East with authentic and accurate knowledge of the
trade conditions under the Portuguese Viceroyalty.
This was Jan Huyghen van Linschoten, who as a boy
had shipped in 1579 from Haarlem to Spain and had
there attached himself to the Dominican monk De
Fonseca who became in course of time Archbishop of
Goa. Linschoten came back from a lengthy service in
Portuguese India with a stock of knowledge and ex-
perience which he was eager to put at the service of
his fellow countrymen. He compiled a book called the
Itinerario, editions of which were presently issued in

English, German and Latin. The effect of this publication was immediate. A Dutch merchant, Cornelius
Houtman, took the *Itinerario* as his guide and, with
four ships and two hundred and eighty-four men,
sailed on April 2, 1595 for the Spice Islands. He returned two years later with a sorry crew of sick and
dying men but, by way of compensation, with a treaty
he had obtained between Holland, as represented by
himself, and the Sultan of Bantam in the western part
of Java. He brought also a cargo which aroused the
envy and avarice of other merchants, who determined
forthwith to embark on what they believed to be a
voyage to El Dorado.

It was out of the enthusiasm thus engendered that
Companies sprang up like mushrooms. Commerce
" von Ferne," " of the distant seas," became the dream
of the Dutch navigators. Most of them planned their
voyages by way of the east, with Indonesia as their
goal.[7] The exception is that notable voyage in which
Will Adams played so important a rôle.

In these days the gossip of Rotterdam speedily became the gossip of the London docks, and one day a
Dutch purser, Melchior van Santvoort, confided to a
chance companion, Timothy Shotten,[8] at Gravesend,
the need at Rotterdam of English seamen. Two of
the richest men of the city, it appeared, were prepared
to invest half a million guilders in an expedition which
was to redound to the profits of their house and in-
cidentally to the fame of Dutch navigation. Some
months elapsed before the opportunity ripened and
during these months Will Adams made several trips
back and forth between Rotterdam and the Thames.
But by June 1598 the expedition was ready and five

ships, well equipped by the two merchants according
to the standards of the time, set sail from the Zuyder
Zee for the glamourous East. The five vessels out-
fitted by the generous and forward-looking Peter van
der Hay and Hans van der Wyck were the *Hoop*, the
Liefde, the *Geloof*, the *Trouwe*, and the *Blyde Bloodschap*, stanch little ships, ranging in size from seventy-
five to something over two hundred tons. Will Adams
was Pilot-major on the *Liefde*, a vessel of a hundred
and sixty tons, manned by a hundred and ten sailors,
surely something more than an adequate crew.
Adams' friend, Timothy Shotten, was on the flagship
of the Fleet-general, Jacques Mahu, and Adams'
younger brother was taken on the *Liefde* as a mariner.

Whatever had been the experiences through which
Adams had passed during his association with the Barbary Company, they were soon driven into the background by the tribulations of this extraordinary voyage. It was about the end of June 1598 that the
" fleete of five saile " left the Texel, a date too late to
make possible the crossing of the equator without en-
countering contrary winds. After two months they
reached the Cape de Verde Islands and soon thereafter had their first brush with the Portuguese, who
proved quite the equals of the winds in contrariness,
refusing even water to the ships and meeting every
overture for peace with treachery. Now and then the
Hollanders succeeded in capturing a few live turtle
for the sick folk on board, but sickness continued to
dog their way all through the Gulf of Guinea.[9] Among
those who succumbed was the Admiral, Jacques Mahu.
In one place the voyagers were received by the negro
king, who in honour of his guests powdered himself

white. On this monarch the sailors lavished more in
the way of provisions than they could well afford, hoping to receive at least the equivalent of their hospitality
in return. But his Majesty produced for the much
anticipated banquet no more than a lean goat and four
scraggy chickens. So the disappointed mariners, on
January 2, 1599, with a favouring wind, made another
attempt to cross the line, making good progress but
suffering horribly from ills both real and imaginary.
Sorely affrighted in passing through millions of tiny
organisms which made the sea appear incarnadine with
blood, one sailor went out of his head and died raving,
while another in his madness tried to bite everybody
within reach. Nobody possessed a sufficiency of warm
clothing, and one man died in agony after enduring
the unskilful amputation of his frozen feet.

At last, early in April, the weary mariners reached
the Straits of Magellan, a region of snow and wind and
biting cold. Here many died of exposure, including
the captain of the *Trouwe*. Others were murdered by
the natives when a landing was attempted in search of
firewood. They stayed in the Straits till September
24, when a great gale scattered the fleet. The *Geloof*
made persistent efforts to find her sister ship, the
Trouwe, but encountered instead the vessel of Oliver
van Noort, who was on the last stage of the first Dutch
circumnavigation of the globe. Supplied by van Noort
with much needed provender, the *Geloof* then returned
to Holland, arriving home in the July of 1600 with a
crew of but thirty-six and these in the last stages of
disease. The *Trouwe* continued on across the Pacific
to India and was there captured by the Portuguese,
though six of her survivors subsequently escaped from

Goa and found their way eventually back to Holland. Of the fate of the *Blyde Bloodschap* nothing is known, but of the remaining vessels of the fleet, the *Liefde* succeeded in passing the Straits and on reaching the coast of Chile was unexpectedly joined by the *Hoop*. Both ships suffered terribly from attacks by natives when they landed in search of wood and water. The *Liefde* lost her captain and twenty-three of her crew, whose heads were carried to the Spanish town of Concepçion, while the *Hoop*, in similar affrays, lost her captain and twenty-seven of the crew. Among these latter was Thomas Adams, Will's dearly loved younger brother. There was, however, little time for grief, since new officers had to be elected by the men. It was under these circumstances that Will Adams was put in charge of the *Liefde*. Yet the unlucky ships still appeared to be between the devil and the deep sea, in peril from Spaniards, Indians, lack of food, bleak coasts and stormy seas, while another terrible winter loomed just ahead. The safest plan seemed to be to continue westward across the Pacific towards the Empire of Japan. Unknown as was at this time this strange land, it appeared to offer fewer terrors than the ills they had already experienced. So, on November 27, 1599, the two ships left the island of Santa Maria, lost a few more of their men in one last effort to replenish their supplies of water, and then continued their course till, on February 23, 1600, a fierce gale, described by Adams as " a wonderous storme of wind as ever I was in," separated the two ships forever. The *Hoop* apparently went down with all hands. The *Liefde* weathered the storm and on April 19, 1600 the tired and weather-beaten crew, of whom only six, beside Adams, could stand upon their feet, came in sight of the welcome coast of Bungo. The ship brought with it from afar something of the destiny of Japan.

The coast of Bungo, on the southern island of the archipelago called Kiushiu, was indeed welcome, but the perils of the *Liefde's* survivors were by no means over. As Adams dropped his anchor in a bight where the waters were almost calm, he perceived a motley crowd on the beach interested in his arrival. There were fishermen, peasants, wayfarers, priests and a number of women, and presently sampans appeared surrounding the vessel filled with islanders eager to catch the first close-up view of the strangers. Adams, Santvoort and five others were brought ashore, while the others, sick and dying, remained on board. It was difficult to prevent everything on board from being immediately stolen by the excited natives, or even to avert from the foreigners acts of violence. But soon a Portuguese priest of the neighbourhood was discovered and brought along to act as interpreter, and though the Jesuit hostility to Dutch and English was as open as that of the Dutch and English to the Jesuits, Adams and his companions were glad enough to avail themselves of the services of the friars. Three men died soon after the landing, and three others on the following day, but the survivors, gathering together a few of the things, including Adams' pocket-compass which had been rescued from the pilferers, awaited the next stroke of their fate.[10]

It came presently in the arrival of an envoy who expressed the desire of the Shogun-to-be, Iyeyasu, to meet the two principal foreigners at his castle in

Osaka. Here a few words are necessary to explain the situation in Japan at the time of the *Liefde's* coming. Two years earlier Japan's greatest soldier, Toyotomi Hideyoshi, military dictator from 1582 to 1598, in succession to Oda Nobunaga, had passed away, leaving his minor son, Hideyori, under the guardianship of his trusted lieutenant, Tokugawa Iyeyasu, and four others. But the Tokugawa, pleading with himself the precedent which Hideyoshi had earlier set in dispossessing the children of Nobunaga, showed no intention of respecting his pledged word and was already preparing to assert his supremacy in civil war. Although Iyeyasu did not actually become Shogun till 1603, he was already in 1600 assuming authority as Regent, gathering together the clans of his supporters, and preparing for the struggle with the supporters of Hideyori. At this juncture he was staying at his great castle at Osaka, the mightiest fortress in all Japan. Hither, such were the orders transmitted, Adams and Santvoort were to proceed immediately.

Of the journey thither it is not necessary to speak in detail. It included twenty days of travel across the Inland Sea to Sakai. These were days which must have been full of interest, not unmixed with anxiety, from the hour when the sailors raised their voices to the *kami* of the sea and turned their vessels, with streamers fluttering at the masthead, towards the north. They would clear the Bungo channel while it was still light, but in the Island Sea the risk was less and there would be liberty to look around and learn from the lips of the Portuguese interpreter something of the significance of the historic shores they passed. So they came to Sakai and thence travelled overland for some ten

miles towards Osaka, Adams on a caparisoned horse
and attended by a bodyguard.

The first sight of Osaka must have been moving and
impressive. It was the greatest city Adams had seen
since he left London, one of the five imperial cities of
Japan and situated among scenes that carry the mind
back to the earliest traditions of Japan. As for the
castle, built by Hideyoshi less than a generation before, and rearing its gigantic ramparts in a great square
more than two and a half miles around, it could not
fail to astonish. The strangers could only see the
outer wall, with its stones of incredible size flaring out-
wards and downwards to the water's edge, and its but-
tressed moles rising towards the golden dolphin which
crowned the keep, and the sky. The Yodo River
washed the castle walls on the north, and a tributary
of the same river defended it on the east. Not only
Adams and his companions but all the rest, without
exception, thought with considerable trepidation of
their entrance on the morrow within the confines of
this colossal fortress. The prisoners, for such indeed
Adams and Santvoort were, were led through one
narrow street after another till in one which seemed
to be but the merest alley, not very far from the main
gateway of the Castle, a door suddenly opened for
them and they found themselves in a place which might
have been a prison or an inn of the meaner sort.

Of the first meeting between Adams and the Regent
imagination must fain have a hand in the description.[11]
When the Englishman and his companion, accompanied
by the Jesuit, passed from the inn yard through the
portals of the Castle, climbed the ramp to the second
gate, and then once again to the inner circumvallation,

they had leisure enough to ponder on the wonders of
this famous structure erected by Hideyoshi. At last,
in the Hall of Audience, whose walls were hung with
weapons of various sorts, they suddenly became aware,
through the removal of the screens, of the presence of
the man in whose hands, and those of his family, the
destinies of Japan were to lie for over two hundred
and fifty years. The seated figure of the Regent made
no immediate impression. Iyeyasu was of medium
stature, of rather rotund form, with a kind of moon
face in which the eyes seemed for most of the time
narrowed to slits. Yet his fellow countrymen had already learned to discount the physical unimpressive-
ness of the man, as well as his miserliness and his in-
elegant handwriting. They had learned to appreciate
the indomitable will and had both seen him and heard
his voice upon the field of battle. They laughed indeed over his habit of taking a hot bath before a con-
flict and of going into battle with a handkerchief
knotted over his head instead of a helmet. But they
knew him also as the seasoned soldier, who had won
his laurels in the service of Nobunaga and had continued his military career under Hideyoshi. The final
decision, which established Iyeyasu as the unques-
tioned master of Japan, was yet to come, but men
recognized already the qualities which, after his death,
made of him a god.

Here then the Regent sat, in his plain dress of dark
brocaded silk, his head-dress with the customary plume
of black lacquer, watching with alert composure the
entrance of the various groups, who pressed forward
to secure his attention. What took place on this occasion between Iyeyasu and the shipwrecked sailors

may be briefly summarized, in part guessed at. The
Jesuit was forward not merely to interpret but also to
accuse the new arrivals of piracy and heresy. But the
Regent was aware of something in the eyes and mien
of Adams, which he did not need to have translated
for him. The fortune which led the Englishman to
bring into the presence of Iyeyasu his pocket-compass
and to explain its use had more to do with his re-
mand in safety than the passionate outburst in
mingled Dutch and English, in which his defence was
presented. " Two strong men " were " face to face,"
though they came " from the ends of the earth." So
the meeting was fraught with much that was to determine the next chapters in the history of Japan. Had
the intercourse thus begun been suffered to continue
unimpeded, still more might have happened such as
would have altered the history of the entire Far East.

We should have to draw very largely on fancy to
make the story of Will Adams in any wise complete,
but there is little difficulty in reconstructing the tale
for the next few months. Another and more leisurely
interview took place with Iyeyasu, this time Adams
being alone, but it was plain that the Regent had much
on his mind at this time besides the fate of a few castaways. Ishida Mitsunari was already collecting the
clans who had supported the falling fortunes of the
Toyotomi house, and Iyeyasu knew that the imminent
campaign was to be no walk-over. Yet he took un-
common interest in the efforts of Adams to explain the
use of the other ship's instruments which by this time
had been retrieved, and there was a new light in his
eye as he watched the sailor's handling of cross-staff,
dividers or astrolabe, or as he listened to the broken

efforts of the Englishman and the Jesuit to make the science of the seaman more intelligible. Perhaps, the Regent's interest was keenest when Adams unfolded the rough chart he had made of the voyage and endeavoured to show the geographical position of Japan in its relation to that of his native land.

This time when Adams was dismissed it was with permission to return to the ship and his Dutch companions, a journey successfully accomplished under guard. Will was received by the survivors of the *Liefde* " with weeping eyes, for it was given them to understand that I was executed long since." The next days were busily employed in the cleaning and refurbishing of the vessel and hearts beat high with the hope that, once the new sails were sewn, they might be able to set out for Europe. They were quite unaware of the fact that they were being guarded more sedulously than ever, though so great was the friendliness of all about them that no suspicion arose as to their being under compulsion to remain.

The priests, who had at first been all for having the castaways put to death as heretics, now showed themselves as eager to get them away from the shores of Japan and made shrewd plans to assist their escape to Nagasaki and thence by the next boat to Europe. But Adams, though as little as ever minded to stay longer in the islands than was necessary, sensed some unspoken menace in devices of this sort, and decided that for him the better part was to remain for the present the Shogun's guest. Meanwhile, the Japanese spoken around him was becoming less unintelligible and he was less than at first dependent on his Jesuit interpreters.

At last there arrived the longed-for permission to sail, but in the unexpected form of a command to take the vessel to Yedo Bay, where Iyeyasu was desirous of yet another interview with the strangers. This order created a good deal of excitement and it was a motley crew in charge of little better than a derelict, which prepared for the journey to Uraga Bay. The seamen patched their rags and trimmed their beards and then committed themselves to the pilotage of the Japanese guards, who did their best to appear something less unfriendly.

Arriving at Yedo, "the Way of the Bay," Adams and Santvoort had leisure to admire duly the new city which the genius of Iyeyasu was creating, to become for the next three hundred years the administrative capital of Japan. They learned doubtless something of the romantic history of the site. Here, in the fifteenth century, a certain daimyo, caught in a shower of rain, had begged from a peasant girl the loan of a straw cloak. The maid had answered him in a cryptic verse which, when it was interpreted, gave Ota Dokwan the ambition to become a poet. He became famed not only for his poetry but also for the not too sumptuous castle which he built among the fishermen's huts of the neighbourhood. Two years before the date of Adams' arrival in Japan, Hideyoshi and Iyeyasu, his lieutenant, had engaged in a campaign against the clans of the Kwanto, or Eastern district. After the capture of the Castle of Odawara, Hideyoshi pointed to the little fishing village on the shores of Uraga Bay called Yedo. There, said he, should be the capital of the Empire. There, with the sea in front and the hills behind, Ota Dokwan had chosen for his

castle the site which was fitted to be the heart of all
Japan. Hideyoshi then offered Iyeyasu the region of
the Kwanto, together with a revenue of two and a half
million *koku*. It was to this place that Iyeyasu returned when he found himself Shogun and the undis-
puted master of Nippon. He had already determined
upon the main outlines of his plan and had engaged
tens of thousands of men to level the hills, fill the
marshes, and prepare the site for residence on the
part of the clan hostages. Above all, he was already
piling up the ramparts of his own castle within the im-
mense moat, which was to enclose in the future the
present Imperial Palace. Much had to be done in
haste and more still left for the leisure of the future,
since the veterans of Hideyoshi's army were on their
way back from Korea, and a *League,* including five
governors of provinces and prominent generals, among
them two Christian generals, Konishi and Ikeda, was
now assuming menacing proportions.

To this Yedo-in-the-making, as guests or prisoners
of a Shogun-in-the-making came the crew of the
Liefde, but it was disconcerting to Adams to find that
he was now separated from his crony Santvoort and
consigned to lodgings in the house of an old soldier
named Magome Sageyu. This man had two daughters
whose presence added much to the Englishman's embarrassment. That the younger of these should be the
innocent instrument of fate, in determining so many
of the issues of Adams' last years, probably at the
time never occurred to the sailor's mind. His thoughts,
so far as we can tell, were still occupied with a speedy
return to his forlorn family in his native land.

But straying thoughts of any sort were dissipated

with the arrival of a messenger, summoning Will
Adams to the palace and the presence of Iyeyasu.
During the mile-long walk from his lodging, with his
interpreter Mitsu, Adams observed all the signs of that
activity which was fast transforming a fishing village
into a great capital. On his arrival at the palace, he
was more than astonished to learn how far his own fate
was to be linked with the Regent's plans. He was informed through the interpreter that he was required to
sell the *Liefde* to Iyeyasu and stay on in his employ,
to build more ships and so further the Regent's plans
for international trade—plans which had been slowly
forming since the first interview with the English
pilot. When he left Yedo Castle, Adams knew himself as one in the grip of destiny, and for the first time
in his life unable to look with any sense of freedom
towards the future.

Of the next events in the story of Anjin Sama it is
impossible to speak except in the sketchiest fashion.
Will reported to Santvoort and the others as hopefully
as he could about the leasing of the *Liefde's* ordnance
and of the probability of their having to stay in the
country for a year or so. But, deep in his heart, he
felt that he was not to escape so easily from the mesh
of circumstance which had involved him. The chief
worry at this time was his relation to Bikuni San, the
younger of old Magome's daughters. That he should
prove unfaithful to his deserted English wife he did
not at this time dream, but he could not fail to note
the beguiling courtesies of Bikuni San. And when one
day Santvoort came in to announce his own marriage
to the daughter of his host, the carpenter, another
piece of hitherto solid ground seemed to crumble be-

neath his feet. Yet there were business matters still
to be transacted between himself and Iyeyasu, and
when the money arrived for the guns and had been
satisfactorily divided among the sailors concerned,
Adams felt that the portion falling to his own share
enabled him to put himself on a better footing with
Magome by paying his way as a lodger.

Whether the buying of the guns had at all influenced
the plans of Iyeyasu cannot be known, but by this
time the issue between him and the forces under Ikeda
Mitsunari had become ripe for settlement. The Regent found it timely to ask the *League* leaders as to
their intentions, and when the result turned out to be
a somewhat defiant reply, mobilization commenced on
both sides. The *League* army consisted of many of the
southern and western clans, but there was no real cen-
tralization of authority or unity of purpose. On the
other hand, Iyeyasu's army was of one mind, and
when he reared his standard of the golden fan and his
white banner with the Tokugawa hollyhocks, many of
the doubtful ones rallied to his side. Men told him
that the gate of the West was shut and he replied
promptly, " I shall open it then with my sword." Some
peasants brought him a basket of persimmons (in
Japanese, *o-gaki*) ; he punned on the word and predicted that Ogaki, the castle then held by the *League*,
would fall into his hands. Without delay he pushed
towards the West and chose as his battlefield Sekigahara, " the Plain of the Barrier," just west of Lake
Biwa and on the main road leading from Yedo to
Kyoto. Here was fought, on September 15, 1600, one
of the great decisive battles in the history of Japan,
a battle which sealed the fate of the Island Empire for

two hundred and fifty years to come. The *League* army, lighting fires on the hillside to guide them, marched out from Ogaki Castle with Konishi Yukinaga in command of the left wing and Ikeda on the extreme left. During the early part of the day it rained hard, but when Iyeyasu got information of the advance, he cried with glee, " The enemy has fallen into my hands." Then the rain changed to a dense fog and the two armies clashed almost before they were visible one to the other. Soon, however, the fog cleared and, amid the sound of drums and conches, firing of match-locks, whizzing of arrows, and the booming of cannon, the battle joined in earnest. It was fought, in spite of the guns, mainly with swords and spears, and so desperately that even Iyeyasu's confidence might have miscarried, had not an entire army corps of the *League* deserted to him in the thick of the fray. Then came a charge along the whole line and, amid dreadful butchery, the western army fled the field. Thousands, some say forty thousands, were slain; many committed *seppuku* when they saw their cause irretrievably lost. Most of the leaders, including Konishi and Ikeda, were pursued, captured and beheaded. These latter, as Christians, scorned the way out by suicide. When at last the victory was assured, the triumphant Tokugawa sat on his camp-stool, ordered his helmet to be brought, and made the memorable remark, " After victory, tighten the strings of your helmet."

The remark describes Iyeyasu's policy to the letter. Although he did not receive from the Emperor his commission as Shogun till 1603, from the date of Sekigahara he was the only ruler known to the majority of the Japanese. To Adams he was " the ould Emperour."

At Yedo, Iyeyasu now pressed with vigour his long cherished designs. The great castle, intended to eclipse the splendid fabric reared by Hideyoshi at Osaka, was now completed. Brilliant pageants were devised to dazzle the crowd. All over the land, daimyates were redistributed and the confiscated estates allotted to members of the Tokugawa family. Every daimyo was ordered to reside for a certain part of the year at Yedo and members of every clan detained as hostages. In these and other ways, the crafty Shogun labored to perfect the instrument he had reason to believe " fool-proof " and capable of much effectiveness even under the weakest of his successors.

It was some time before the victorious Iyeyasu was at liberty again to see much of the Englishman, but during these days and weeks much was happening to occupy Adams' time. The *Liefde* was slowly rotting in the Bay and her former crew was at about the same rate dispersing in various directions. Two of them— Conway and Otwater—had been executed for claiming sole ownership of the vessel and its cargo. Several of the rest had escaped overseas from Nagasaki. But Adams and Santvoort still remained the Regent's guests, albeit they knew well that the word " guest " was but a synonym for captive. If the question be asked as to what Adams did in this little oasis of time, the answer must still be given with some indulgence in guesswork. Yet we may think of him as practising fence with old Magome Sageyu, as making small models of ships to float upon the water and catch the breezes of Uraga Bay, as making the acquaintance of all and sundry who visited Magome's home, including some Spaniards and Filipinos, who brought word as to the possibilities of the Nagasaki trade. Beyond all in importance was the slowly ripening consciousness of a relationship to Bikuni San which, treacherous as it seemed to the memory of an English wife and mother, was in moments of cool reflection, under the circumstances, only the natural result of an enforced propinquity. In truth, it was Bikuni who did most of the wooing, for Adams held back not only out of respect to his pledged troth but also because he would not offer himself as a son-in-law to Magome except as the soldier's equal, a two-sworded samurai by the grace of Iyeyasu himself.

It was this last consideration which governed his attitude towards the Regent when, after successive meetings, he found himself the recipient of a demand for ships. The way had been well prepared. Iyeyasu had asked him as to his religion and Will had answered with the sailor's simple creed, " I said in God that made heaven and earth." He was asked as to the possibilities of voyages to the north and Adams told of all the expeditions of which there was knowledge ere he left England.[12] He expatiated also on the opportunities offered, on the basis of maps he had made, and conversations he had had with the old Japanese sea-dog, Shongo Sama. At last, the Shogun came bluntly to the point. Would Adams build ships for ventures Iyeyasu had in mind? Adams as bluntly made request for his two swords that he might marry the daughter of Magome. For a while they sparred with one another. " What of my ships? " asked the one, and, " What of my swords? " replied the other. Naturally the battle of wits and wills ended in a mutual agreement. Iyeyasu looked confidently forward to the

opening of a trade, such as should confound the Dutchmen of Hirado, while Adams went home reflectively to
ask his soldier host for the nowise reluctant hand of
his younger daughter.

Very shortly after, with his two swords promptly delivered from the Castle, and with them the promise of
a daily grant of rice from the Regent's own store, and
sundry other favours, Will Adams of Gillingham found
himself a samurai of Japan, the husband of a samurai's
daughter, busily engaged with paper and a piece of
charcoal sketching out the lines of Japan's first foreign-
built ship, " in all respects as our English manner is."
One cloud still vexed his horizon, apart, of course,
from such shadows on his conscience as came from the
memory of Mistress Adams in England, and that was
whether it were fitting for a samurai to trade, since he
was firmly resolved on handling at Yedo an agency for
the commerce carried on from Nagasaki.

The ship that gradually took shape before the eyes
of its builders was not a large one, but it was in many
respects different from those familiar to the Japanese.
It was built for sailing only and not for rowing. Its
body was rounded instead of narrowing to the long
keel, which ordinarily ran from stem to stern. Instead
of the usual wide opening astern made for the more
convenient management of the rudder, the vessel was
planked up to the deck line and there was no elevation
of the deck astern as was commonly the case. The
general effect was of something stanch and strong, and
intended for voyages beyond the limits of the archipelago. The firs and cedars, hewn under Adams'
direction in the neighbouring hills, had all been specially selected for a vessel which the builder expected,

in any event, to survive himself and perhaps keep the
name of Anjin Sama alive in the land. When, on rare
occasions, Iyeyasu came down to watch the growth of
the ship into a thing of beauty, the desire increased
in his heart for more ships—ships to sail to Mexico
and the Indies, to Malacca and the Californias. Who
could predict the end?

Will Adams was now in the way of settling down as
one in most particulars a Japanese. He had been created a *hatamoto*, or minor daimyo, with an estate in
the fair region of Hemi, yielding ten thousand *koku*
of rice, and with ninety husbandmen to till his fields.
The Lady Bikuni bore her lord, first a little son whom
Will named Joseph, out of far-away memory of the
Bible hero who had been sold into slavery in a foreign
land and wedded to a woman of alien race. A year
afterwards a little girl was added to the family. Will
might well have named her " Forgetfulness," since
thoughts of the home land were getting fainter and
fewer with the passing months, but she seems to have
been named Susannah.

There is not much else with which we can fill the
record of the next succeeding years. Much of Adams'
time was spent at Hemi, for Iyeyasu was an exacting
master, particularly in the case of those upon whom
he had bestowed his favours. The Tokugawa had become Shogun in reality in 1603, by actual commission
from the Emperor, and during the two following years
he spent most of the time consolidating the political
instrument which, as already mentioned, was to outlast
his own life by a quarter of a millennium. Then in
1605, without at all relinquishing the substance of

power, he caused his son Hidetada to be appointed Shogun in his stead, while he sat back, not too remotely, to watch the functioning of the machine. Hidetada was by no means the man his father was, but outside his attitude of hostility to the " Kirishitan," he was not a ruler to be despised. As one who arrived on the battlefield of Sekigahara too late to render much service, Hidetada was esteemed as something of a laggard, but he may be summed up fairly enough as " a hard, painstaking, conscientious plodder."

Several years later, when the supposedly abdicated Shogun one day crossed the path of Hideyori, the son of his predecessor Hideyoshi, at Osaka, Iyeyasu recognized instinctively the need of entering again the world of affairs to avert disaster from his house. For Hideyori, who had once been his ward, and was now entering upon the period of manhood, had still many friends in the south, who were ready to rally to his cause, when it became clear that the ex-Shogun had no intention of respecting the lad's inherited rights. So the last years of Iyeyasu's life were like the first, years of warfare and intrigue.

But for these years between 1605 and 1611, the Tokugawa head was fairly well assured of the permanence of his clan control, and so could give himself to the carrying out of more personal designs. One of these led to further cultivation of the talents of Will Adams. Will wrote later to his " Unknowne Frinds and countri-men " of Iyeyasu that " beeing in such grace and favour, by reason I learned him some points of jeometry, and understanding of the art of mathematickes, with other things: I pleased him so, that what I said he would not contrarie." He adds: " At which my former ennemies did wonder; and at this time must intreat me to do them a friendship, which to both Spaniards and Portingals have I doen: recompencing them good for evill."

Such toleration was not common in these days, and it may well have been a surprise to the Spaniards that an Englishman, who had played his part in the repelling of the Armada, should have been willing to ease their relations with the Shogun, and this on the brink of one of the fiercest religious persecutions in history.

No less beholden to Will's good offices were the Dutch, who knew more about the founding of the *London East India Company* than they permitted to reach the Englishman's ears, and at the same time did whatever they found possible to capitalize his favour at court. So Adams was back and forth at Yedo not a little and went even further afield on Iyeyasu's errands. The Shogun continued his interest in the shipbuilding, and the launching of the first vessel of eighty-two tons was so successful that Iyeyasu must of necessity commission Adams to build a larger. The result was that after Will had tested his handiwork in a voyage or two in the smaller vessel, a bigger one was built of some hundred and twenty tons. "In this ship," wrote Adams later, " I have made a voyage from Meako (Kyoto) to Eddo (Yedo), being as far as from London to the Lizards or the Land's End." It is to be noted that Anjin Sama still retained his English standards of distance. The story of the second vessel is somewhat involved. As nearly as we can follow the somewhat tortuous language of the letter already quoted, Iyeyasu lent this bigger ship to the Spanish Governor of the Philippine Islands, in order that the latter might

sail, with eighty of his men, to Acapulco, in Mexico.
Apparently the loan followed the shipwreck, off the
Japanese coast, of a great Spanish vessel, the *San
Francisco*, in which the Governor was just about to
sail for the Americas. Adams says that the wrecked
ship was of " about a thousand tunnes " and that about
three hundred and fifty men were saved and thirty-six
drowned. It was the loss of this vessel which prompted
Iyeyasu's offer of Adams' ship, " with a great present
and with an Embassadour to the Emperor (Iyeyasu)
giving him thanks for his great friendship: and also
sent the worth of the Emperour's ship in goods and
money: which shippe the Spaniards have now in the
Phillippines." [13]

There is no doubt that during these years, with activities at Hemi and Yedo, Adams was a very busy
man. Whether he was a happy man is not so certain.
Old memories would not down and when the arrival
of a foreign ship, or the receipt of news from Europe
awakened the call of blood and race, there would come
upon him an almost overwhelming fit of nostalgia.
With knowledge that the way back lay so invitingly
open, all that he possessed and loved in Japan suddenly
came to weigh upon him like a mass of lead hung
around his neck. He had given too many hostages to
fortune to expect peace through flight. He knew that
whichever way he turned, he would face spectres such
as were not easily exorcised. Nevertheless, from
time to time, the temptation to shake the bars of his
prison, if only to test their strength, was beyond his
power to resist. So he writes: " In the ende of five
yeeres, I made supplication to the king to goe out of
this land, desiring to see my poore wife and children

according to conscience and nature." The request was in vain. Iyeyasu " was not well pleased " with it and ordered the petitioner to " byde in the land." A little later, when news came that certain Hollanders were at hand, it " rejoyced us much, with hope that God should bring us to our countrey againe, by one meanes or other." So he renewed his supplication and " boldly spake myselfe with him," with the same result, though Will pleaded that he could do much to bring the traffic of English as well as Hollanders to the Empire. The Shogun remained still as adamant to the proposal.

The climax came in 1611, when opportunity came to transmit a letter to his " Unknowne Frinds and countri-men," through the agency of certain Dutch factors at Bantam. It seems that two copies of this letter were sent, in case one or the other should miscarry. The epistle was directed to the " Worshipfull Fellowship of the Merchants of London trading into the East Indies." It is a memorable document, in that it had much to do with the historic effort to establish trade intercourse between England and Japan in the early seventeenth century. A few words of this letter may be quoted: " Therefore I do pray and intreate you in the name of Jesus Christ to doe as much as to make my being here in Iapon knowen to my poor wife: in a manner a widdow, and my two children fatherlesse: which thing only is my greatest griefe of heart and conscience." How deeply he had pondered in exile on days that were no more is poignantly revealed in the ensuing words: " I am a man not unknowen in Ratcliffe and Limehouse, by name to my good Master Nicholas Isaac, and William Isaac, brothers, with many others; also to Master William Jones, and Master

Becket. Therefore may this letter come to any of
their hands, or the copy; I doe know that compassion
and mercy is so that my friends and kindred shall have
newes that I doe as yet live in this vale of my sorrow-
full pilgrimage; the which thing again and again I do
desire for Jesus Christ his sake." Again, at the close:
" Thus, in briefe, I am constrained to write, hoping that
by one meanes or other, in processe of time, I shall
heare of my wife and children: and so with pacience I
wait the good will and pleasure of Almity God. Therefore I do pray all them, or every one of them, that if
this my letter shall com to their hands to doe the best,
that my wife and children, and my good acquaintance,
may heere of mee; by whose good meanes I may in
processe of time, before my death heare newes, or see
som of my friendes agein. The which thinge God turn
it to his glory. Amen. Dated in Iapon the two and
twentieth of October 1611. By your unworthy friend
and servant, to command in what I can, William
Adams."

In all this there is no word of Bikuni San. Was
there conscious and deliberate hypocrisy? Or did Will
feel that to no other than God Himself was explanation
possible? We can but record the external activities of
the man, without attempting to lay bare the workings
of his heart and conscience. In any case, these contacts with Europe, few and far between as they were,
surely reopened the old wounds and removed for ever
the expectation of any ultimate anodyne save that of
death.

We must now make a digression from the personal
story of Will Adams to tell of the founding of the

London East India Company, the notable event which brought other Englishmen to the shores of Japan. Yet in truth there is no real digression, since Adams had a capital part in inducing the Company to send its agents to the Sunrise Empire. If the story of the enterprise in Japan turned out to be but brief, little more indeed than one of lamentable failure, it has to be remembered that the brevity and the failure alike were due to the refusal of Sir John Saris to follow the advice of Anjin Sama. Had our hero been but permitted his own way, not only would English trade have become in Japan a settled affair but the entire history of Japan and the Far East would in all probability have been changed.

Ere the end of the sixteenth century, commercial circles in England had become increasingly dissatisfied with the condition of their overseas trade. It was small consolation to know that the Papal Bull of 1493 was being successfully defied by the Dutch. The Dutch in their turn had begun to claim a monopoly of the East Indian commerce and Shakespeare's dream of "a new map with the augmentation of the Indies," so far as Englishmen were concerned, seemed destined to remain unfulfilled. The Dutch monopoly in the Spice Islands was particularly galling and Englishmen complained: "The Dutch have gained all the foreign freight, whilst our ships lie still and decay or go to Newcastle for coals."

Yet, then as now, a specific grievance was needed to bring dissatisfaction to a head. This appeared when the Hollanders raised the price of pepper from three shillings to eight shillings a pound. Then the London merchants became themselves so peppery with rage that a meeting was called, on September 22, 1599, with

the Lord Mayor in the chair, to discuss the matter.
At this meeting it was decided that only by the for-
mation of a Joint Stock Company could the situation
be met. At once over a hundred sturdy and indignant
citizens set down their names to a subscription which
presently aggregated over thirty thousand pounds.

The new-born Company had many storms to weather
ere it received the Royal Charter. It became plain
that if the Company were to function, reaching out to,
and receiving wealth from, the seventeen listed realms,
a much larger subscription must be raised. So, at last,
Queen Elizabeth, on December 31, 1600, in her state-
liest manner, issued the famous Charter " for the
Honour of our Nation, the Wealth of our People, the
Increase of our Navigation, and the Advancement of
lawful Traffick to the benefit of the Commonwealth."
It conceded the solemn right of trading with all
countries beyond the Cape of Good Hope or the Straits
of Magellan for a term of fifteen years. Interlopers
were to be suitably punished with forfeiture of their
ships and cargoes. Thus the creation of the Company
was made the occasion for a kind of counterblast to
Pope Alexander's Bull, with added defiance of the too
successful Hollanders. Until 1612 the accepted plan
was that of Separate Voyages, by which the shareholders received a dividend on the profits of the ships sep-
arately. But in the reign of James I the fifteen year
Charter was superseded by one which ran " for ever,"
though the canny Scots monarch qualified his liberality
by providing for revocation, should the traffic not prove
profitable to himself and the realm.

So the *London East India Company* started on its
historic career. The earlier coat-of-arms showed a pic-

ture of three ships under full sail, with the motto, *Deus Indicat,* in which the reader will detect a punning reference to India. It was not till 1698 that this coat-of-arms was changed to the better known shield, with its lion supporters, and the familiar legend, *Auspicio Regis et Senatus Angliae.*

It must be confessed that the first adventures of the Company were not startlingly successful. An illustration is to be found in the voyage of Captain George Weymouth in 1602. The captain offered for the sum of five hundred pounds to take his ship to Cathay by the Northwest Passage and so save the tedious journey round the Cape of Good Hope. For this he made large preparation, spiritual as well as material. Not only did he lay in a stock of " hides to make the mariners' cassocks, breeches and gowns," but he also engaged " John Cartwright, of London, Preacher," to act as chaplain, at a stipend of three pounds a month. Only half of this magnificent sum was to be paid if they failed to reach China and, as a matter of fact, on the failure of the expedition, the unfortunate parson was not only robbed of the moiety of his promised salary but was asked to return " the gowne and apparel " in which he was expected to grace the Chinese court. In brief, the shareholders lost their money and Queen Elizabeth's letters were undelivered.

We may scarcely regard the voyage of Sir John Saris to Japan as in the same category with that of Captain Weymouth. Yet, in view of what might have happened, had Adams' advice been followed, it too must be set down a failure. Saris had already acquired much experience in the East Indies, going out first with Sir Henry Middleton in 1604 to Java. When Middleton

left Bantam, Saris stayed behind as a factor for the
Company in the island from which the Portuguese had
been driven by the Dutch in 1596, but in which the
English too had succeeded in establishing a factory.
It was here that Saris remained till 1609, living under
the rather patriarchal conditions then in vogue, all
under one roof, taking their meals in common, obliged
to be in bed at an early hour, with daily prayers and
rigid rules against dicing, excessive drinking, and
" brabbles." He must have fretted considerably under
these regulations, since he quarreled with a good many
people from first to last, and earned the reputation of
being " self-opinionated, suspicious and of shallow
judgement."

It was on April 18, 1611, that Sir John started on
his most memorable voyage, as commander of the
Clove, with two other ships, *Hector* and *Thomas,* in
company as far as the Spice Islands. He bore with
him a special letter from King James for delivery to
the Emperor of Japan. By August he was five leagues
off the Cape of Good Hope, and a month later was
running up the east coast of Africa by the Mozambique
Channel. At Mocha, over a trivial matter of preced-
ence, he quarreled definitely with Middleton and this
brought about the latter's return to England forthwith.
Saris proceeded to Bantam, arriving on October 24 and
staying till the following January. Then he sailed
away in the *Clove* for the Moluccas, experienced the
usual amount of opposition from the Dutch, and departed for the Empire of Japan.

Now it so happened that just about the time of
Saris' sailing from Java, Adams was addressing letters
thither to his " good and loving friend," Augustus

Spalding, in which a strong plea was made for the
speedy sending of one of the English Company's vessels. He wrote that he had received two letters from
England shortly before; one from the Governor of the
Company, Sir Thomas Smythe, and one from " my
good friend, John Stokle." In each of these, mention
is made of the sending of a ship, and Adams was eager
that his own experience should be of use to the Company. "I doo prayse God for it," he wrote, " who
hath geven me favour with the Emperour, and good will
to me, so farr as that I may boldly say our countrymen
shall be so welcome and free in comparrison as in the
river of London." But he is anxious that the English
traders make no mistake. It is useless to bring cloth,
since in Japan at this time the price of cloth was " so
good chep as in Ingland." Moreover, at the time the
Dutch were making but small profit on their lead, steel,
mirrors and drinking glasses. The thing was to bring
plenty of spices and use Japan as a half-way house to
China. " Then shall our countri mak great profitt, and
the worshipful Indiss Company of London shall not
hav need to send monny out of Ingland, for in Japan is
gold and silver in abundance, for with the traffic heer
they shall hav monny to serve theer need." Above all,
Adams advised the sending of the ship to Yedo, where
the Shogun held his court, rather than to the southern
island, which was dominated by the daimyos not in
sympathy with Iyeyasu's policy. He writes: " Now,
once, yf a ship do coum, let her coum for the esterly
port of Japan, lying in 35 d. 10 m., where the Kinge
(Hidetada) and the Emperour (Iyeyasu) court is; for
coum our ships to Firando (Hirado) whear the Hollanders bee, it is farr to ye court, about 230 L., a wery-

soum way and foul. The citti of Edo (Yedo) lyeth in
36, and about this esterly part of the land thear be the
best harbours and a cost so clear as theayr is no sholdes
nor rokes ½ a myll from the mayn land. It is good
also for sale of marchandise and security for ships, forr
which cass I have sent a pattern (chart) of Japan, for
which myself I hav been all about the cost in the
shipping that I have made for ye Emperour, that I hav
experyence of all yt part of ye cost that lyeth in 36 d."

Adams took occasion in this letter to thank Mr.
Spalding for " the frindly token of a byble and three
other bookes " and to urge that whoever came to Japan
should make enquiry for him under the name of Anjin
Sama.

Had Saris received this letter, " written in Japan in
ye island of Ferrando, the 12 of Jeneuari 1613," the
story of the Orient might well have been different, for
the better or the worse, who shall say? Yet it is possible that the obstinate English captain might still have
clung to his opinion that Adams was but a common
sailor, " only fit to be master of a junk," and so kept
to his ill-judged and ultimately disastrous course. In
any case, Sir John started from Bantam two days after
Will Adams had put pen to paper at Hirado and did
not sight land in the Japanese archipelago till the 11th
of June when, bearing N. N. E., he suddenly found
before him " many small rockes and hummockes," and
beyond the " hummockes " the island now known as
Mishima. " Next day," says Saris, " we steered north
by west and had sight of two hummockes without the
point. Then wee steered north-north-west and soone
after came foure great fisher-boats aboord, about five
tunnes apeice in burthen, they sailed with one saile,

which stoode like a skiffe saile, and skuld with foure
oares on a side, their oares resting upon a pinne
fastened on the toppe of the boat's side, the head of
which pinne was so let into the middle part of the oare
that the oare did hang in his just poize, so that the
labour of the rower is much lesse than otherwise it must
be; yet doe they make farre greater speed then our
people with rowing, and performe their work standing,
as ours doe sitting, so that they take the lesse roome."
With these fisher-boats Saris made agreement that they
should pilot him to Hirado, where they arrived on the
11th day of the month. There was naturally much
curiosity concerning the English vessel, which some at
first mistook for the ship from Macao. Presently the
Clove was visited by the old daimyo of Hirado and his
nephew and, since these were attended by some forty
boat loads of retainers, it may be taken for granted
that Saris' not too even temper was a little frayed by
the reception. King James' letters, or at least one of
them, were handed to the daimyo, but that dignitary
declined to open the missive till the arrival of Anjin
Sama, an indication of Will's importance in the land
which the English captain had done well to heed. Had
Saris taken the hint, he would have saved himself much
trouble. He did indeed write Adams a letter, asking
his attendance as speedily as possible, and while the
letter was on its way he manifested no little impatience.
The waiting, however, was relieved by visits paid to
the *Clove* on the part of the Hirado traders and others
in the vicinity. One was from the Dutch factor, Hen-
rich Brouwer, who came partly from the desire to spy
out the intentions of the newcomers and partly, it may
be believed, out of genuine courtesy. It was, however,

at this time that the Hollanders gave Saris the bad
advice, which later led him to establish his factory at
Hirado, under the very eye of the Dutchmen, rather
than at Yedo, as both Adams and Iyeyasu desired.

But the majority of the visitors were Japanese, men
and women, the latter, Saris sententiously observes,
" of the better sort." Some of the women were Christians and sufficiently unsophisticated to mistake a picture of Venus and Cupid, " which did hang somewhat
wantonly set out in a large frame " in the Captain's
cabin, for a representation of the Madonna and Child.
To Sir John's consternation they fell down and worshipped it " with shewes of great devotion." Among
the men were, in addition to the " King," several noble-
men of high station, who came aboard with their retainers, wives and children, in such numbers that there
was no room on deck for the sailors to move. Altogether, though Saris got much entertainment from the
feasting, singing and instrumental music with which his
stay provided him, he was anything but sorry when,
on the twenty-ninth of July, Adams at last appeared.
Later, in " a veary larg letter wrot from Japan . . .
and sent home in the *Clove* 1614," Adams refers to
the letter of Saris, asking his presence in all haste. He
adds: " Ye which so sooun as I had received his
letter, I made no dellai, being at that tyme at the
courte, being distant from the place of the ship's arrival 250 llgs." But it had taken Anjin Sama seventeen days to go from Suruga, where Iyeyasu was holding his court, to Hirado, and when he arrived Sir John
somewhat testily reminded him that he had been awaiting his coming some forty-eight days. Yet the General entertained his fellow countryman in friendly

fashion and held long conferences with him, in the presence of the merchants, as to the prospects of the English adventure. Will was the soul of caution. " I am glad," said he, " Sir John, that you have come, but in respect of the ventures by the Worshipful Company I am not sure you have gone the right way about it. You have here, of course, as much opportunity as the other merchant traders from Europe, especially if you follow my advice and that of the Shogun. But, to begin with, the things you have brought are not just now the most vendible of commodities. You have, for instance, brought quantities of cloth, and you should know that these past four years cloth is almost a drug on the market, with an over supply out of Holland, Nova Spania and Manila. You have also brought ivory and knew not that the Hollanders have here more than can be sold, with the price fallen very low. Calicoes, too, of which you have large store, are as cheap here as in England, since the country has abundance of cotton. Metals, too, such as lead and tin, are no dearer here than abroad. Even the pepper and cloves with which you have laden yourselves from the Spice Islands are little used in Japan and command no high price."

Sir John looked a little taken aback, but Will went on to say that the English would fare no worse than the rest, and much better if Saris would come as speedily as might be to Suruga to hear what the " ould Emperour " had to propose. Saris was the better minded to take this advice, much as he disliked playing second fiddle to Adams, when several days later the daimyo, by this time a little tired of entertaining strangers, came to ask what was the bulk of the

presents which the General intended to take with him
to Yedo. He expressed his willingness at the same
time to transport them to Osaka and to have at that
port the horses and palanquins necessary to convey
them the rest of the journey.

Perhaps, there was in this a gentle hint on the part
of the daimyo, whom Saris calls Foyne, that some of
these presents might well be left behind for local distribution. In any case, Sir John, with the aid, no
doubt, of Adams, proceeded to a division of the spoil,
setting aside presents to the value of about eighty-
seven pounds for Iyeyasu himself, half as much for
Hidetada, about a third of this for each of the two
chief secretaries, and so on, in a gradually descending
scale. Altogether the value of the gifts Saris took
with him amounted, for those days, to the respectable
sum of nearly two hundred pounds.

After this due apportionment of presents, the Englishmen started on the long journey to interview
Iyeyasu. With them were seventeen men of the Company, and the experienced pilotage of Adams soon
brought the expedition through the Straits of Shi-
monoseki and into the smooth waters of the Inland
Sea. " We were rowed through," says Saris, " and
amongst divers islands, all of which, or the most part
of them, were well inhabited, and divers proper
townes builded upon them; whereof one called Faccate
hath a very strong castle, built of freestone, but no
ordnance nor souldiers therein. It hath a ditch about
five fathome deepe, and three as broad round about
it, with a draw-bridge, kept all in very good repaire."
Saris landed and dined in this town, which was about
two days' sail from Hirado, but he advises others who

might come after him to pass through without regarding " those idle rabblements." He was, however, interested in the woman divers, who lived on their boats along the coast and got their living by diving for fish. He noted also a junk of some eight hundred or a thousand tons' burden, sheathed in iron and guarded by many soldiers against too close observation. When he tells us that she was built " in a very homely fashion, much like that which describeth Noah's ark unto us," we cannot but reflect that in this instance the Japanese had taken a lesson in shipbuilding from Korea and were reproducing vessels like those which had wrought such havoc among the transports of Hideyoshi.

On August 27 the travellers arrived at the great city of Osaka, having been transferred from the bark to smaller boats about six miles from the city. Saris was filled with admiration at his first sight of this famous town and has left us the following interesting description:

" We found Ozaca to be a very great towne, as great as London within the walls, with many faire timber bridges of a great height serving to passe over a river there as wide as the Thames at London. Some faire houses we found there, but not many. It is one of the chiefe seaports of all Japan; having a castle in it, marvellous large and strong, with very deepe trenches about it and many drawbridges with gates plated with yron. The castle is built all of freestone, with bulwarks and battlements, with loope holes for smal shot and arrowes, and divers passages for to cast stones upon the assaylants. The walls are at the least six or seven yards thicke, all (as I said) of freestone, with-

out any filling in the inward part with trumpery, as
they reported unto me. The stones are great, of an
excellent quarry, and are cut so exactly to fit the place
where they are laid, that no morter is used, but only
earth cast betweene to fill up voyd crevises if any be."

It may be remarked, in passing, that Hideyoshi's
son, Hideyori, was living in the castle at the time of
Saris' visit, all oblivious of the fate which the next two
years were to bring to him and his.

On the following day the Englishmen, after some attempt to introduce their commodities to the notice of
the Osaka folk, left by boat for Fushimi. Thence they
started by road for the Castle of Sumpu, in the province of Suruga, whither Iyeyasu had retired when, in
1605, he relinquished the active duties of the Shogunate to Hidetada. Iyeyasu had always been fond of
Sumpu, from the day when, many years before, he had
received the province as a gift from the hands of the
master-soldier, Oda Nobunaga.

On arriving at the great gate, Adams announced his
presence and that of his guest, requesting that the
news be immediately transmitted to the old Shogun.
The visitors were evidently not unexpected, for the
soldiers very shortly returned with permission for Saris
and Adams to enter, while their companions were requested to await their superiors in the guardhouse. So
the two Englishmen followed their guide along a series
of dim corridors, in which the so-called " nightingale
floors " gave ample warning of their approach. Suddenly they found themselves ushered into a large apartment, almost as dim as the corridors, and which at
first seemed void of human presence. The gold-flecked
screens, behind which, doubtless, armed men were

lurking, gave startlingly the effect of sunlight, though
no ray penetrated from the outside. The visitors were
gratefully conscious of the relief thus afforded from
the glare of the open air, though at this date the extreme summer heat had begun to abate. Then
presently they looked up and became aware of the ex-
Shogun's presence. He was a little fatter than when
Adams had first encountered him and his eyes a little
more narrowed. Though his body was for the most
part motionless, he gave the curious impression of being intensely alive. He had evidently been taking
stock of his visitors before they had become aware of
him.

Iyeyasu beckoned them to come closer and gave permission to Adams to speak. Will in turn asked leave
for Saris to read the letter from King James, tactfully
referring at the same time to the presents the ambassador was charged to proffer. With a vast assumption of dignity Saris read the letter, though his elocu-
tion was wasted on the Shogun. But Adams gave
Iyeyasu the sense of the august epistle and promised
presently to have it rendered into the *kana*, in order
that the chief secretaries, with due regard for style,
might render it into the proper ideographs. These
preliminaries transacted, the Tokugawa made the conversation general and, through Adams, asked a multitude of questions regarding geography and world affairs, with special reference to trade opportunities in
the neighbouring seas. The queries flew thick and
fast: " What about Sakhalin? ", " What about
Yezo? ", " What about Kamchatka? ", " Is the Northwest Passage navigable? ", and the like. Poor Sir
John, who had never been so interrogated since he was

a schoolboy, answered as well as he was able, but
lamely on the whole. Iyeyasu was not long in con-
trasting him unfavourably with the Englishman by his
side whom, thirteen years before, he had rescued from
death.

Yet the Shogun, in his own interest, was not the less
eager to come to some agreement with the agents of
the London Company. And here Adams was elo-
quently persuasive in Iyeyasu's support. " Think what
it will mean," said Will, " for the English traffic if,
while the Dutch are limiting themselves to the favour
of the southern daimyos, you, Sir John, engage to bring
your wares to Uraga Bay and the actual capital of
the Empire! "

Sir John was silent. Was his conscience troubling
him because of secret engagements already made with
the crafty Hollanders at Hirado? Or did he doubt
the power of the Tokugawas to maintain their sway?
Was he persuaded that Japan's future lay with the
Christian daimyos of the southern island rather than
with the war-lord of the Kwanto?

At any rate, the expostulations of Adams were in
vain. The utmost Saris would promise was that, if
Iyeyasu, in conference with Adams, would draw up a
treaty between the Shoguns and the East India Company, he would give the document his best consideration. So Sir John Saris went out from the presence of
Iyeyasu and back to his lodging in the town.

A few hours later Adams received an imperative
summons to pay another visit to the castle. Iyeyasu
was at first in an irascible mood, but when Anjin Sama
promised to use his best powers of persuasion with the
captain of the *Clove,* he softened and promised to

have the suggested treaty ready next day for Saris'
signature at the house of the chief secretary. In closing the interview, the ex-Shogun exclaimed: " I will
give him better than he could ask or believe possible.
Yet I fear the man is a fool and will not accept." Will
was rather inclined to agree, but held his peace.

The meeting at the secretary's house—surely in its
possibilities one of the most momentous in the history
of diplomacy—took place on the following day. The
result was the drawing up of a *Charter* constituting one
of the most liberal trade agreements ever proposed
between East and West. Had it been accepted and
acted upon, how much trouble and display of belliger-
ency on the part of the Occident against the Orient
might have been saved!

The main provisions of the *Agreement*, which was
actually signed by Iyeyasu, on October 1, 1613, are as
follows:

1. It provided that the *Clove* might carry on trade
of all kinds without hindrance, while subsequent visits
by English ships would be similarly welcomed.

2. Ships might visit any ports in Japan they chose
and, in case of storms, put into any harbour.

3. Ground would be given in Yedo for the erection
of factories and houses and, in the event of the return
of the factors to England, they would be permitted to
dispose of the buildings in any way they wished.

4. If any Englishman committed an offence on
Japanese soil, he should be punished by the English
general " according to the gravity of his offence."
Thus the principle of extra-territoriality was recognized in the Far East, long before the period of Western treaties with China.

The extraordinary liberality of these terms, due, not
to foreign pressure but the foresight of Adams, has
only to be contrasted with the results wrung from one
of the last of Iyeyasu's successors through the visit of
Commodore Perry, to be appreciated. It is clear that
Saris had no excuse for misunderstanding them, however obstinately bent on following the counsel of the
Hollanders. For four days he stayed at Adams' house
at Uraga, and all this time Will was wrestling with
him and urging the acceptance of the Agreement as
speedily as possible. At the end, the utmost Saris
would concede was a curt, " I will consider it and let
you know." [14]

Later on we shall have the story of the English captain's " great refusal," and of the tragical decade of
failure on the part of the London factors at Hirado.
We shall also have occasion to note how the stubborn
folly of one English seaman frustrated what the foresight of another had rendered possible. For the
present we must be content to mark the immediate
impression which Saris' hesitation made upon two of
the chief actors in our story.

Iyeyasu was still engaged in consolidating the position of his clan in respect to the Shogunate. Taking
a lesson from the fate which had befallen his predecessors in the Bakufu, he determined that no weak
links in his own line should imperil the chain of power
he himself had forged. Partly to ensure this, as already noted, he had placed, years before, the supreme
authority in his son's hands. For the like reason, he
is said to have formulated the creed of the Tokugawa
house in the so-called *Legacy of Iyeyasu*. Many
formidable obstacles lay in his path, such as only the

completest self-confidence could overcome. There was the loyalty of the southern daimyos to the house of Toyotomi, even then encroaching on the main island to the west, and rallying itself about the person of Hideyori at Osaka. Then, there was the situation arising from the presence and propaganda of the Portuguese friars, and of late from the competitive zeal of quarrelsome Spanish friars from the Philippines. And, once again, there was the commercial ambition of the Dutch and their settlement in the south, where their traffic was enriching not the Shogun but his enemies. A solution of these manifold difficulties was to be found, thought Iyeyasu, in a new traffic, carried on by men not too friendly with either Portuguese or Dutch, and who were willing to trade under his own immediate patronage, and even unite with him in carrying out grandiose schemes of adventure in Yezo and Kamchatka and across the ocean. It burned in the Shogun's heart like hidden fire that, should the English captain repudiate the proffered alliance and permit himself to be hoodwinked by the Dutch, it might become the part of statesmanship to close the portals of the Empire against the foreigners altogether and, by one stroke of policy, counteract alike the ambition of the rebel daimyos, the designs of the missionaries and the intrigue, actual or threatening, of the European traders. How this policy was eventually to be adopted, with its consequences bad and good, is a story which lies beyond the limits of our own. Nevertheless, the shadow of its *dénouement* lies darkly across this part of the career of Anjin Sama.

The indecision of Saris had indeed, at this point, a determining influence on the personal fortunes of Will

Adams. The coming of the *Clove*, and its now imminent departure for the home land, *Agreement* or
no *Agreement*, had for Will its own peculiar temptation. The homesickness, to which he had now for
some years been a stranger, returned. Was not this
the providentially ordered opportunity for him to escape a foreign bondage and see again the country of
his birth? Particularly if the *Agreement* were ratified,
would not the Company be glad to recognize his services in the matter and reward him with an honourable
place in the traffic about to be inaugurated?

Thus, while Saris was still in the neighbourhood,
looking gift-horses in the mouth, Adams made still
another effort to see Iyeyasu on private business. The
ex-Shogun, irritated by Saris' procrastination, and a
presentiment of refusal, was not easy of approach.
More than once Will was left to cool his heels in the
guardhouse, while this or that secretary assured him
the Tokugawa was too busy to see him. At last one
morning found Iyeyasu in a better mood. So Adams
made himself " soumwhat bold " and entered the
august presence. Invited to approach the dais, he took
out of his bosom the broad seal which gave him title
to the lands at Hemi and, laying it at the feet of
Iyeyasu, made his request to be released from service.

Iyeyasu looked seriously, and not a little sadly, upon
his well-tried henchman. He asked, " Are you so desirous of leaving me and returning to the land of
England? " " Most desirous," replied Adams, in a
low voice. What the ex-Shogun said further we do
not know, but we may imagine it ran somewhat thus:
" I should do wrong, my friend, to detain you against
your will. Much as I hoped to have you always in

my service, I could not now do violence to your desire.
I would, however, that you tarry till other shipping
come. There is much I am anxious still for you to do.
But you must take your own path. And so, Farewell." The old Shogun dismissed him hastily and
Adams went, a prey to strangely conflicting currents
of feeling. What he would do with his recovered
liberty, should he choose to use it, he did not know.
Now that he had it, it pleased him little.

What followed immediately is again largely hypo-
thetical, but it requires no extravagant exercise of
fancy to think of Adams as at this time entering
upon the bitter fruit of his " great renunciation." No
further word had come from the ex-Shogun, beyond a
reminder that it might be well to pay a visit to Hidetada at Yedo. This was done, with no particular result, for the reigning Shogun was a somewhat lumpish
individual, who was never likely to use initiative, unless it were in persecuting the Christians. The will of
Saris, too, had now stiffened into a deliberate resolve
to reject the proposals of Iyeyasu. Adams was not a
little disgusted to learn how the Englishmen had dis-
ported themselves at Kamakura, and had given great
offence by climbing into the head of the Daibutsu.
There, after the manner of modern Philistines, they
had succeeded in inscribing their ignoble names. A
day or two after, Adams joined the General on the way
back to Hirado, by way of Kyoto and Osaka. So at
last they reached the little island which was destined
to be the rock against which the efforts of the London
Company to establish trade with Japan were to be
broken. Will mused sadly on the dismal prospect and

then returned to take stock of his personal fortunes.
Since the last conversation with Iyeyasu his mind had
been like a weathercock, responsive to every variant
gust of feeling. At one moment he longed with unspeakable longing to make the break complete and
see the last of the shores of Japan. Then he thought
of the Lady Bikuni, of Joseph, of the estates at Hemi,
of his friends and acquaintances in Japan, and immediately his hardly won liberty turned to dust and
ashes in his mouth. Again, since coming to Hirado,
several circumstances added their weight of doubt to
the strength of his desire. Differences with Saris had
multiplied. Adams could not get out of his head
" dyvers injeries doun against me veri strang and un-
looked for." Moreover, he had been approached by
the chief factor of the Company, Richard Cock, with
the offer of so many pounds a month in case he should
conclude to stay and share in the interests of the enterprise. These considerations, indeed, were small, when
placed beside the true love he had for his Japanese
wife and children, but they helped to turn the scale.

Strangely enough, at the very time he was realizing
the strength of his affection for the Lady Bikuni, he
seems to have been inditing a letter to his English wife,
in the conviction that the *Clove*, when presently it
sailed, would bear, not himself but a letter. So mar-
vellously complex is the mind of man. Perhaps he
was trying to forge a defensive armour for himself
against the manifold temptations of the occasion.
Here are parts of this letter:

" Loving wife, you shall understand how all things
have passed with me from the time I last indited a
letter, though, such are the fortunes of life, that I know

not whether you received my newes or no. You shall
know that Captain John Saris arrived in the *Clove* not
many months since and has during these many weekes
past been engaged in dyvers negotiations with the
Prince of the land, all of which we trust shall turn
out to the welfare of our High and Mighty King James
and His realme. . . . I am sending herewith the
twenty pounds which was loaned to you by the Worshipful Company. I pray you to return to them the
money with grateful thanks for myself as well as from
you for their deed of Christian charity in lending you
the money. I hope soon to send more if, as I believe
to be possible, the Company should offer to take me
into their service in these islands. . . . More I have no
leisure to write at present. I bequeath you and your
affairs to the tuition of God. May He bless you and
keep you in body and soul from all your ennemies forever and ever. Amen. Youre unworthie husband,
William Adams."

The letter, except at the close, is not overcharged
with emotion, but one may think of many things which
must have passed through the Pilot's mind before he
made his ultimate decision. These, however, are for
the novelist to describe rather than the historian.
Whatever the spiritual struggle, Will Adams decided to
cast in his lot for the time to come with Japan, and
with the family and friends he had there made his own.

What has still to be told may strike some readers
as an anticlimax. It happens, however, not infrequently that while the heroic faculties have to be
marshalled to the front for the making of a great decision, those faculties, retired to the background, are no
less needed for the maintenance of the decision after

it has been made. In any case, the stream of Will
Adams' existence, from this time onwards, so far as
all outward appearance is concerned, flows placidly
enough towards the bourne which is the common destiny of us all.

But, ere we come to this more or less peaceful ending to the narrative of a strenuous life, it is proper to
gather up some threads of story, which up to the
present have been left floating a little loosely.

First, we take our leave of that rather disappointing
adventurer, Sir John Saris. His last days in Hirado
he spent with his chief factor, or " cap-merchant,"
Richard Cock, with whom he negotiated for the re-
tention of Adams in the service of the Company. He
was still annoyed at the course things had taken and
in the *Remembrance* which was left for Cock's instruction, Saris made some ungenerous remarks about Will,
who was " only to be used as linguist at corte, when
you have no imployment for hym at sea." The document goes on to say, most unjustly: " It is necessarye
you stirre hym, his condition being well knowne unto
you as to myselfe: otherwayss you shall have littell
service of hym, the countrye affording great libertye,
wheareunto he is much affected. The forsed agreement
I have made with hym as you know could not be
eschudd, the Flemmings and Spaniards making false
proffers of great intertaynment, and hymselfe more
affected to them then his owne natyon, we holye destitute of language."

It is but fair to Cock to say that he by no means
took Adams at Saris' estimate. The General was a
vain and narrow-minded man, who was bound to re-
sent the superior qualifications of Anjin Sama. The

Clove sailed from Hirado about the end of November
and reached Bantam a month later. Then sails were
hoisted for England about the middle of February
1614, and seven months later, on September 27, Sir
John let down his anchors in the waters of Plymouth
Harbour. His homecoming, however, brought him into
no haven of repose spiritually. For, first of all, the
Captain had to meet charges that he had carried out
" a great private trade " for his own advantage, and,
several months later, when his ship had been brought
round from Plymouth to the Thames, a charge was
filed to the effect that he had brought back with him
" certain lascivious books and pictures . . . to the
great scandal of the Company and unbecoming their
gravity to permit." One wonders whether, among
these scandal-causing pictures, which were promptly
burned, was found that one of Venus and Cupid which
the simple-minded Christians of Japan had mistaken
for the Madonna and Child. It appears, again, that
soon after Saris' return to England he married, but
whether this brought him further trouble or no we do
not know. Sir John lived more than thirty years after
the return of the *Clove,* occasionally consulted on matters Japanese by the officers of the Company. He
died, leaving no issue, in 1646.[15]

We have already referred to Adams' engagement by
the *London East India Company.* Over its terms
there was much dispute. As originally drawn up by
Saris, the contract commences as follows:

" Whereas ye R. honourable compayne, ye mar-
chants of London trading into ye East Indyes, of there
greate love and affection to you, Capt. Addams, have
appointed and set out this shippe called ye *Clove* for

Japan; bilding there hoopes uppone ye foundation of your long experyence in these partes, for the settling of a benyficiall ffactorie. And having since my arrival not onlye obteyned the Emperor's grant with large privaliges for ye same, but also procured your freedome, which till this present could not be obteyned. It now resteth what course you will take; wheather to retorne for your counterey or remaine heare ye companyes servant, in what manner you hould yourselfe best able to doe them service: what sallory you will have; and in what manner to be paid."

The Company offered eighty pounds a year to Adams, who replied that he would not consider under a hundred and twenty pounds. Eventually, it was agreed that the remuneration should be one hundred pounds a year, paid at the end of two years, or at such time as news arrived of the safe homecoming of the *Clove*. Only, meanwhile, Adams desired " that yf he stood in neade of twentie pound str. to lay out in apparell, or any other necessaries, that he might be furnished therewith."

So the bargain was closed and signed by Adams in his own behalf, and witnessed by Richard Cock, Tempest Peacock and Richard Wickhamon on behalf of the Company. It was about this time that Will Adams wrote to England a rather pathetic letter which betrays something of his disquietude of soul. After apologizing for his failure to return in the *Clove*, a decision he explains as due to "som discourtissies offred me by the generall . . . which injuries to wryt of them I leave; leaving to others, God sending the ship hom, to mak rellacion," he continues: " Sinc the tym I saw your wourship, I hav passed great misseries

and trowbels." But the battle was over now and he is
unwilling to write particulars. " God hav the prayss,"
he says, " to whom it doth belonge, that hath delivered
me out of them all." That he has not torn the memory
of England altogether out of his heart is plain from
the wistful messages of greeting to such dimly remembered personages as " My good frind Mr. William
Bourrall, shipwryt, who I heer is on the Company, and
to my good Mr. Nicholas Diggines," to " thank him
for his former love to me."

The question will occur, What did Will Adams do
in return for his hundred pounds a year? The little
company of seventeen Englishmen, with their three
interpreters and two servants, could not have had a
very strenuous time, considering the small amount of
business they transacted. But it is evident that Captain Adams was really being paid for his experience
and the value of his advice in the business of pushing
into notice the English wares. It was he who knew
the advantage of sending presents to the Shogun. He
knew also what the Shogun most desired to have. For
instance, he puts in a request that there be sent for
" the Emperour " " soum Rousse (Russian) glass of
the gratest sort: so much as may glasse him a roum
of two fadom four square, and what fine lames skenes
(lamb-skins) you will and two or three peces of fyne
holland, yf it be more I leav it to your discression:
with three or four payr of spaktakle glasses." He was
furthermore in touch with the general needs of the
people and spoke with authority, when he advised the
sending as merchandise of " soum thousand barres of
steill four squar, in length soum eight or nine foout;
which goods the Hollanders have brought and sold to

the Emperor at fifty-one sterling the picoll, which is Inglish waight 125 powndes."

It is interesting to note that Will's responsibilities to the Company did not prevent the resumption of the old feudal life at Hemi. Iyeyasu readily forgave his temporary defection and the family was soon again settled on the estate, growing yearly more lovely, in the vicinity of Yokosuka. We have one charming glimpse of that life in the *Diary of Richard Cock* who, soon after Iyeyasu's death, was called upon, in behalf of the Company, to visit Yedo for the purpose of securing renewal of the " privileges." Under date of September 26, Captain Cock writes as follows: " We departed towards Orengava this morning about 10 o'clock and arrived at Phebe (Hemi) some two houres before night, where we staid all that night: for that Capt. Adames' wife and his two children met us theare. This Phebe is a Lordship geven to Capt. Adames pr. the ould Emperour, to hym and his for eaver, and confirmed to his sonne, called Joseph. There is above 100 farms, or housholds, uppon it, besides others under them, all which are his vassalls, and he hath power of lyfe and death over them: they being his slaves; and he having as absolute authoretie over them as any *tono* (king) in Japan hath over his vassales. Divers of his tennants brought me presents of frute: as oringes, figgis, peares, chistnutts, and grapes, whereof there is aboundance in that place."

Next day the diarist continues: " We gave the tenants of Phebe a bar of coban [16] to make a banket after our departure from thence, with 500 gins to the servants of howses, the cheafe of the towne accompanying us out of their precincts, and sent many ser-

vants to accompany us to Orengava (which is about
8 or 9 English miles); all running before us on foote
as honeyer to Captain Adames. After our arrivall at
Orengava, most of the neighbours came to vizett mee,
and brought frutes and fysh, and rejoiced (as it should
seeme) of Captain Adames retorne."

Yet it is obvious, even from the above quotation,
that Adams during these years was often away from
the quiet routine life of Hemi. From 1615 to 1618,
he made three considerable voyages which, since the
salt was in his blood, may have gone far to appease
his restlessness. The first was an unsuccessful attempt
to journey, in the interests of the Company, to Siam.
He started out from Hirado with something of his
youthful ardour. If he might not discover the Northwest Passage, an ambition he never entirely abandoned,
he might at least behold one more of those strange
oriental lands such as had claimed the major part of
his life. But, two days after leaving, a great storm
arose which, for the space of three days, threatened
the destruction of the ship and the loss of all on board.
Counting officers, mariners, merchants and passengers,
there were forty souls on board and these were kept
baling out the water from the compartments of the ship
till they were almost dead with weariness and fear.
They begged Adams on their knees to save their lives
by any course he might devise. As two officers of the
Company, Richard Wickham and Edmund Saris, were
aboard, Adams put the matter up to them. Provided
they abandoned for the present the plan of reaching
Siam, there were two alternatives. One was to proceed to China, from which coast they were not more
than twenty leagues distant. This, however, was

deemed unwise because of the bitter hostility which, since the time of Hideyoshi, had existed between Chinese and Japanese. The other possibility was to run in for shelter to one or other of the islands known to the Japanese as the Ryukyu Islands and to the Chinese as the Loochoos. It was decided to adopt the second plan, greatly to the relief of all on board, and in three days they reached the archipelago. The natives showed the crew and passengers " marvellous great frindship," and Adams was glad enough of the opportunity to unload the cargo, replace the mast and trim the ship, before proceeding again to the south. Unfortunately, when they were now in good shape and ready to start, the monsoon had already passed and it was clear that for this season it was too late to proceed to Siam. So in the end they returned to Japan.

In the next year, 1616, Anjin Sama made his second venture, and this time reached Siam, after a steady and prosperous voyage. On his return, to his great joy, he found two other English vessels, the *Thomas* and the *Advice,* arrived a few days before his own coming. But, if there was joy in meeting other Englishmen, there was great grief for Adams in learning that his noble patron, the friend of so many years, Iyeyasu, was no more. The end had come on June 1, 1616, only a few days after the death of William Shakespeare on the other side of the globe. Will would fain have been among those who saw the ex-Shogun laid to his rest at Kuno, but later he was able to travel north to Nikko when, in 1617, Hidetada laid his illustrious sire in the tomb, amid the plashing cataracts reduced to clouds of blown spray and mist, and the waving of stately trees—a tomb to be still later superseded by the gorgeous shrines erected through the piety of Iyemitsu.

The death of Iyeyasu brought in its train a multitude of changes, for Hidetada, as already intimated, was cast in a meaner mould than his father, and in no way inclined to be generous with the traders. It became necessary for Adams to journey with Richard Cock all the way to Yedo, to secure such privileges for the future as had already been granted to the factors. There ensued a great deal of going and coming amid much troublesome negotiation. In the end, the traders felt themselves much disadvantaged by the accession of Iyeyasu's son.

The actual engagement of Adams by the Company terminated with the close of 1616, but Anjin Sama made two more voyages, this time to Cochin China. The first journey was necessitated by a brawl which had occurred there between the natives and the factors whom Richard Cock had despatched three years before. No trade had followed and the men had not been heard from. Then came the news that one of them, Mr. Peacock, had been killed. In consequence of this untoward event, some one had to go to investigate and, though the Company was willing to send William Neilson with him, Adams preferred to go alone, "desiring the protexion and favour of all mightie God." What the occasion of the second visit to Cochin China was, in 1618, is not known, but it seems to have been Adams' last.

Perhaps it was just as well, in some respects, that he was away from the atmosphere of the Court during those last stormy years of Iyeyasu's career. From the time of the battle of Sekigahara in 1600, as we have seen, one life had stood between the Tokugawa and the complete fulfilment of his ambition. It was Hideyori, son of the great Taiko Sama by his favourite wife, the Lady Yodo. It was on the conscience of Iyeyasu that he, as Hideyori's guardian, had sworn an oath to secure for his ward succession to the dictatorship. But from the beginning he had no such intention. Indeed, it was to secure the perpetuity of Tokugawa rule that Iyeyasu created his formidable administrative machine, with its complicated system of fiefs, hostages and spies. To this end, particularly, he had nominally resigned to his son the Shogunate in 1605. For some years thereafter, however, the danger of disturbance was but slight. The partisans of the Toyotomi family were quiescent and Hideyori, a minor, was living with his mother in Osaka Castle. Then, one day, we are told, Iyeyasu visited the castle and found that which left him " enveloped in darkness." Here was a fine, upstanding youth of seventeen, who was evidently looked up to by the daimyos of the west and south. Here, too, were the piled-up riches which Hideyoshi had left, cast, suggestively enough, in the form of golden war-horses. From this moment, Iyeyasu began the weaving of a new web of intrigue. First, he filled the castle with women, by whom the heir of Hideyoshi was to be debauched, and with spies, who reported to Yedo all that went on within. Then, when these plans failed, Iyeyasu tried to ruin his enemy by forcing on him extravagant expenditures of every sort. The great image of the Buddha, made by Hideyoshi, had been ruined by an earthquake. It seemed therefore easy to bring about Hideyori's impoverishment by compelling him to rebuild the image and the temple

which enshrined it. When all this was done, without
entailing the desired result, a quarrel was picked over
an inscription on the temple bell. This consisted of
but four innocent ideographs signifying, " May the
State have Peace and Prosperity." But certain priests
were suborned to testify that the real meaning was a
reference to Hideyori as the *Rising Sun* and to Iyeyasu
as the *Waning Moon*. The wolf of the fable was
bound to find excuse for his assault upon the lamb.
New demands were now made that Hideyori, or his
mother, the Lady Yodo, should leave Osaka Castle,
and take up their dwelling at Yedo as hostages. It
was soon after the last refusal of Hideyori to acknowledge himself as the Tokugawa's vassal that the
first campaign was launched against the Castle. Iyeyasu was not unequal to the task of finding further
ground for his really unprovoked attack. Hideyori had
been entertaining Jesuits at Osaka, and there was
documentary proof, discovered or invented, to the effect that the Jesuits were plotting against the Tokugawa supremacy. The *Winter Campaign,* however, as
it was called, was not a success and, on its failure,
Iyeyasu made the astonishing proposal that the rivals
should now make peace with one another and that, seeing they were at peace, the outer parapet of the Castle
should be demolished and the moat filled up. Iyeyasu
even lent troops to carry out this disinterested piece
of work, and the zeal of the troops far outstripped the
limits of anything to which Hideyori had at first consented. When, in the supposed interests of this sus-
piciously new-born friendship, the Castle had been
thus far weakened, Iyeyasu commenced the *Summer
Campaign* of 1615, against which Hideyori found him-

self shorn of his old strength. Yet, so valiant was the
defence, that at one moment Iyeyasu despaired of victory and even gave orders to one of his retainers to
cut off his head. Fire, however, and treachery accomplished what the bravest resistance was unable to avert.
The Castle surrendered on June 9, 1615. Hideyori
committed *seppuku,* and every member of the house of
Toyotomi, down to the six-year-old son of Hideyori,
was put to death by the common executioner. Adams
refers to this campaign in the last of his surviving
letters, naturally leaning towards a favourable interpretation of his patron's policy, as follows:

" In the yeear of our Lord 1615 heer was great
warres: for Quambabaccodono (the Lord Kwambaku,
i. e., Hideyoshi) a two yeeares before his deth had a
soone which untill this, being the 24 yeeare of his age,
and having aboundance of riches, thought himselfs
strong with divers nobles to a rooss with him, which
was great likly. Hee mad warres with the Emperour,
allso by the Jesuits and Ffriers, which made his man
Fiddayat Sama (Hideyori) beleeve he should be favoured with mirakles and wounders; but in fyne it
proved to the contrari. For the old Emperour (goeth)
against him presently, maketh his forces reddy by sea
and land and compasseth his castell that he was in;
although with loss of multitudes on both sides, yet in
the end rasseth the castell walles, setteth it on fyre,
and burneth hym in it. Thus ended the warres."

Iyeyasu only lived to enjoy his triumph for a year,
but he had succeeded in his purpose of transmitting
the Shogunate to his descendants. Hidetada now commenced his personal rule, and it was soon clear that
the favour which Will Adams and others had enjoyed

with the Shogun was to be sensibly diminished. Indeed, the government policy was now distinctly antiforeign. First of all, there was manifested a set determination to eradicate the Christian religion as a thing subversive to the State, and this inaugurated, as related in a previous chapter, one of the most terrible and persistent persecutions in all religious history. Adams wrote, in the same letter from which we have already quoted:

" His (Iyeyasu's) son ragneth in his place, and hee is more hot agaynste the romish religion than his ffather was: for he hath forbidden thorough all his domynions, on payne of deth, none of his subjects to be romish christane; which romish seckt to prevent everi wayes that he maye, he hath forbidden that no stranger merchant shal abid in any of the great citties. On such pretence many jessuits and ffriers might seket (secretly) teach the romissh relligion. Thies are the casses of our Inglish ffactorie and all other strangers are not suffred abov in the countri."

So the foreign traders shared in the disabilities imposed upon the missionaries, and the policy was gradually unfolded which led presently to the expulsion of the Portuguese and the limiting of the Dutch to the tiny settlement of Deshima, raised from the bottom of Nagasaki harbour and connected with the mainland by a causeway.

The burden of this critical time weighed particularly on the English factory at Hirado. Here the Dutch did their best to render the venture unprofitable, by lowering their prices beyond the possibility of competition. Richard Cock made not a few mistakes on his own account. Ere long, Richard Wickham wrote home that

unless the merchants opened up trade with the Moluccas and with China, or engaged in plundering expeditions like the Dutch, " the Japan trade was not worth
continuing." This last suggestion, that the policy of
piracy might be adopted to recoup the merchants for
their losses by commerce, was even accepted. In company with the Dutch, the English factors made raids
on Manila and elsewhere. But the policy proved unprofitable and when, in 1619, the Company fortunes
had so far declined that the factors were mobbed in
the streets by Dutch and Japanese alike, it was clear
that the end was not very remote. The sight of British prizes being brought into the port of Hirado by the
Dutch must have caused the iron to enter deeply into
the Englishmen's souls.

At last, from the Oriental headquarters of the Company in Batavia, came the letter to " Mr. Cox and the
rest," ordering the dissolution of the factory. That
this letter was signed by " Your loving Friends, Richard Fursland, Thos. Brockenden, Aug. Spalding," did
not diminish the humiliation. So it came to pass that,
at noon on December 24, 1623, the English factors of
Hirado sailed away on the *Bull*, and the curtain was
rung down upon the story of a great opportunity made
possible by the efforts of an English sailor, William
Adams, but rendered " frustrate and vagabond " by
the obstinacy of another, John Saris. Happily, Will
Adams was not alive to hear of the ignominious departure of the *Bull* with its melancholy company. Yet one
wonders whether, from some purgatorial or paradisai-
cal sphere, the two seamen may not sometimes have
looked down upon the scenes of their terrestrial adventures. If so, one wonders again whether Anjin

Sama resisted the temptation to mutter, " I told you so," to his stubborn fellow countryman.

Master Will had both foretold the *débâcle* and had seen it on its way, but he had in these last years ceased to concern himself overmuch with the affairs of the Company. He still dreamed of his great scheme of proving the feasibility of the Northwest Passage, but he was now to embark on a still longer voyage, that which comes to all in its due season.

The spring of the year 1620 came in with unusual magnificence. Never had the cherry trees bloomed more sweetly or the sun shone more warmly on the fields of Hemi. Yet when the last call came, Will was absent from home, in Hirado, living in " the poor house with an old St. George's Cross for cullers." But, at Hemi or at Hirado, his last thought was of the beloved woman who had held him with her love during the years of his exile as with hooks of steel. In the satisfaction of this thought Will Adams sank back and expired, about noon on May 6, in the year of our Lord 1620.

On December 13, 1620, Mr. Richard Cock, chief factor of the Company at Hirado, wrote a letter to the Governor and Committee which contains the following passage: " Our good friend Captain Wm. Addames, whoe was soe long before us in Japon departed out of this world the vi of May last; and made Mr. Wm. Eaton and my selfe his overseers: geving the one halfe of his estate to his wife and childe in England; and the other halfe to a sonne and doughter he hath in Japan. The coppie of his will, with another of his inventory (or account of his estate) I send to his wife and doughter, per Captain Martin Pring, their good frend well knowne to them long tyme past. And I have delivered one hundred pounds sterling to divers of the James Royall Company, entred into the pursers book to pay two for one in England, is two hundred pounds sterling to Mrs. Addames and her doughter, for it was not his mind his wife should have all in regard she might marry an other husband, and carry all from his childe; but rather that it should be equally parted between them; of which I thought good to adviz your worship. And the rest of his debts and estates being gotten in, I will either bring, or send it per first occasion offred, and that may be most for their profitt, according as the deceased put his trust in me and his other good frend Mr. Eaton."

The *Inventory* commences as follows: "In the Name of God, Amen. 1620, May the 22nd. day. The Inventory of the estate of the Deceased, William Addames, taken at Firando, in Japan, after his death, pr. me Richard Cock, and Mr. Wm. Eaton, factors, in the English factory at Firando, in Japan, left by testament his overseears, viz., of all the monis, debts, merchandize, and moveables, being as hereafter followeth." [17]

In money Adams had about five hundred pounds at the time of his death to divide among his heirs, but, of course, the estate of Hemi, regarded as an heritage apart, remained for his son Joseph, of whose subsequent life it must be regretfully confessed that we know nothing. The Lady Bikuni, who survived her husband thirteen years, was also suitably provided for.

Every visitor to Japan, if the excursion be at all possible, makes the ninety mile journey northward

from Tokyo to Nikko, to gaze upon the splendid
shrines erected to the memory of Iyeyasu, through the
piety of his grandson Iyemitsu. Even before the visitor leaves the train he is fain to note the glorious avenue of cryptomerias which was all that the pious
poverty of one of the daimyos could contribute to the
magnificent memorial. Soon thereafter he enters those
impressive gateways, the Kara-mon and the Yomei-
mon, " All-day-gazing gate," to find himself face to
face with the most wonderful architecture of the Tokugawa period. The buildings, lavishly, perhaps too lavishly, bedight with lacquers of gold, vermillion and
black, become a hundred-fold more impressive because
of their setting amid the majestic forests of the moun-
tain region. Nor is this all. The visitor has still to
climb by upwards of two hundred steps to the actual
tomb, sublime in its simplicity, where lie the mortal
remains, possibly represented by a single hair, of the
great first Tokugawa Shogun. All this is unquestion-
ably Iyeyasu's meed of honour.

But, by comparison, it is not a little sad to realize
how few are the foreign visitors, who take the trouble
to look up the little monument which stands in front
of the Okichi San Fudo, in the neighbourhood of the
Mitsukoshi Department Store. Still fewer seek the
lovely summit of the hill hard by the old heritage of
Hemi-mura, overlooking the Bay of Yedo and Gold-
borough Inlet. In the very shadow of that hill in 1854
was anchored the fleet of Commodore Perry, who had
come to wrest from the successor of Iyeyasu the *Treaty
of Kanagawa*. Yet at this time, no soul seems to have
shown any interest in, or any knowledge of, the story
of Anjin Sama. Nevertheless, here it is that the first

Englishman in Japan chose a spot for the last repose of himself and his Japanese wife. It was hither the gallant Elizabethan was borne by his sorrowing tenantry. It was here that the people of Yedo erected memorial stone lanterns in recognition of his services to the Shoguns and their realm. Thirteen years later, the sod was again disturbed to receive the tired body of the Lady Bikuni. She had loved Will for twenty years of their life together, with a love that was stronger than death. Then for thirteen years, still loving, she had remained faithful to his memory. Now, at last, they were united in death, as they had been united in life.

At the top of a short flight of some six steps, separated by only a few feet from the memorial lanterns, rise the two simple *haka* which constitute the Anjinzuka, or Pilot's Mound. Around these shafts, as around the fir-trees of Takasago and Suminoye, we may see in fancy the liberated spirits hovering in the gladness of their reunion. The grasses and shrubs gradually encroached on the burial place and in time there was nothing visible to bring the passer-by to a halt, or tempt him to a moment of reflection on the story of three centuries ago. Gradually arose in the neighbourhood the great docks and shipyards of Yokosuka, where, without ceasing, the hammers rang upon the clanging anvils, while Japan set to work to create for her modern needs fleets beyond anything the shipwright of Chatham and Limehouse had ever dreamed. All these years there were few to think of the man who built for Iyeyasu his first ships and fired the imagination of the Tokugawa with visions of adventures on the sea.

It was not till 1872, on another May day, like that
on which Will Adams died, that Mr. James Walter re-
discovered the lonely and forgotten graves. Perhaps
it was then to have been anticipated that, at some still
future date, a grateful Occident, mindful of Anjin
Sama's influence on the Japan of his day, would build
another monument to that memory, if only to atone for
the long neglect.[18]

So it came to pass that, in 1905, in the presence of
Prince Arthur of Connaught, who had come to Japan
to present the *Order of the Garter* to the Emperor
Meiji, a new memorial was unveiled on the site of the
old homestead of Hemi, now become a suburb of
Yokohama. It remains a worthy reminder and symbol of the alliance which at that date existed between
two great Empires, about which Will Adams had
dreamed and one he had laboured earnestly to realize.[19]

NOTES

1 On this occasion messages of greeting were sent to England from the Premier and other members of the Japanese Cabinet.

2 Nicholas Diggins was " a shipwright of repute, who later built and repaired many ships for the East India Company in its early days " (Diosy).

3 Laughton in his *Defeat of the Spanish Armada* (pp. 329–340) identifies Adams with the " Captain William Adams " of the *Richard Duffield,* one of the ships used for the transportation of victuals to the fleet.

4 The Marriage Register of St. Dunstan's, Stepney, under date of August 20, 1589, has the entry: " William Adams and Mary Hyn," but the date seems too early. In the Register of Gillingham there is an " Elizabeth Adams," who has often been taken to be Will Adams' wife. Others have taken Mrs. Adams' name to have been May, or Mabel.

5 That Adams did not altogether neglect his English wife is shown by the fact that he not only repaid this twenty pounds, but that at other times he sent the sums of fifty, seventy, and sixty pounds, through the Company.

6 Following the union of the two Crowns of Spain and Portugal, and the accession of Philip II, came the Declaration of Independence by the Netherlands in 1581.

7 On the entry of the Dutch into the trade of the Far East, see Ch. V of Dr. J. C. Beaglehole's *The Exploration of the Pacific,* London, 1933. The Dutch boats were better built and better served than those of the Portuguese.

8 Timothy Shotten had already circumnavigated the globe with Thomas Cavendish, whom Adams calls " Candish," as the name was then pronounced.

9 At one time in this part of the voyage the men were reduced to eating " the calves' skinnes wherewith the ropes were covered."

10 During these days of waiting Adams and his comrades fully expected to be " crossed " (crucified), which is " the manner of dealing with pirates and thieves and such like in this country."

11 Not altogether, for Adams gives some interesting details of the meeting in the *" Letters."* This first interview with Iyeyasu took place on May 12, 1600.

12 We may imagine the eyes of Adams lighting up with the question as to the N. W. Passage. "Yes, verily," he said in answer, "the people of his countri did still not cees to spend much monny in discoveri theareof."

13 But the courteous Spaniard is said to have sent back to Iyeyasu an even better ship as a return present.

14 On the whole history of Iyeyasu's negotiations with the London Company, see *The History of the English Factory at Hirado,* by Dr. Ludwig Riess, in the T. A. S. J., December 1898.

15 The story of Sir John Saris may be gathered from *The Journal of the Clove,* now in the India Office, London; *Purchas his Pilgrimes,* Part I, 334–384; and the *Diary of Richard Cock,* Hakluyt Society.

16 The *coban* (or *koban*) was a piece of gold valued by Dr. Kaempfer as worth twenty-three and a half Dutch guilders.

17 The original of this Will is said to have been formerly in the possession of the East India Company's Office, London, but I am informed by Mr. W. T. Ottewill, Superintendent of Records at the India Office, that "repeated searches have established the fact that it is not now extant." I am informed also that the English copy of the Will is in Folio 21, Register No. 24 (1621– 6) of the town section of the Court of the Commissary of the Bishop of London.

18 The *Japan Weekly Mail* of May 27, 1905, has the following interesting information respecting the Tomb of Will Adams at Yokosuka:

"Ever since Mr. James Walter discovered, in 1872, the tomb of the Kentish pilot, Will Adams, at Hemi-mura, near Yokosuka, he has been keenly interested in all that appertains to the first Englishman to visit Japan.' Mainly through Mr. Walter's efforts the tomb was restored some years ago, and now that the place has again fallen into ruins Mr. Walter is moving to secure its complete renovation. Through the cordial coöperation of Sir Claude MacDonald, Governor Sufu, and the Minister of Home Affairs, permission has been obtained to open the tomb to see whether it is merely a cenotaph or a proper grave, Dr. Riess having contended that Will Adams' remains really rest at Hirado. On Tuesday arrangements for the tomb-opening were completed, and Sir Claude MacDonald travelled from Tokyo with Mr. Okada, Secretary to Governor Sufu, and was joined at Yokohama by Mr. James Walter and Dr. Wheeler. At Dzushi Lady Mac-Donald, Governor Sufu, and Mr. Page met the train, and accompanied the party. Arrived at Hemi-mura, the work of excavation was begun, but the virgin rock was reached and nothing had been found. Then an ancient inhabitant of the village vouchsafed the information that 22 years before the tomb had been opened and an urn removed, which urn was re-interred to the right of the present excavation. Search will be continued there, but meanwhile the exploration party had to leave to catch their train. A piece of old brass turned up during the digging, which was handed to the British Minister. We believe that the Japanese Government intend to restore the tomb, and make it the centre of a public park."

[19] The story of Will Adams may be pieced together from his *Letters*, printed in *Purchas his Pilgrimes*, Part I; Rundall's *Memorials of the Empire of Japan*, Hakluyt Society, 1850; Hildreth's *Japan*, 1855; *The Diary of Richard Cock*, Hakluyt Society, 1883; and Arthur Diosy's *In Memory of Will Adams*, T. A. S. J. 1905.

IV

RANALD MacDONALD OF OREGON

On June 27, 1848, a young man of twenty-four made a decision which to-day might almost be considered comparable with a resolve to venture a journey to the moon in a rocket. The young man was one Ranald MacDonald, who a year earlier had bargained with Captain Edwards, of the whaler *Plymouth,* to be put off as near the coast of Japan as could be managed at the moment requested. The captain had agreed, believing that he would never be called upon to fulfil his promise. But on the day mentioned above, when the *Plymouth* was about five miles off the coast of Hokkaido, then more generally known as Yezo, young Ranald had demanded that the bargain be carried out. It is the purpose of this study to tell something of the story of this apparently crazy adventure, of the daring adventurer, and of the influence that adventure had upon the subsequent history of Japan and her relations to the United States of America.

Ranald MacDonald cannot be said to have been the first *American* in Japan, quite in the sense in which we describe Will Adams as the first of *Englishmen.* There were Americans in the service of the Dutch who had visited Nagasaki even before the close of the eighteenth century. A few months before MacDonald's arrival in the country as a voluntary castaway some of the crew of the *Lawrence* had been shipwrecked on the Japanese coast. Some of the crew of the *Ladoga* had deserted their vessel to seek their fortunes in the Sunrise Empire. But these Americans, when ultimately deported, left barely a name behind them, whereas the name of our hero is associated with a great deal that has to do with the relations of Japan and America.

There is another reason for hesitating over the name *American,* since Ranald MacDonald was born under the British flag, and Oregon attained Territorial status and a Territorial Government under the *Stars and Stripes* only in 1848, when the runaway was already on the other side of the Pacific.

Yet, through Ranald's inheritance from a Chinook Indian mother, a circumstance which by itself would have made him a truer American than the majority of us, and through his later choice and residence, he becomes sufficiently an American to justify our description of him. With whatever qualification we choose, we may say that Ranald MacDonald was the first American to leave his stamp upon the people and country of Japan.

But before applying ourselves to the details of his romantic story, it will be proper to suggest something of the situation in Japan in the decades immediately preceding the epoch-making visit of Commodore Perry. The Tokugawa Shogunate, which in our last study we saw in the heyday of its authority, was now exhibiting many signs of decline. Indeed the intimations were rather rapidly succeeding one another of imminent collapse. First of all, there had been the writing of the *Dai Nihon Shi,* or " Great History of Japan," by the

Prince of Mito. This important book carried the thoughts of men back into those far-off periods of Japanese history, when the Emperors ruled as well as reigned and when the institution of the Shogunate was unknown. Then, as a reaction against the *Kangakusha,* or School of Chinese Learning, which had been dominant in the seventeenth century, arose a School of Japanese Learning, the *Wagakusha.* In this, enthusiastic nationalists of the type of Motoori, Mabuchi and Hirata stressed the same facts of history and appealed for a return to the older ideals as established in the *Great Reform* (Taikwa) of the seventh century. Almost coincidently we find a diffusion of Dutch influence, through which a number of young Japanese urged the reversal of the isolationist policy of the Shogunate, in order to make way for new ideas in medicine and politics. A Japanese writer even fixes the beginnings of the New Japan at the date March 4, 1771, when two students, Sugita Gempei and Maeno Ryutaki, obtained leave to dissect the body of an executed criminal, in order to compare the result with the anatomical charts the Dutchmen had brought to the country. The influence of this spirit of research was felt much earlier than 1771, but it was only gradually that the substance of the new learning percolated into the minds of men, and these only an elect few among the ignorant mass. As an example of the way in which the new knowledge was sometimes applied, we may take the story of Unagami (1771-1825) who, when travelling with a friend, each penniless and hungry, came to a farmer's house, where they prepared their way by first visiting the cowshed and surreptitiously sprinkling a drug on the cow-fodder. Then they knocked at the farmer's door and asked for tea. While this was being got ready news came from the stable that one of the cows was suddenly taken sick. Without delay, the travellers announced themselves as physicians after the Dutch method, and proceeded to administer an antidote which, since they themselves had supplied the poison, effected an astonishingly rapid cure. The delighted farmer rewarded their skill with a present of money, which was sufficient to carry them on to similar exhibitions of their medical knowledge in other communities.[1]

A fourth influence may be said to be closely related to the one last named. It is that of the men whom we may call the Japanese martyrs of the new era, men who suffered and died to bring about the reopening of Japan and the restoration of their country to the status of a "courteous nation." Speaking of these men in connection with the accomplishment of the Restoration, Prince Ito has said: "No inconsiderable amount of credit, however, must in this respect be given to patriots and servants such as Rin Sahei, Kwazan Watanabe, Choei Takano, Shozen Sakuma, and others." How the knowledge of these obscure heroes filtered out from Japan may be illustrated in the charming sketch of Yoshida Torajiro, which Robert Louis Stevenson has given us in his *Familiar Studies of Men and Books*. Stevenson had learned of this devoted patriot from his friend, Mr. Masaki, and he concludes an eloquent appreciation with the words: "Only a few miles from us, to speak by the perspective of the universe, while I was droning over my lessons, Yoshida was goading himself to watchfulness with the stings of the mosquito; and while you were grudging a penny income tax, Kusakabe was stepping to death with a noble sentence on his lips."

Of all this "small, transfigured band" I like best Takano Nagahide who, after gaining some sort of a medical education through contact with the Nagasaki Dutchmen, set out to labour prodigiously, by writing and teaching, for the reopening of Japan. He wrote fifty-one separate works in two hundred and thirteen volumes, sometimes on subjects he knew little about, but always with the desire to enlighten the ignorance of his people. One small volume, however, is worth all the rest. The *Yume Monogatari*, or "Story of a Dream," has won undying fame, though at the time it brought only imprisonment, and ultimately death. In this work, under the semblance of a dream, he spoke earnestly of the good time to come, when Japan would once again open her hospitable portals to the outside world. Arrested for sedition, Takano was lodged in prison, but later, on the burning of the jail, he disfigured his face with saltpetre to prevent recognition and resumed his career as teacher. The end came on September 29, 1850, when, betrayed by one he had benefited, Takano found the house surrounded by police and, after a brief resistance, calmly took the high samurai way out of life by *seppuku*.[2]

This was only a few months after the stay of Ranald MacDonald in the Islands. I mention it here specially because it illustrates the fact, too often obscured, that, if there were efforts made from without to force the portals closed by the policy of the Tokugawas, there were also those within who were working for the same end and ready to suffer and die in the effort.

But, in addition to the influences already referred

to, as driving a nail here and there into the coffin of
Bakufu rule, there are two or three others which must
be mentioned, in order that we may appreciate the
particular place Ranald MacDonald holds in the history of the time.

The most important of these was the gradually increasing pressure exerted upon Japan by the ships of
Europe and America, for the purpose of forcing the
reopening of the country to foreign trade. For after
the time of Will Adams, the outside world by no means
ceased to be interested in the Far Eastern Empire.
The Dutch trade, carried on from Nagasaki, continued
for many years to be lucrative. In 1640 the returns
of the *Dutch East India Company* showed a profit of
over a million guilders. Yet before the end of the century, the Age of Gold had given place to the Age of
Brass, as copper had now become the chief export.
About this time, too, the hopes of England revived
and an expedition was fitted out in 1673 which, after
touching at Bantam, came to Nagasaki. The captain
showed a copy of the treaty which had been offered
to the English Company by Iyeyasu in 1613, without
saying a word as to its refusal by Sir John Saris. When
it was reported that King Charles II had been married
to a Portuguese princess, trade was immediately refused, in spite of the plea that the English were no
Papists. Naturally, this expedition was a total failure,
but hopes for the restoration of trade were not at once
given up. With the passing of the eighteenth century
the Dutch profits were much reduced, and the *London
East India Company* Directors reported that the export
trade to Japan would never amount to anything. Captain Broughton, with the *Providence,* surveyed Japa-

nese waters in 1795–6–7 and touched on the southern point of Matsumae. But a little later the *Providence* struck on a rock off the coast of Formosa and was lost, though Broughton and his crew were saved and taken on to Macao. It was also in 1797 that an English ship, commanded by Captain Stuart, but sailing under American colours, and chartered by the Dutch, visited Nagasaki—the first contact with Japan of the United States. Still another English vessel, under Captain Torey, was sent in 1803 to Nagasaki by the merchants of Calcutta, but was ordered to quit Japan within twenty-four hours.

From the beginning of the nineteenth century much activity was displayed by Russia, with a view of breaking through the restrictive measures of the Shoguns. A special mission, sent in 1805 under Captain Krusenstern to offer trade, was repulsed and the presents intended for the Shogun refused. Then in 1810-11 we have the dramatic story of Captain Golownin and his capture after a landing in the Kurile Islands. The Russian sailors found the Japanese intensely nervous over reports of foreign naval activity in northern waters for two or three years past, and particularly anxious to learn the fate of certain fishermen who, as it was supposed, had been carried off by Chwostoff. It was in July 1811 that Golownin, who had landed men merely to fill their water-casks, suddenly found his party surrounded by a body of armed men. They were taken prisoners, bound and carried to Matsumae. During more than a year's captivity in Japan, while the prisoners were for the most part treated kindly, they suffered from tedious interrogatories, suspicions of the absurdest sorts, and not least from the desire of the Japanese to learn as much of the Russian language as was possible. The record of these experiences is given in Captain Golownin's two volumes on *Japan and the Japanese,* comprising the Narrative of a Captivity in Japan.[3] On one occasion the captives made their escape, but without bettering their condition. They were rather glad than otherwise to be recaptured. At last, word was transmitted to them through Nagasaki that if the *Diana* would put in to the port of Hakodate, the Captain and his party would be suffered to depart. This plan was carried out in September 1812 and ended for the time being the curiosity of the Russians respecting Japan.

We might well have taken the story of Captain Golownin in detail, to illustrate the contacts of the outside world with Japan in modern times. But we use it here merely to show the gradual weakening of the policy of isolation, in the face of European and foreign pressure generally. At the time, this pressure only increased the determination of the Yedo Government to maintain the policy of exclusion, but it was obvious to many, both within and without the Empire, that a change was imminent.

Perhaps, the aspect of foreign pressure which worried the Shoguns more than anything else was that which appeared from happenings in China, particularly those which followed upon the war between England and China in 1839 and upon the signing of the *Treaty of Nanking* in 1842. The old fable of the shell-fish which, retiring for safety within the shelter of its shell, woke up to find itself upon the fish-monger's stall, labelled *1 sen,* kept recurring more and more to the official mind at Yedo.

All these events, to which it has been necessary to refer in order that we may the better understand what followed, have a very definite connection with the efforts, now becoming more numerous and insistent, by which the American Government sought to establish relations with Japan. Since the discovery of the Hawaiian Islands in 1778, the establishment of Astoria, the development of the Northwest fur trade, and the westward movement of the nation generally, the commerce of the United States had begun in earnest to seek the Pacific. It was convenient for the ships which summered at Nootka Sound and wintered at Honolulu, to put in the intervening months in some profitable venture in the ports of China, with sandalwood from Hawaii to provide the heathen with incense, and with furs from the Hudson Bay Company to ward off the inclemency of a Chinese winter. So, long before the middle of the nineteenth century, American ships were finding a haven at Canton, where they traded in all sorts of things, good and bad, with the *hongs* who managed the foreign commerce of the Middle Kingdom. When at last, in 1844, the United States Government followed up the *Treaty of Nanking* with a treaty of its own, there seemed no limit to the expansion of American business in the Far East.

But there was one great difficulty. The long voyage across the Pacific to Canton or Shanghai often found ships caught in the *Kuro Shiwo,* or Black Current, off the coast of Japan, and sorely in need of wood and water, if in no actual danger of shipwreck. We know of certain cases in which Japanese fishermen, caught in that current, were borne right across the Pacific to the shores of North America. We can form no estimate of the number of seamen from this side of the ocean, who have left their bones on the coast of the Far Eastern archipelago. Perhaps, to start with, there was but little thought of much trade with Japan; but in the interests of humanity as well as of trade with China, it seemed highly desirable that the rigorous policy of seclusion, into which Japan had retreated since early in the seventeenth century—a seclusion which even barred the way of return to Japanese themselves who might be cast upon a foreign shore—should come to an end by agreement between the Sunrise Empire and the outside nations.

For many years, little or no progress was made towards this end. It is true, as mentioned above, that as early as 1797 a ship, under American colours, the *Eliza* of New York, commanded by Captain Stuart, had made its way to Nagasaki, but this was by arrangement with and in the employ of the Dutch. Holland, subject to the French during the Napoleonic wars, was unable at the time to carry on the permitted commerce with Japan in its own ships. The following year, 1798, another American ship, the *Franklyn,* also sailing under the Dutch flag, made the same voyage. And, once again, in 1799, a vessel from Salem, this time under charter by the East India Company, came to Japan and, as Dr. Nitobe narrates, left footprints on the sands, " soon to be washed away." [4]

The first real effort on the part of the United States, in an official way, to bring the two countries into amicable relations with one another was that by Commodore Porter. In 1815, the same year that Decatur's squadron was sent to the Mediterranean, he wrote to Secretary Monroe suggesting the sending to Japan of a similar squadron in the interests of the whaling fleet. Seven years later, John Quincy Adams urged that " it was the duty of Christian nations to open Japan, and that it was the duty of Japan to respond to the demands of the world, as no nation had a right to withhold its quota to the general progress of mankind." [5] Ten years later, President Andrew Jackson went a step further by furnishing to Mr. Edmund Roberts, American Minister to Muscat and Siam, letters to the Emperor of Japan and instructions as to the opening of commercial relations. These instructions were renewed in 1835, but unfortunately Mr. Roberts died at Macao in 1836 without having had opportunity to discharge this part of his mission.

Before another governmental effort was made along these lines, we have the picturesque incident of the sending of the *Morrison* by Mr. King, some distorted report of which served to inspire Takano Nagahide to write the *Yume Monogatari*. Mr. C. W. King, an American merchant of Macao, conceived the idea of breaking through the obstacles imposed upon foreign intercourse by the Bakufu, by taking on board his ship, the *Morrison*, some shipwrecked Japanese sailors with a view to their repatriation. Included in the ship's company were the three well-known missionaries, Peter Parker, S. Wells Williams, and Charles Gutzlaff. But the Yedo authorities refused the bait, fired upon the vessel and compelled its withdrawal.

No more efforts were made till 1845, when a New York Congressman, Mr. Zadok Pratt, brought before Congress a resolution to the effect that " immediate measures be taken for effecting commercial arrangements with the Empire of Japan and the Kingdom of

Corea." The resolution was tabled, but it seems to have made some impression on the Administration, for, shortly after, Commodore Biddle, with an East Indian squadron, was ordered to see what could be done in the way of effecting entrance to this obstinately secluded realm, " yet not in such a manner as to excite a hostile feeling; or a distrust of the Government of the United States." Even this cautiously planned approach was repelled, not without incidents which might have had serious results but for the Commodore's patience. The Japanese delivered to Biddle an explanatory edict which declared: " We are aware that our customs are in this respect different from those of some other nations, but every nation has a right to manage its affairs in its own way."

It was shortly after this, on May 27, 1846, that the *Lawrence* was wrecked off the coast of Hokkaido and her eight survivors, of whom one was possibly killed in an attempt to escape, were incarcerated, to be later deported to Batavia on the annual Dutch ship. The second crew, consisting of fifteen men from the *Ladoga,* six Americans and nine Hawaiians,[6] who had deserted their ship on account of allegedly bad treatment, did not arrive till shortly before the landing of Ranald MacDonald.

This has been a lengthy introduction to our main subject, but it was necessary to have the background against which to place the career of MacDonald. We are now free to take up the main features of his personal story.

Ranald MacDonald was the son of Archibald MacDonald, a Hudson Bay factor, and his Chinook wife, " the Princess Sunday," daughter and heiress of " King

Com-Comly." The boy was born at Fort George, now known as Astoria, in Clatsop County, Oregon, in 1824, probably in the month of February. The vicissitudes of his infancy were predictive of the wanderings of later years. Ranald's mother, the Chinook princess, died at " salmon-running time " when the baby was but a few months old, and the fort itself was transferred to the site of the present Vancouver, Washington, the same year. In the following year the child, who since his mother's death had remained in the care of an aunt, Car-cum-cum, found a new foster-mother in Jane Klyne, whom Archibald MacDonald married in September. Then in the following year, 1826, the family removed to Kamloops, in the present Province of British Columbia. Here Ranald stayed off and on till 1830, visiting his Chinook relations in the intervals. Up to his tenth year he was kept in ignorance that his maternal grandfather was no other than " King Com-Comly." [7]

The factor's family was still by no means settled, for the Columbia River fur trade necessitated frequent changes of residence. Fort Langley, Fort Colville and Fort Vancouver are mentioned as among the places to which the little Ranald and his brother Angus were borne, sometimes by water in bateaux, but often in two baskets suspended on either side of a horse's back.

Meanwhile, the more academic education of Ranald was proceeding, sometimes at the hands, we trust not too literally, of his father, and during the winter of 1833-34 with Mr. Ball of Vancouver, who had established the first school in the Pacific Northwest. In the fall of 1834, Ranald went further afield to a school, founded under the auspices of the Hudson Bay Company, at Fort Garry, now known as Winnipeg. The trip by pony over the Athabasca Pass, when the snow was deep and the cold severe, was the hardest experience the young traveller had as yet encountered.

By this time Archibald MacDonald was beginning to think he had done almost enough for his children. He was strongly opposed to making what was called " Handsome provision " for them and, as he put it, " I am myself for being off with them as soon as possible." He did indeed assign Ranald " with certain indescribable fears " to the care of Mr. Frank Ermatinger, on the understanding that " I cannot afford to make a gentleman of him." He also commended him to the headquarters of the Company, on the footing of an apprentice clerk. But, in 1843, we find him writing in a vein of paternal discouragement: " For all I shall do for him again he may just crawl through life as the Black bear does—lick his paws."

Truth to tell, Ranald MacDonald showed no great disposition to lean on his father, or on any one else, for support. His biographers give us the glimpse of " a high-minded, visionary, quixotic youth," for a time fretting away his soul on the high stool of a bank in St. Thomas, Ontario, with his hot Indian blood combining with the restlessness of his Highland forebears to stretch his bonds to the bursting point. Even thus early, his roaming eye seems to have caught sight of the lure of Japan. Some time in 1836, a Japanese junk had been cast up on the shores of the Queen Charlotte Islands and the survivors had been taken in charge by Dr. McLoughlin, the Hudson Bay representative at Vancouver. These were the castaways Mr. King endeavoured to restore to their native land by sending the *Morrison,* after they had gone all the way around Cape Horn to England and thence to Macao.

Stimulated by this incident, Ranald MacDonald gained the conviction that across the Pacific lay the land of his maternal ancestors, since the Indians of the Northwest coast and the Japanese were evidently, to his mind, of one stock. There grew up in his heart the determination to test this belief by his own experience, and on the other side of the Pacific to learn something of Japan and the Japanese. So we next find him deserting the counting-house at St. Thomas to make his way, by a route sufficiently circuitous, to the land of his dream. He journeyed on foot to the Great Lakes, at St. Paul joined one of the Mississippi river boats as a deck hand, and presently from New Orleans made his way to New York. Thence, in 1842, while his father was considering making the journey to New York to discover his whereabouts, in order to bring the runaway to his senses by setting before him his claims as the heir of " King Com-Comly," a letter arrived from Ranald dated from London. It seems that the young rover had sought in vain for an American ship to take him to Japan, and had suddenly embraced the opportunity to visit Europe. Archibald MacDonald did actually make the visit to New York, but, ere he arrived, the elusive Ranald was in San Francisco, then known as Yerba Buena, though without calling on Mr. Rae, the representative of the Hudson Bay Company. According to his own account, our hero had in the interim made a voyage in a slaver which, when chased by a British man of war, established a clean record by throwing overboard its cargo of " white ivory." He had also made a voyage to Calcutta which ended off the coast of California, where the crew were sent ashore and the vessel scuttled. It is a little difficult to fit in the dates properly at this stage of our story, but there seems to be no reason to doubt that Ranald may have made several voyages from San Francisco before bringing up at Lahaina,[8] on the Island of Maui, in the Hawaiian group, in the fall of 1847. From hereabouts he wrote to his father: " I again shipped for another Cape Horn voyage with the intention of being discharged at some of the islands of the Spanish main. These intentions I have altered, and as Captain Edwards was going to China, and from there to the Japan sea, I thought it a good opportunity to crown my intentions; that, if I went with him, I should be discharged before he left the sea. He tried to persuade me to give up the adventure, but I am going."

Here then we find Ranald MacDonald on the threshold of his great adventure. " But I am going "— these are the curt words which betray the resolve of the man. The actual object of the journey is somewhat veiled. To one unacquainted with Ranald's musings on his ancestry, it would seem a journey inspired merely by the spirit of adventure. From *The Seaman's Friend,* of Honolulu, quoted by Mr. Lewis, we get the following impression of Ranald from a shipmate. He says he was " a man of about five feet, seven inches; thick set; straight hair and dark complexion. . . . He was a good sailor, well educated, a firm mind, well calculated for the expedition upon which he embarked. His intentions were to stay at this island (Yezo) and learn some of the Japanese language, and from there go down to Yeddo, the principal city of

Nipon, and, if the English or Americans ever open trade with the Japanese, he would find employment as an interpreter. He had other intentions which I never mention only in a secret manner." [9]

We may now take up the story as gathered from Ranald's own words, in the *Journal* which, after the writer's vain efforts in his lifetime to find a publisher, was printed in 1923 for the Eastern Washington Historical Society, under the joint editorship of Mr. William S. Lewis and Naojiro Murakami. The story of the long delay, before it was possible to make this *Journal* known to the world, is a pathetic one, though in part the fault of the author himself. Had Ranald MacDonald prepared his narrative for the press immediately after his return, when the interest in the reopening of Japan was at the flood, there is little doubt that it would have been eagerly accepted by the publishers. But in 1853 he left the original manuscript with a friend of his father's, Mr. Malcolm McLeod, at Ottawa, and then proceeded to the Northwest coast, where he remained, without communicating with Mr. McLeod, for nearly twenty-five years. Meanwhile, the Ottawa lawyer had edited and to some extent rewritten the *Journal,* but had not succeeded in finding a publisher. It was not till 1887 that the second draft of the manuscript was made, and the third, revised by the author, was made as late as 1891. In that year some serious effort was made to interest a publisher in Montreal and the book was advertised as forthcoming under the title of *A Canadian in Japan.* But once again the attempt proved a failure. In 1893 three copies of the revised draft were made, and renewed efforts made to secure publication in England, Canada, or the United States. But still no publisher was willing to take the risk of producing the book, except at the author's expense, and Ranald MacDonald was quite unable to raise the requisite sum. The same year, however, a newspaper man, Mr. L. C. P. Haskins, of Eastern Washington, went so far as to print a few pages in the *Pioneer* of Kettle Falls, Washington, in the hope that the public interest would demand the whole. But, alas, the first American in Japan was not destined to see the record of his great adventure. In the summer of 1894 Ranald MacDonald made the voyage over seas less charted than those of the Pacific. There is not only pathos but irony in the fact that in these years of Japan's great advance towards westernization, while books, many of them of slight value, about the Island Empire were pouring forth from the presses of the world, two copies of MacDonald's *Journal*, unused and probably unread, were lying in the Public Library at Spokane and in the Provincial Library at Victoria B. C., unable to find contact with the outside world.[10] It was not till 1905 that Mrs. Eva Emery Dye, of Portland, Oregon, used some of the Victoria material for the production of her *MacDonald of Oregon*, and a good deal later, in 1923, that Mr. William S. Lewis edited the *Journal*, with annotations, for the Eastern Washington Historical Society.

Now let us pass from the book to its story, the record of a journey as intrepid as was ever made into the world of the unknown. We may pass over all that part of the *Journal* which describes the author's boyhood, when " the British flag covered my cradle," and the adventures of his early manhood, already sufficiently indicated. We start at that memorable day in Lahaina,

Hawaiian Islands, when he came upon his former Captain, Lawrence B. Edwards, of the *Plymouth,* and made the curious bargain which Captain Edwards, for his own part, never dreamed he would have to carry out. While in all other respects Ranald MacDonald's agreement was of the sort common on the whaling ships, it included the promise that the young adventurer was free " to leave the ship off the coast of Japan wherever and whenever " he might desire. He exacted also the pledge that the Captain should teach him the usual methods of making observations. To this end he obtained for himself a quadrant and a nautical almanac. So in the spring of 1847 MacDonald found the dreams, over which he had so long been brooding in various parts of the world, beginning to be realized. The *Plymouth* sailed in company with the *David Paddock,* but " one was taken and the other left," for the *David Paddock* was wrecked on July 20, off the coast of Sakhalin, though all hands were happily saved.

The immediate destination of the *Plymouth* was Hongkong, but on the way thither quite a few adventures were experienced. In the neighbourhood of a rock in mid-ocean which Ranald calls French Frigate Shoals, there was encountered the worst storm of the voyage and Captain Edwards was forced to make for the Island of Gregan for repairs, as well as for wood and water. Here they came upon a naked white man who a little later presented himself only in a shirt and revealed himself as one Liverpool Jack. Apparently there were white sailors, shipwrecked men or deserters, not a few scattered throughout the Pacific, for Liverpool Jack spoke of another whom he called Spider Jack, living about a mile to the north of him. The two had been there from fifteen to twenty years. Ranald Mac-Donald conversed with the exiles, but was not inclined to put implicit faith in their stories, though they spoke confidently of a great store of buried treasure in the neighbouring island of Pegan.

Heavy weather was experienced again in the China Seas, but the *Plymouth* managed to reach Hongkong in safety and was there laid up a month in preparation for the whaling. Then she started northward, by way of the Ryukyu Islands, for the Sea of Japan. In the vicinity of the Island of Quelparte the whalers occupied themselves leisurely with the fishing. " Whaling," writes Ranald, " was so easy in the Japan Sea; the fish were so numerous that we had no occasion to chase them with our ship; we had nothing to do but to lower our boats, harpoon them, and bring them alongside for stripping. In the forepart of the season we took several whales. Towards the latter part of it—the fish having run north—we sailed into the Channel of Tartary, where we captured four whales."

With the vessel nearly full of whale-oil, Ranald Mac-Donald now felt he had done his duty by Captain Edwards and prepared to carry out his own personal plan. He writes: " At length, on June 27, 1848, the ship then being full and lying off the coast of Japan, about five miles from the nearest island, I asked the Captain to let me leave the ship. With much reluctance, he consented, according to our bargain. I then bought from him a small boat, specially made for himself, rigged for sailing, a quadrant—for I could take an ' Observation ' for latitude and longitude—provisions for thirty-six days, etc. I also assigned to him, in trust, the balance of my share in the whaling adventure, say about six hundred dollars."

So our hero, against the pleading of Captain Edwards, stepped into his newly acquired boat to say good-bye to his comrades of the Pacific voyage. He had placed in his tiny shallop his box of books, a little stationery, some clothes, his precious quadrant, but no chart. He himself cut the rope which still bound him to the *Plymouth,* heard from the ship's deck the " God bless you, Mac," of the sailors, and so severed the last link between himself and the North American continent. The whaler went its own way, dipping her flag, the Stars and Stripes, more than once, as though reluctant to say the final farewell, while Ranald dipped, once only, his own small pennon and steered away into the dense fog which seemed a symbol of his dark and uncertain fate.

Presently, however, there loomed out of the fog a reef, on which the breakers were pounding. So, to avoid the rocks, Ranald worked round to the leeward of an island, afterwards known as Kotonto-mari, disturbing the sea-lions in his course. He landed on an islet called Rishiri, which he presently discovered to be uninhabited. Here he spent a couple of days, among ducks and geese and other waterfowl, but without a sign of human beings. These two days of Robinson Crusoe-like existence gave him the desired opportunity to prepare for a landing on some larger island, where he might reasonably expect to encounter the natives. So, after landing most of his stores, he practised upsetting his boat and righting it again, till he was fairly certain he could do it at will. Then, on the first of July, he set his little sail towards the northern tip of the island of Yezo, now Hokkaido, and there on the following day, when near enough to the shore to see the ascending smoke of a village, and in the sight of a few Ainus who were engaged in fishing, he went through the carefully rehearsed action of capsizing his craft. The plan worked excellently. He was soon rescued, together with his boat, and such of his stores as remained afloat. Then he was carried to a large house, where he was enabled to change his wet clothes for dry and was given a pair of Japanese sandals. He was also offered some *saké*, which his hosts described by the curious term of " grog-yes," probably a reminiscence of speech with the shipwrecked crew of the *Lawrence* some two years before.

Next day, Ranald's rescuers, whom by now he had learned to recognize as Ainus rather than Japanese proper, especially because of their long beards and generally hairy appearance, took him, with such flotsam and jetsam as had come to hand from the boat, to the nearest military station. This was Soya, a place about twenty miles from the point on which the landing had been effected. Before starting, however, as MacDonald informs us, the kindly fishermen performed their customary religious rites, offering *saké*, fish and rice to Heaven and Earth and the gods of fire and the sea. It is interesting to note that, even at this early stage, the budding philologist was at work, trying to catch the exact pronunciation of the syllables he heard, and endeavouring to identify some of these with the language of the North American Indians with whom he had been acquainted.

The Ainus and such Japanese as had now appeared were equally curious as to himself and his whence-abouts. They produced a map and endeavoured to obtain from the stranger information as to the probable whereabouts of the vessel from which he had escaped. Ranald speaks of this map as " the only purely Japanese map I ever saw," and did his best, for his own part, to find out the position of the principal towns and cities. His guards—for there was now no question as to the relations between himself and his hosts—were kind and even generous, but at the same time evidently bent upon preventing any attempt to escape. They also carefully examined everything which was in the prisoner's possession, sketching and measuring things in detail, as well as taking the most careful measurements of his own person.

The journey from the place of landing was resumed early in August and Ranald MacDonald must have presented a remarkable appearance, dressed in a cotton kimono several inches too short for him and marching between two lines of watchful Ainus. But he was permitted to smoke and was allowed attendants who were proud to carry his pipe or tobacco box, or the *hibachi* at which at need he obtained a light. When the company reached a village, curtains of striped cotton were placed along either side of the street, to hide the foreigner from the too curious gaze of the populace. But the precaution was ridiculous since the tall foreigner was easily able to look over the top of the screen.

They came at length to the point from which it was intended to embark for Matsumae, and the farewell taken of the Ainus was quite touching, men, women and children coming down to the water's edge in great numbers to make their adieux. Ranald was now for the first time enabled to use that expressive Japanese

word, *Sayonara* (Farewell), which was the last word
he was to utter, more than forty-five years later.

The start by junk was to the American sailor especially interesting, for the men, to his great admiration,
did some real sculling and sang as they worked. The
only drawback to the voyage was that Ranald had to
sit cross-legged in the covered part of the boat, with
little or no opportunity to stretch his limbs. The
officers in charge were two-sworded men and not likely
to allow to their prisoner overmuch in the way of freedom. The first stage of the journey, however, was
only a short one, since to make the main voyage it was
necessary to have a larger vessel and a fair wind. For
these they had to wait and, meanwhile, on shore there
was plenty of courtesy shown, but no large measure of
liberty allowed. There was also endless enquiry as to
the strange lands overseas, their size, the character of
their inhabitants, and the like. But at last came the
expected junk when, with renewed *Sayonaras* for those
left behind, the captive and his guardians turned again
to the south. The junk was covered with cotton sheet-
ing painted with what seemed to Ranald to be imita-
tion portholes, in reality the *mon,* or heraldic pattern
of the daimyo of Matsumae. The length of the journey
was uncertain, possibly a couple of weeks, so Ranald,
" cribbed and thought-weary in the solitude of my
prison on the ever-rocking sea," lay in a small cabin
towards the stern of the vessel or, on occasion, enjoyed
the run of the deck. He gives a good account of the
junk and notes particularly the religious services held
at sunrise and sunset before the altar, with the oft-
repeated Buddhist prayer, *Namu Amida Butsu,* and
the telling of beads.

The journey down the western coast of Hokkaido was in those days a considerable voyage, and it was the beginning of September by the time our travellers reached Matsumae. Decked out with a special array of small flags, and with the lances of the soldiers fixed upright around the poop, the junk presented quite a picturesque appearance on its arrival and attracted to it a big crowd of fishing boats. Unfortunately for Ranald, he was compelled to remain under cover all the time, and so was unable to see the outside world except through a chink in the partition. Among the officials who came down to meet the junk were some who were evidently of high rank. When at length one of these was brought into the presence of Ranald, his first word was *Nippon-jin* (Japan-man), indicating his belief that the prisoner's somewhat Indian features betrayed a Japanese origin. After this preliminary exclamation there followed a good deal of dumb show, with the trying out on the foreigner of words picked up from various quarters. From these Ranald did indeed gather that a still longer voyage was in store for him, namely, to Nagasaki.

But, before this could be arranged, there was the disembarkation and the examination in Matsumae. Amid a great crowd MacDonald was placed in a *norimono,* or palanquin, while the populace stood around gazing as at a new kind of wild beast. Then, with the *norimono* closed, without even a peephole, the bearers started forward at a smart pace, only pausing at one village or another to give place to another relay. During these enforced stops, food was brought to the prisoner, but he was not allowed to dismount till after midnight, when they came to a building with the walls well protected by spikes of bamboo and iron. Within this building Ranald was comfortably settled, provided with fire, kettle, and cup and saucer, and welcomed by one whom he took to be the Governor. To his great surprise he saw two English letters, a J and a C, scribbled with charcoal on the wall. Noticing his surprise, his host directed his attention to some more writing on " a stanchion in the middle of the room, supporting the ridge-pole of the roof." There, to his startled gaze, appeared the names, *Robert McCoy, John Brady,* and *John*—the rest was indecipherable. By pronouncing the word *America* and by drawing his hand significantly across his throat, the official gave Ranald to understand that certain Americans had preceded him in Japan and that, probably in attempting to escape, had been slain. Later it was learned that fifteen sailors, eight Americans and seven Hawaiians,[11] had indeed been MacDonald's predecessors in a Japanese prison. As already noted, they were men from the whaler *Ladoga* [12] who had deserted their ship, dissatisfied with their treatment, and had drifted ashore near Matsumae. Since they were suspected of being spies, they were confined in the prison where Ranald found the mysterious initials, but there had been no throat-cutting. One of the Americans had died of disease, or perhaps of the medicine prescribed to cure him, and one of the Hawaiians had committed suicide by hanging himself. The rest had already been transported to Nagasaki, where MacDonald was destined to meet them and sail with them on the *U. S. Preble.*

Ranald evidently took the exhibition of the American names and the gesture of his jailor as advice to be good, for he accepted his fate quite philosophically, and even managed to retain as a souvenir the bamboo spoon provided for him as well as a wooden fork which one of the *Ladoga* deserters had made and left behind. He was indeed becoming quite used to Japanese food and clothing and beginning to be able to express his wishes to the guards. As a mark of special favour, they allowed him to have his Bible and, as a tribute to its sacredness, even made a special shelf on which it might be placed. The rest of his things they kept under seal to offer as exhibits in the enquiry at Nagasaki.

On October 1 they were ready for the next stage of the journey, as it turned out the last for MacDonald in Japan. The junk was a large one, but the prisoner was put in a small, grated cage, the grating of which, at Ranald's request, was subsequently removed. But he was not permitted to go on deck and, while he was able to study the manners and customs of the soldiers and sailors, at their meals and prayers, he was not able, except by surreptitious peeps, to see much along the coast through his porthole. One advantage, however, he had, that while quite a number on board the junk were seasick he was not only immune but well able to enjoy the fish, fruit and rice provided for meals. So at last, sailing along the *east* coast of the main island (at least so the *Journal* informs us, though the *west* coast route would seem to be the shorter), they came in due course to the outer harbour of Nagasaki.

Here a great concourse of officials came to meet them, and among these a high military chief, whose name is not very recognizable from the spelling of the *Journal*. A preliminary examination was held in the middle of the cabin, with the two chief officials and their "pale-faced secretaries" sitting behind their books, maps and writing materials. Ranald was fortunate in being provided with an interpreter, Moriyama Iyenosuke, who figures much in all dealings with Americans, from the examination of the *Ladoga* crew to the negotiations with Commodore Perry. He was an astute personage, described later as "one who spoke tolerably good English but understood only as much as he wanted to." At any rate, he proved a good friend to MacDonald, especially in the matter of slurring over our hero's profession of the Christian faith, which was unlawful and punishable with death.

Ranald himself describes Moriyama as follows: "He was, by far, the most intelligent person I met in Japan. He had a pale cast of thought, piercing black eyes which seemed to search into the very soul and read its every emotion. He spoke English pretty fluently and even grammatically. His pronunciation was peculiar, but it was surprisingly in command of combinations of letters and syllables foreign to the Japanese tongue. He was my daily companion—a lovable one—ever afterwards during my sojourn in Japan. When with me he always had books in Dutch, and a Dutch and English dictionary. The Dutch factor at Nagasaki, John Levyssohn (Joseph Henry Levyssohn) told me that Murayama (Moriyama) spoke better Dutch than himself. The books were on different subjects, but principally on the commerce and customs of European nations." It may be well understood that Moriyama, who was studying Latin and French as well as English and Dutch, was a great comfort and support to Ranald MacDonald at this crisis of his affairs.

A sympathetic interpreter was certainly a great boon at this juncture, for the officials at Nagasaki were bent on probing to the very depths of the stranger's soul. They asked him his nationality and were puzzled to learn that he was not exactly himself clear on the matter, being both British and American. They asked him of his father, mother, brothers and sisters, of his ship and its whereabouts and his reason for leaving it. Then, soaring in a moment from earth to heaven, they enquired as to his belief in God, professing themselves satisfied with his, or rather his interpreter's, answer. After this, Ranald was taken from the junk, placed in a small boat moored to a bridge of boats, and so conveyed to the main harbour, where he was able, at closer range, to survey the town. Nagasaki, he tells us, was a city of about ten thousand houses, with wide streets paved in the middle with stone. At the entrance to the harbour was the fatal spot called by the Dutch Papenberg, where in 1638 took place a hideous massacre of the Christian population. A little nearer was the island called Deshima, connected by a causeway with the main part of the island, and serving practically as a prison for the Dutch merchants, who had been permitted to remain after the expulsion of the Portuguese. Three large Chinese junks, armed with cannon, were in port, and a whole swarm of smaller Japanese craft. The party with their prisoner landed at a jetty with steps of stone, passed under a massive *torii* into the city, through files of soldiers, and then Ranald found himself deposited in a *norimono* and

borne past houses and gardens, great and small, till
they reached the residence of the Governor.

Here, with thousands of spectators to watch the foreigner's entrance, a new and still severer inquisition
was preparing. This time there was a Dutch interpreter to give Ranald assurance and the benefit of his
advice, but the guards who stood about, handling their
swords and daggers, looked very grim and expectant.
Nevertheless, MacDonald kept his poise and, to show
that he was not afraid, ate freely of the rice, pickles
and fish, which were set before him. At this point his
friend Moriyama appeared and bade him be of good
courage, at the same time explaining that it would be
necessary to place his foot upon a certain image on a
plate to prove that he did not worship " the devil of
Japan." It was fortunate that the interpreter thus
camouflaged the fact that to place the foot upon the
picture of Virgin and Child was to abjure Christianity.
For if Ranald did not suspect the real character of the
symbolic act he declared aloud that he did not believe
in images, and so passed the crucial test. He did make
difficulty, however, about squatting on the floor as did
the other occupants of the office, and he refused absolutely to *kotow* to the Governor as everybody else
did. It was probably with some trepidation that, with
all the others prostrate, Ranald stared for fifteen
seconds at the Governor, face to face. Later, he asked
Moriyama what the Governor had said and received
the answer, " He said you must have a big heart."

Now the questions came fast and thick, and the
answers were written down by the secretary as soon
as interpreted. Once again, after the usual queries as
to name, place of birth, and so on, came the enquiry

as to his belief in God. But this time a more definite answer was demanded as to what he believed about God. Ranald immediately, mindful of the catechism days of his youth, began the recitation of the *Apostles' Creed* and got as far as " And in Jesus Christ, His Only Son, our Lord; Born of the Virgin Mary . . .", when the interpreter hastily stopped him with a whispered, " That will do! That will do! " Ranald was wise enough to stop, for he was here, unwittingly, stepping on dangerous ground. The examination soon after came to an end and the prisoner, now not at all doubtful as to his status, was carried in another palanquin to a room, neat enough and clean, but partitioned off with bars four inches thick and the same distance apart. Outside was a small garden, with a stone wall all about it, about six feet high, and topped with broken glass. The apartment to which Ranald was confined was just seven feet by nine, provided with brazier, cup and teapot, and the floor covered with mats of rice-straw. Here, not without some comforts and relaxations, MacDonald was destined to stay for just seven months.

It is not necessary to do more than summarize the incidents, which were really not particularly numerous, of these months. The prisoner was well fed, provided with most things he asked for, though for some time not his Bible, and visited by about nine persons who acted, more or less, as his interpreters. When he mentioned anything he needed, they would look up the word in a Dutch-English dictionary they possessed, and with patience and some measure of good luck, would presently arrive at the approximate meaning of his request. About twenty days after the last men-

tioned inquisition, Ranald was again taken to court
and interrogated on most of the old issues and such
new ones as could be thought of. The officials were
particularly desirous of having pointed out to them, on
a map which they produced, the exact spot where
Ranald had left the ship, all about the vessel's course,
and everything that could be told about the whale-
fishery. A few days after this, a still further examination was held at the Town Hall, before the Dutch
factor, Mr. Levyssohn. On this occasion it was
brought out that the Dutch ship, the *Josephine Cath-
erine,* had already departed and that, if it were decided
to liberate and deport the American, another year
would probably have to elapse. The examination concluded with the establishment of a reasonable degree
of friendliness on either side.

These were the months during which a school for
the teaching of English was for the first time, and
under the strangest of imaginable circumstances, set
up on Japanese soil. For, now that the situation was
to a certain extent stabilized, the prisoner accommodating himself to his captivity and the officials concluding that they had discovered everything they were
likely to learn, Ranald MacDonald received a number
of inquisitive pupils, fourteen all told, who came to
him almost daily for instruction. He writes:

" Their habit was to read English to me one at a
time. My duty was to correct their pronunciation and
as best as I could in Japanese, explain meaning, con-
struction, etc. It was difficult to make them catch
some of our sounds, especially the consonants, and
some of the combinations particularly were impracti-
cable to them. For instance: they cannot pronounce,

except very imperfectly, the letter L. They pronounce
it R. So that they rendered my name Ranardo Mac-
donardo, with a strong burr of the R. They also had
a habit of adding an I (short I) or O at the end after
a consonant. As to the vowels there was no difficulty.
They have all the full ore rotundo sound and are all
pronounced, even the final E." Of course, the teacher
was at the same time learning from his pupils and he
adds: " Without boast, I may say that I picked up
their language easily, many of their words sounding
familiar to me—possibly through my maternal ancestry." [13]

Among Ranald's visitors were a few priests, probably Shinto. At any rate he picked up from them
something as to their faith, though he mistakes the
Shin in *Shin-to* (Way of the Gods) for Way instead of
translating the *To*. He got a rather high idea of both
the creed and the morals of the native religion and
describes it once as " more Christian in its beatitudes,
in many respects, than Christianity itself (so-called)
in the world since its primal purity."

One incident from these almost daily interviews led
to tragic consequences, though not for Ranald. The
captain of the guard was very anxious to break through
the rule which had hitherto confined MacDonald's
audience to the men. So he asked of Ranald permission to bring his wife and daughter to see the foreigner. They came, with three of their attendant
women, saw, but evidently did not conquer. Ranald
writes, rather ungallantly: " I cannot say that they
were beautiful; nor, on the other hand, that they were
ugly. Their general expression of countenance was
that of smiling good nature and artlessness calculated

to make a favourable impression." Yet these "giggling " women, who " shuffled in and out, and squatted in such a manner that they looked more like moving bundles of clothes than anything else," brought upon the head of their introducer, the captain, the most summary of all repercussions. When, shortly after, Ranald noticed his absence and enquired the reason, he was informed " that his head had been chopped off —that was how they expressed it—for breaking the law forbidding what he had done in bringing women to my prison." It was evident that in this " first English school " the Japanese officials did not intend to encourage co-education.

Only a few other incidents broke the humdrum monotony of MacDonald's long confinement. He got back his Bible and again the guards, observing his reverence for the sacred volume, made for it a special shelf, a *tokiwari*. He gained permission to have meat once a week and as there was neither beef nor mutton was well content to get pork. So Sunday became his pork day, or perhaps the other way about. In course of time he learned of the presence of other foreign prisoners in the neighbourhood, largely because he found the soldiers using terms which they could only have picked up from the vocabulary of British or American sailors. When, however, he was asked to translate such terms as " shiver my timbers " into Japanese, he had to confess his limitations as a teacher of English.

In compensation, he learned plenty of Japanese, though he spells *Hara-kiri* (more politely called *seppuku*) sometimes *Harra-karri* and sometimes *Harri-karri*. His translation of the term as " happy dispatch " has stuck, though it appears to have been anticipated by Mrs. W. Buck some eight years before. Ranald gives a somewhat detailed and not too inaccurate account of Japan's feudal system and at any rate recognized the existence of an Emperor as well as Shogun, a kind of double rule which was not understood in America till long after the *Treaty of Kanagawa*.

It is evident that, as the weeks went by, Ranald MacDonald, in spite of his too narrow quarters, was becoming increasingly *en rapport* with his Japanese associates. He remarks again on his own resemblance to them in feature, saying: " In look, facial features, etc. I was not unlike them; my sea life and rather dark complexion, moreover, giving me their general colour—a healthy bronze. I never had a cross word with any of them; and I think I passed rather as a favourite amongst them—eliciting, ever and anon, the compliment of the Governor as to my ' heart.' " He adds: " Enjoying a well-guarded liberty in their social life, and a perfect toleration of creed, except as to that form of Christian faith known as Roman Catholic, banned, for reasons of State, over two hundred years ago—(I speak of the time I was then there)—they had nothing to complain of."

Into the even tenor of this monotonous, but not too uncomfortable, existence came a red letter day, New Year's Day (not yet the adopted New Year's Day of the Japanese), January 1, 1849. The occasion was marked by the sending of a present from the Dutch factor, Mr. Levyssohn, consisting of " a bottle of exquisite coffee, some small loaves of wheat bread—also more precious still to me—sixty-eight numbers of the

London Atlas newspaper, and *Weekly Dispatch,* the whole with his polite card of compliments." It may be imagined what a feast there was in this thoughtful gift for the lonely and surely sometimes homesick exile, both for body and mind.

Yet at this time, so far as outward appearances go, he seems to have been happy rather than otherwise, especially as the Governor was good to him and his pupils were making rapid progress under his instruction. He writes: " They improved in English wonderfully, for their heart was evidently in the work, and their receptiveness, quick and comprehensive aptitude in learning was, to me, extraordinary; in some of them phenomenal."

Then suddenly his peace was shattered, about the end of April 1849, by the sound of cannon shot. It was impossible at first to learn the reason for the intrusion. Ranald thought possibly it merely signified the arrival of a new Governor. But presently the guards informed him that a foreign ship had arrived in port and that the shots had been fired to summon the troops from the interior. At the same time military curtains, which Ranald mistook for sham forts, were put in place, and a good deal of target practice started.

From Moriyama, Ranald soon obtained more precise information as to what was happening. It appeared that the foreign ship was no other than the *U. S. Corvette Preble,* under Commander Glynn, and that the Commander had come to take off from the islands the sailors now in confinement. Glynn had for two years been cruising in the North Pacific and now took advantage of the presence of the Dutch at Deshima to make his demands upon the Shogun. He knew nothing at this time of MacDonald's presence at Nagasaki, so that the rescue of our hero was only incidental to the repatriation of the other Americans. It may be imagined that there was an unwonted state of excitement when the palanquin arrived to take MacDonald to the Town Hall, where the new Governor and the old Governor stood side by side to see the transfer of the marooned men. Ranald at this time got his first sight of his compatriots and, with some complacency, contrasts them, in their ordinary sailor dress, and looking pale and thin, with himself, in his "best Japanese dress, plain and respectable."

The men were made to kneel before the Governor while, by means of the interpreter, they were given the information that they were now at liberty to leave the land. The actual transfer, however, had to be made through the good offices of the Dutch factory, the only contact with the outside world recognized by the Japanese Government. So, in separate palanquins, singing their sailor chanteys, the men were borne, through an avenue of the gaping populace, over the covered bridge which connected Nagasaki with the Dutch settlement of Deshima to the factory. Before leaving the bridge they were searched and immediately after found themselves the guests of Mr. Levyssohn. "This is a Christian house," their host announced and told them it was not necessary for them to kneel. Ranald describes the feast that followed with a good deal of gusto: "We were entertained with a good dinner, with knives, silver table service, chairs, pork, bread, etc.— all of which we duly relished, with a parting cup of best Dutch Java coffee, and then with a true 'Cheery men,

Oh! ' embarked on the good ship *Preble;* warmly wel-. comed; and with her noble Captain and right good crew, sailed for freer and more genial shores."

The rest of Ranald MacDonald's adventures, following upon his departure from Japan, must be condensed into a few paragraphs. He made his formal statement, duly taken down, to an officer on board the *Preble,* and this is now among the documents published by the State Department. As, however, there had been no official demand for his return to America, Ranald felt at liberty to leave the *Preble* in Chinese waters. He writes: " I, a penniless waif on the ocean of life, took ship again before the mast. Thence, after many adventures, the world over, including Australia during the first ' gold-diggings,' I returned, after several years, to my native land, or rather to that portion of it (British Columbia) which had been left to the Old Flag by the Oregon Treaty. Of this portion of my life—matter for a book, and of some public moment as pioneer work, in close connection with my old and ever good friend, Sir James Douglas, first Governor of that Colony—I shall not here speak."

On his way back to British Columbia, Ranald visited the family home at St. Andrew's, but, alas, not in time to see again his father. Archibald MacDonald had died shortly before the return of his errant son. So Ranald set out to join his half-brother Allen in British Columbia. Here we find him engaged in a variety of undertakings, working at the ranch on Bonaparte River, running pack trains to the gold mines on the Upper Fraser River in the Cariboo country, labouring with others to find and make easier routes to the promise of El Dorado, running a ferry (at a dollar a head) across the Fraser at Lilloet, and interesting himself between times in the mining prospects of the Horsefly Country. During these years he was respected among the rough characters, whom the gold rush had attracted to the Cariboo country, as well as esteemed by the respectable. On more than one occasion he was a guest at the residence of the Governor, Sir James Douglas. His physical prowess, too, was recognized by more than one of the " bad men " of the period. A certain prize-fighter named McCune, having been thoroughly worsted in a duel with single-stick between himself and MacDonald, remarked that " he wouldn't have cared a damn if he had been beaten by a white man, but that he hated like hell to be beat by a siwash." After which Ranald was commonly known in the district as " Siwash " MacDonald.

Later still, after some experience in running a stage line in British Columbia, keeping an hotel at Hat Creek, working in his cousin's trading store at Kamloops, he moved over, about 1882, into what was then Washington Territory and settled down near the old Hudson Bay station of Fort Colville. Here he lived a life which often enough interested itself in attractive, but for the most part unprofitable, ventures. In the intervals he occupied himself with the compiling of his *Journal.* As time went on, it was a great grief to him that no one was sufficiently concerned about his story to encourage its publication.

Several accounts have been collected by his biographers of visits paid to the aging pioneer from time to time. According to an account first published in *Harper's Weekly* of July 18, 1891, and reproduced by Mr. Lewis, Mrs. Elizabeth Custer, widow of the famous

General, came to see him at Fort Colville in 1890. She found a courtly old gentleman whose manners and high-flown language belied his rather shabby appearance. Later on her reference to him as " a prince of paupers " made him very indignant and drew from him the remark that although on this occasion he had appeared carelessly garbed, and with moccasins on his feet, he had in his chest " clothes in which I could have appeared before the crowned heads of Europe." Mrs. Custer found the old man living in a motley crowd of dogs and chickens and half-breed children (the children of Duncan MacDonald, Ranald's cousin), but she was much impressed by his story and his stately manner.[14]

Nearly three years afterwards Mrs. Holly, of Kettle Falls, describes a visit made to her by Ranald, then sixty-nine years of age. She gives the following account of him: " His hair, worn rather long, was gray, thick and curling; he wore a full beard, cut rather short, but not close, which was quite gray and also very curling. His features were rather rough-hewn, but the high cheek-bones and rather large and flat nose (with peculiarly wide nostrils) were the only features which would appear to show his Indian ancestry. His complexion, while dark, was not more so than that of many men who have spent much of the time in the open. His rather small and deep-set eyes were gray and peculiar in that the gray iris was encircled at the outer edge by a distinct line of hazel brown." [15]

A little more than a year later the wanderer's life reached its earthly close. He was at this time feeling the infirmities of age, complaining of deafness and pains in the joints. He breathed his last while on a visit to the house of his niece, Mrs. Jennie Lynch, daughter of his younger half-brother, Benjamin, near Toroda, on Kettle River, Ferry County, Washington, about seventy-five miles from the old Fort Colville. His last word was the beautiful Japanese word of farewell, *Sayonara,* a word which seemingly at this juncture came floating to him naturally out of the gulf of the years.

The remains of the old pioneer, writes Mr. Lewis, " are buried in a neglected Indian graveyard near Toroda, Washington; a spot unmarked by any monument and known and remembered by only a few relatives and friends." It is to be hoped that some day those who are interested in the story of American-Japanese relations will place on this spot some suitable memorial of one of the most significant episodes in the American-Japanese history of the last century. In such a case the words of Stevenson might very properly be borrowed:

> " This is the line you grave for me:
> ' Here he lies where he longed to be;
> Home is the sailor, home from the sea,
> And the hunter home from the hill.' "

One cannot better conclude this brief sketch of the career of Ranald MacDonald than with a couple of paragraphs from the concluding chapter of the *Journal*: " It is long, nearly half a century, since my adventure here sketched: Yet even now, after the vicissitudes, varied and wearing, of my life, I have never ceased to feel most kindly ánd ever grateful to my fellow men of Japan for their really generous treatment of me. In that long journey and voyage from the extreme North to the extreme South—fully a thousand miles—of their country; throughout my whole sojourn of ten months in the strange land, never did I receive a harsh word, or even an unfriendly look. Among all classes, a gentle kindness to the fancied castaway—the stranger most strange—pervaded their general regard and treatment of me. From the time I landed on the beach of Tomassey in the Straits of La Perouse, when Inoes (Ainus) took me gently by the wrist, one on each side, to assist me to the dwelling of their employer, while others put sandals to my feet, to the time of my joining the United States Slope of War, *Preble,* it was ever the same uniform kindness. Truly I liked them in that congenial sympathy which, left to itself, unmarred by antagonism of race, creed, or worldly selfishness, makes us all of Adam's race ' wondrous kin.' . . . In my old age; while living out, still in sweat of brow, the fast falling evening shades of life, in my native home-land of the Columbia, after having, in my wanderings, girded—I may say—the Globe itself, and come across peoples many, civilized and uncivilized, there are none to whom I feel more kindly, more grateful, than my old hosts of Japan; none whom I esteem more highly." [16]

NOTES

1 See *T. A. S. J.*, August 1913, p. 475.

2 See H. H. Gowen, *A Precursor of Perry.* University of Washington Chap-books, 1928.

3 Captain Golownin, *Japan and the Japanese.* London, 1853.

4 I. Nitobe, *The Japanese Nation*, p. 259.

5 I. Nitobe, *ibid.*, p. 263 ff.

6 So Nitobe gives the figures; MacDonald himself says 8 Americans and 7 Hawaiians.

7 For the life of Ranald MacDonald the main source is his own *Journal,* which has been edited by Mr. W. S. Lewis and Mr. Murakami, from the MS. in the Spokane Public Library, for the Eastern Washington State Historical Society, Spokane, in 1923. My quotations from the *Journal* are, by permission, from Mr. Lewis' edition. The story of Ranald MacDonald is also told by Mrs. Eva Emory Dye, of Portland, in her *MacDonald of Oregon.*

8 MacDonald's Ls are written, I find, by examination of his correspondence, made like Ss. Hence the "*Sahina*" (for *Lahaina*) which appears in Lewis and Murakami.

9 Lewis and Murakami, pp. 43–44.

10 In the Provincial Library at Victoria B. C. there is a bundle of MacDonald's Letters to Malcolm McLeod and there are also three tin boxes, under the name of McLeod, which contain, among other things, a duplicate copy of the MS. of the *Journal* and a typed copy of the same. These came to the Library with the effects of Dr. McLeod.

11 See Note 6.

12 MacDonald, naturally followed by his editors, invariably writes *Lagoda* for *Ladoga.*

13 Lewis and Murakami, p. 226 f.

14 Lewis and Murakami, p. 49 ff.

15 Lewis and Murakami, p. 61.

16 Lewis and Murakami p. 265.

V

TOWNSEND HARRIS

The First American Envoy

During my visits to Japan there have been few places to which my feet have been more compellingly drawn than the little temple known as the Zempukuji, in the Azabu ward of the city of Tokyo, not so very far from the present American Embassy. It is at this spot that the American Consulate was first established in Tokyo, then called Yedo, and here the American flag, made for the occasion by a woman of Japan, was first displayed in what is now the capital of the Empire. The patriarchal ginko tree which has grown to colossal proportions, still bursts forth with its myriad fan-shaped leaves in spring and falls in golden showers in autumn. For a thousand years this little temple had existed, but it acquired a new title to reverence when it was made the dwelling place of the first American representative in Japan, Townsend Harris. It is of Townsend Harris that one inevitably thinks when he stands in the quiet precincts of the Zempukuji. As recently as 1931, a celebration was held at this shrine by joint representatives of Japan and the United States. On this occasion, Baron Masuda, who as a boy of thirteen had obtained the position of an office-boy at the Consulate, gave his reminiscences of seventy years before and, more japonico, recited a poem containing the lines:

> " Well I remember
> The old man with ruddy face,
> Stroking his white beard,
> Who argued vehemently,
> Such was his sincerity." [1]

In my last study the impression must have been given that the shadows of imminent doom were closing slowly down upon the power of the illustrious Tokugawa Shoguns. When Commander Glynn steamed away in the *Preble*, bearing with him the recovered castaways, it was clear that the fabric which Iyeyasu had reared with so great care was badly shaken. At the same time, new hope was aroused in the United States that the fast closed doors of Japan were now about to be opened for international trade and intercourse. New voices were heard demanding the establishment of a coal depôt on the Japanese coast. Glynn himself was forward in the plea that the necessary steps should now be taken by " naval officers of tact " to complete the negotiations already begun. So in June 1851 Commander Aulick was sent by President Fillmore. His non-success, however, and his subsequent recall may be taken as implying that his " tact " was not of the right quality. Soon after, backed by memorials from the merchants of the Atlantic coast, Aaron Haight Palmer appealed for action by the President and Secretary of State, even advocating a blockade of the Bay of Yedo. Then came the final push at the closed door, already well-nigh forced, through the famous expedition of Commodore Perry, who as

" the last executor of Columbus " entered the Bay of Uraga on July 7, 1853. He was in command of four ships of war and with a letter from the President. His mission was to be, if possible, one of persuasion, but there can be little doubt that in the last resort he was prepared to employ force. As the *New York Herald* of the time puts it, a little ironically: " The Japanese expedition, according to a Washington correspondent, is to be merely a hydrographical survey of the Japanese coast. The 32-pounders are to be used merely as measuring instruments in the triangulations; the cannon-balls are for procuring the base lines. If any Japanese is foolish enough to put his head in the way of these meteorological instruments, of course, nobody will be to blame but himself if he should get hurt." The general inclination in America, in spite of all the agitation for the reopening of Japan, seems to have been to view the matter not quite seriously. The *Baltimore Sun,* for instance, said of the enterprise: " It will sail about the same time with Rufus Porter's aerial ship." Dr. Edward Everett Hale wrote: " The funeral of Bill Poole or the filibustering operations in the Gulf of Mexico have (naturally) awakened more interest among the people than has the opening by peaceful diplomacy of the Italy of the East to the intercourse of the world." And, for one last illustration, Dr. Nitobe comments on the whole matter: " Looking through a number of newspapers and periodicals of the time, I am struck with the absence of public sympathy covering an enterprise of which the United States can be so nobly and justly proud." [2]

Perry's instructions were quite sufficiently clear: to obtain such an understanding as would make for friend-

ship, commerce, access to coal and other needed supplies, and humane treatment of shipwrecked sailors.
Between the two visits in 1853 and 1854, President
Pierce had succeeded President Fillmore, but there was
no difference between the two administrations in point
of view on this subject. Yet neither appreciated the
affair as it concerned the internal situation in Japan.
Neither President realized the difficulty that existed
even in approaching the Emperor to whom the letter
was addressed. Nor did either know how little the
Shogun was in a position to act with anything like decision, breaking through the Tokugawa tradition of
receiving letters from the outside world only through
the Dutch at Deshima, and that of consulting the feu-
datory princes as to the policy to be pursued. The Yedo
Government was indeed placed a most humiliating
position, especially as yielding to the concessions first
demanded made further concessions inevitable wh.
the American fleet, reinforced, should return. Dr. S.
Wells Williams, in his *Diary* for July 14, 1853, had a
clear vision of the predestined result when he wrote:
" This closed the eventful day, one which will be a date
to be noted in the history of Japan, one on which the
key was put into the lock, and a beginning made to do
away with the long seclusion of the nation."

Perry sailed away to his winter quarters in China,
promising to return for an answer to the President's
letter in the following spring. In the meantime gloom
hung over the Empire of Japan to an extent which has
never been realized in the United States. The Shogun
and his officials, who naturally had to bear the brunt
of the American pressure, found themselves between
the devil and the deep sea, with the American demands

to deal with on the one hand, and a powerful party in Kyoto urging the Emperor to press the Shogun to declare war without delay against the foreigners. The death of the Shogun Iyeyoshi, eight days after the departure of the " Black Ships " seemed but the first of those bitter fruits of a restored internationalism which the Japanese nation was fated in the near future to taste. The new Shogun, of course, had to carry on the distasteful policy of dealing with the intruders and soon learned, as the outer world could not possibly learn, what the gathering hostility of Kyoto and the clans in sympathy with the Emperor's anti-foreign policy meant to himself and his house. Letters were sent to all the daimyos asking for an opinion as to whether the American fleet should be repelled by force or whether a temporizing policy should be pursued. The answers showed a large majority in favour of immediate hostilities; only a small minority preferred to admit provisionally a measure of foreign intercourse. After the signing of the *Treaty of Kanagawa* the excitement, so far from dying down, actually seemed to increase, and in 1855 the Shogun ordered the Prince of Mito to put all the coasts in a state of defence. It appeared quite clear to most of the officials at this time that the visit of the American fleet was but the preliminary reconnoitring in preparation for a campaign of conquest.

If such was the impression made upon those whom we may call the intelligentsia, it will readily be understood that the terror of the common people was still more genuine and intense. Here, to the fear of the cannon and ships of Commodore Perry, was added the fear of foreign magic. It was commonly believed that

American sorcery was potent to draw forth the souls of young girls from their bodies to become the prey of kidnappers. Many felt themselves obliged to send away their wives and daughters to the interior to save them from destruction. A document of the time runs as follows: " The American ships which have come to the sea off Kanagawa are reported to have sailed for and entered the port of Shimoda. This may mean that the foreigners might land and stroll about here and there and therefore all are warned that the doors and windows of the houses must be tightly closed, that they must also close their shops and hide their merchandise in order to prevent foreigners from entering. Moreover, if anyone has cows, he must hide them from the foreigners. Women and children must naturally never leave their houses and, if the foreigners come to look at them, the greatest caution must be taken that this will not be allowed to happen."

The poor Shogun had fears less fantastic and more serious than these, and, as we have seen, was in a tight place. Only a timely demise, hastened as some believe by violence, saved Iyeyoshi from having to grasp one or the other horn of his dilemma. His successor, whom Brinkley calls a " witling," would have needed more *finesse* than he possessed to avoid a show-down. When Perry returned, on February 13, 1854, with ten ships and two thousand men, there was nothing for the Shogun's ministers to do but advise their master to " agree with his adversary quickly," whatever might be the situation in Kyoto. The *Treaty of Kanagawa* was the result, satisfactory enough from the American point of view. On this important event I

may be permitted to quote a paragraph from my
" *Outline History of Japan* ":

" It did not take long now to establish such contact
with the government as to bring about the desired result. The first meeting was appointed for March 8.
It is amusing to note that, in landing, the American
officers, in anticipation of a substantial feast, took
their knives and forks with them. They resented
greatly the flimsy banquet which gave them no opportunity to use these weapons. On March 31, a day forever memorable in the history of the Pacific, Japan
gave her adhesion, through the Bakufu, to the ' first
formal treaty with any western nation.' The Commodore was evidently very much possessed with the
importance of the occasion and showed a certain his-
trionic ability to utilize the opportunity. When he
landed at Yokohama for the ceremony, first went two
gigantic negroes carrying the American flag; then followed the Commodore and his officers in full uniform;
after these came the band playing Yankee Doodle;
and lastly were the sailors with naked cutlasses guarding the presents. Perry may be excused for being a
little rhetorical at the time, but his declaration that ' if
the Japanese came to the United States, they would
find the navigable waters of the country free to them,
and that they would not be debarred even from the
gold-fields of California,' does not to-day have about
it the ring of an inspired prediction." [3]

So the *Treaty* was signed to the satisfaction of the
Commodore. He, of course, could not know that it
had not behind it the force of the Imperial assent, nor
did he know that the presents, with the exception of
the Madeira, whiskey, champagne and perfumery,

would be left to the " mildew, rust and neglect " of the Shogun's godowns, where Dr. Griffis says he saw them as late as 1872. For the harassed Shogun the signing of the treaty was far from being the end of the trouble. In the same year came Admiral Stirling with a demand for a similar treaty with Great Britain. The Dutch followed soon after with the demands presented by Donker Curtius. In October 1857 came Admiral Pontiatine to press the claims of Russia. Then the Dutch returned with a demand for the inclusion of Nagasaki as well as Shimoda and Hakodate as treaty ports. But by this time, the subject of our sketch had arrived in Japan as Consul General, and it is to his story that we must now in the main confine ourselves.

It is possible that at this point the question may be asked why Harris rather than Perry has been chosen as the representative of American diplomacy. The answer is, first, that the Commodore's visit to Japan was comparatively brief and, secondly, that the Kanagawa *Treaty* is of comparatively little significance, except as an entering wedge, when considered in reference to the *Commercial Treaty of 1858* negotiated by Townsend Harris. Moreover, while Perry had the " Black ships " behind him to enforce his demands, Harris was left almost unnoticed and unsupported by his Government, struggling along in the face of illness and against the procrastination and opposition of the Japanese officials. Without depreciating the work of Perry, it is but fair to affirm that Harris' work was incomparably greater. We may well approve the statement of J. H. Longford that the story of Townsend Harris' labours is one of " marvellous tact and patience, of steady determination and courage, and straightforward uprightness in every respect." In the light of one particular incident some may think meet some qualification of this praise, but the judgment I believe to be substantially just.

Townsend Harris was derived from Welsh stock, which crossed the Atlantic with Roger Williams and settled first of all in Massachusetts. His father, Jonathan Harris, moved to Sandy Hill, Washington County, New York State, where he rose to be a magistrate. He gained his living by making hats, and found pleasure, with some profit, in introducing to his neighbourhood the grafting of fruit-trees. Jonathan Harris had six children, and Townsend, who was born in 1804 and named after his grandmother, Thankful Townsend, was the youngest of the five boys.

The child's education, except for the very competent instruction of his mother, was limited to that provided by the primary school and the Academy. Townsend regretted to the end of his life his lack of a University education, and it was the sense of this deficiency which stimulated his later interest in the educational institutions of his native state. He became, it will be recalled, the President of the Board of Education of New York, and will always be remembered as the founder of the Free Academy which developed into the College of the City of New York.

From 1817, when Townsend was thirteen years of age, he engaged in business in New York City and so continued till 1848. Outside of his business he was a home-keeping young man with little indication of his later disposition to roam the world. He started work in a dry goods store and then entered into partnership with his elder brother in the importing of china and earthenware. From this he drifted into the business of a general importer. During these years he has been described as " a typical old-time New Yorker," often to be found in the Clubs to which he belonged, but at the same time devoting himself earnestly to civic affairs, working enthusiastically with the Democratic Party, and teaching in Sunday School regularly. The only sign of his future bent is to be seen in his devotion to the study of foreign languages and literatures.

Harris may be said to have laid the foundation of his success as a negotiator in the successful conduct of his business. If, as Dr. Griffis says, " Trade was not the law of Townsend Harris' life, but its necessity only," yet his business career proved an excellent apprenticeship for the years of bargaining which were to come, since, especially in the Orient, bargaining constitutes an important part of a diplomat's experience. At the same time, his fondness for the languages and literatures of France, Spain and Italy had a broadening influence which lifted him above the lower interests of a merchant's life. As to this, Dr. Griffis says that " he had access to the best libraries, and his memory, naturally retentive, was trained to system. His power of prompt recollection was noteworthy."

The question has sometimes been raised why Townsend Harris never married. The usual, and probably the correct, explanation, is that he refused to think of association with any other woman while his mother, to whom he was deeply attached, remained alive. It will therefore be readily understood that when the inevitable separation came, through Mrs. Harris' decease in 1847, Townsend found himself bereft of much of

the interest his life had hitherto held. It was the deso-
lating sense of an irreparable breach that turned his
so far stay-at-home existence in New York into a kind
of restless *wanderlust*. So in 1849 he sold his business,
threw over the habit of years, and began his travels.

His first journey, as soon as the settlement of his
mother's estate had been completed, was westward to
California, a journey at this time of considerable
length and difficulty. Harris, however, set out in a
vessel of his own, one in which he had acquired a
half interest, presently to be transformed into a complete ownership. On arrival at San Francisco, and
after buying out his partner, he started on a sea cruise
which was to last for six years. In his *Diary* for
Christmas Day 1856, Harris notes that he had spent
the Christmas of 1849 in the North Pacific Ocean, that
of 1850 at Manila, that of 1851 at Pulu-Penang, that
of 1852 at Singapore, that of 1853 in Hongkong, that
of 1854 at Calcutta, and that of 1855 in Ceylon. In
all these, and other, places he found much to interest
him. In China, for example, he interested himself
much in the resources of Formosa, and even made a
proposal to the Secretary of State that this island
should be purchased by the United States.

It was probably this interest in American foreign
policy and politics that prompted the choice of Harris,
to be the first envoy to the Empire of Japan. He was
recommended by Commodore Perry and by Secretary
Seward and appointed by President Pierce. With his
thirty years of experience in commerce in New York
and his six years of actual contact with the peoples and
problems of the Far East, he seemed the ideal person
to carry on and complete the work which Perry had

commenced in Japan. The letter announcing his appointment reached him in China on July 31, 1855, and includes the following passage: " A principal motive of the President in selecting you as Consul-general for Japan was the hope that by your knowledge of Eastern character and your general intelligence and experience in business you would make such an impression on the Japanese, as would in time induce them to enter into a commercial treaty with us."

Harris returned to the United States for his formal appointment in August 1855 and found that he was expected to negotiate a treaty with Siam on his way out to his post. So he left New York on October 17 by way of Europe, and at Penang was joined by the Dutch secretary who was to share his exile, Mr. C. J. Heusken. The two then sailed for Bangkok where the desired treaty with Siam was successfully negotiated. Then came the voyage to Japan in the *San Jacinto*.

The arrival at Shimoda on August 21, 1856, was anything but encouraging. Harris' *Journal* for that day reads as follows: " August 21: Anchored in the harbour of Shimoda. Found there was practically no inner harbour, room for three small boats being its limit; and that the outer harbour was nothing more than an open roadstead." More discouraging than the appearance of the harbour was the attitude of the Japanese officials, which made it impossible for him to effect a landing before September 3. It seems there was a misunderstanding as to the language of the *Treaty of Kanagawa*. Article XI, according to the American version of the Dutch original, was to the effect that consuls or agents might be permitted to reside in Shimoda, eighteen months after the signing of the treaty, if *either* of the two governments deemed such an arrangement necessary. But the Japanese text of the article read that a consul was only to be sent, when *both* countries were agreed upon the step. It is clear that Japan had not expected the Kanagawa *Treaty* to involve any attempt on the part of Americans to reside in the land. Only a short time before, two Americans, Reed and Daugherty, had endeavoured to effect a landing at Shimoda for a load of merchandise, from which they expected large profits, but by orders of the Shogun had been compelled to leave. The officials doubtless felt the same measure could apply to others, even though coming with the credentials of a consul. At any rate, for several days they refused to budge from their position and pleaded with Commodore Armstrong to take away the unwelcome agent, or at least bear to the President an explanatory letter. The Commodore replied that he could only receive letters through the Consul. It was, as Harris records, " an extraordinary situation " such as could only be relieved by patience. But at last, on September 3, the new envoy was able to leave the warship and bestow himself in the little temple of the village of Kakizaki, on the opposite side of the harbour of Shimoda, which had been hastily prepared for his residence. Here, on the following day, he hoisted the first American consular flag displayed in Japan, and from the rocky top of the peninsula of Idzu watched, with a strange feeling of loneliness, the departure of the *San Jacinto*. Now, to use the words of one of his diplomatic successors, Roland Morris, " he was in the midst of an utterly strange and alien civilization, suspected and distrusted by all those around him, his only medium of communication the faithful Heusken, his Dutch interpreter."

In the *Journal* for September 4, 1856 Harris writes: " Slept very little from excitement and mosquitoes, the latter *enormous* in size. . . . Flagstaff erected; men form a ring around it and, at two and a half P. M. of this day, I hoist the ' First Consular Flag ' ever seen in this Empire. Grim reflections—ominous of change —undoubted beginning of the end. Query,—if for the real good of Japan? " There was reason for misgiving, for the Japanese still insisted that the Consul should pack up his effects and return to the United States.

Still, since possession is nine points of the law, when Townsend Harris commenced on September 5 to open packages and arrange their contents, fixing up an old belfry to accommodate his four pairs of pigeons, he had a right to feel that the danger of a forcible removal was over. Yet after a week he was still far from feeling at home, though fairly well settled. He writes in his *Journal* of " a flare up " he had with the officials, and adds that they " told me some egregious lies in answer to some requests I made." It is cheering to note that exactly a year later, September 11, 1857, he wrote in a very different vein as follows: " I am happy to state that my relations with the Japanese authorities are of the most agreeable kind. By pursuing a mild, yet firm course, I have broken down, one after another, a great number of absurd regulations calculated to restrain my liberty, yet in so doing I have not in any case caused unpleasant feelings. With the exception of the limit of seven *Ri* to which I have voluntarily confined myself for a short period, I am as free as I would be in the city of Washington. I have never been molested or annoyed in any way by the people, and although my house has more than twenty doors, not one of which has either lock, bolt or bar, I have not been robbed of the most trifling article in a year's residence here."

These two passages in juxtaposition with one another afford an admirable illustration of the advance made by Harris in a single year in gaining the confidence of the Japanese. But it must be remembered that conditions in 1857 were very different from those which existed in 1856. Mr. Gubbins gives a very accurate picture of the situation at the time immediately following Harris' arrival when he describes it as " unwelcome to the Japanese who had not expected the enforcement of the stipulation." He adds: " They accordingly boycotted him. He could get no trustworthy information. If he asked for anything, it was withheld as being ' contrary to the honourable country's law '; and his letters were not answered because ' it was not customary to reply to the letters of foreigners.' "

So the days and weeks which followed upon Harris' settlement at Kakizaki were more than a little trying. They were days and weeks in which trivial things often assumed an importance of portentous proportions. There was the typhoon, not quite a trivial thing, of September 23, which gave the Consul apprehension that the consulate would lose its roof and which placed the flagstaff at an angle of 65 degrees with the ground. There was the sight of Oshima to the eastward, belching out its smoke and causing a few tremors now and then which recalled to his retentive memory the story of the great earthquake and tidal wave of three years earlier.[4] And, added to fears of this sort, was the treading on a big nail which gave him a painful foot for many days thereafter.

There was not at this time a sufficiency of diplomatic duty to fill in all the time, so we find Harris looking up, with some touch of homesickness, and within the limits of his seven *Ri*, some of the familiar flowers of the home land. We find him trying to patch up his " wretched stove " to prevent the household from being completely smoked out. On another occasion, we find him planting " four rows of Irish potatoes," with great expectation. And on Sundays, when he always declined to transact official business, we find him reading regularly the Prayer Book services of the Episcopal Church and trying to imagine himself back amid the familiar scenes of New York.

Now and then, events of more than usual importance occurred to break into the monotony of life. For example, on October 30, he had the unique privilege, up to the present, of receiving in his house the Governors of the two adjacent districts: Inouye, Governor of Shinano, and Okado, Governor of Bungo. It was a meeting all the more significant because it aroused hopes of accomplishing some real and definite arrangement of the sort he had come to negotiate. A few days later, on November 9, the entire community was excited by the arrival of a Russian corvette, under Commodore Possiet and Commander Korsakoff. With these, and the other officers, Harris had some very pleasant social interludes, and it was with great regret that he bade them farewell on December 14, though their departure enabled him to send off a large packet of mail. The Consul found himself in thorough agreement with the Russians that Shimoda was not a suitable port, and that it should be exchanged for some other at the earliest possible opportunity.

It is evident that the loneliness of Townsend Harris, though alleviated for the moment, was by this departure actually exacerbated. There is a touch of pathos in his insistence upon permission from the authorities to fire a salute on Washington's birthday. In the words of Mr. Dooman, one of the secretaries later in the American Embassy, " Allowed to see nothing of what was going on in this country (Japan), he was allowed to peek through the doors once in a while, and although he saw a tremendous hurry and bustle, he knew nothing whatever of their causes; he ascribed it to the unwelcome presence of himself in Japan and he believed that the confusion and excitement which he saw from time to time were due to the demands which he was making. We now know how far this was from the truth."

Truth to tell, Harris did not bear all this with the angelic patience which has been sometimes ascribed to him. The Japanese accounts make not infrequent reference to his nervousness and quickness of temper, though sometimes, no doubt, the nervousness was more apparent than real. Baron Masuda, looking back over seventy years, said at the celebration of 1929: " When he (Harris) did not go out on horseback, he used to walk the long verandah back and forth, and I remember the noise he made with his shoes. As a little boy I wondered what he was doing that for." Occasionally, the impatience was genuine enough and led to actions

which might easily have had very serious consequences. For example, one day, annoyed with the
slow progress of the negotiations, which were at the
time on foot for the framing of the *Commercial Treaty*,
he became very angry, picked up the *hibachi*, or
brazier, and hurled it against the *shoji*, or sliding partition. The room was filled with smoke and ashes and
the situation must have been a tense one. But the
Governor of Shimoda, with great self-restraint and
presence of mind, raising an arm to shield his eyes
from the dust, managed at the same time to convey by
signs his orders to the attendant samurai that they
were on no account to draw their swords. For there
were quick tempered men among the Japanese as well
as among the foreigners. The Governor's action
saved the situation, and probably altered the whole
course of American-Japanese relations. Nearly a year
later, when the understanding between Harris and his
Japanese associates was much more complete, we find
a letter written by the Governor of Shimoda to the
Government at Yedo, dated December 22, 1857, containing the following passage: " Since there were some
points in the American Consul's petition to which we
could not give our consent, we wanted to talk over the
particulars with him, but he became angry and refused
to listen to our words. We did not understand what
he was saying but, pointing his fingers at the Japanese
officials who were present, he seemed to be rebuking
them in a loud and excited manner. Furthermore,
when he saw the attendants bring in tea, he waved his
hands and with a sweeping motion hurled them away.
This, most likely, meant that he did not desire any
tea. Since his conduct resembles that of a lunatic, if

we insist upon consulting with him, it would make matters worse.   Therefore we cannot make known our
desires and clarify the particular points of disagree-
ment.   Thus our conversation had to be postponed."

Of course, this is only one side of the story. Harris
had, as we have already seen, much reason for impatience.   His feelings have plenty of excuse in the
dilatoriness of the Japanese, which was not only the
expression of the Oriental temperament but also a
more or less deliberate effort to evade an embarrassing
decision.   But the Consul had even more solid grounds
for his impatience in the strange absence of news from
his own Government at Washington.   Harris was himself a rather prolific letter-writer, sometimes, it would
appear, from lack of anything else to do.   He tells us
that some of his letters were sixteen pages in length
and, though the opportunities for sending them away
were few and far between, he wrote many of them.
But he got no replies.   It looked very much as though
the State Department, after taking strong measures to
force the presence of a representative on Japan, had
completely overlooked the fact that a representative
had been sent, in the person of Townsend Harris.   In
his *Journal* for May 5, 1857, the Consul writes as follows: " I have not heard a word from Washington
since I left the United States, say October 1855.
What can be the cause of this prolonged absence of an
American man-of-war?   Where are the English?
Where are the French?   And, above all, where is the
Russian consul? . . . I am only nine days from Hongkong, yet I am more isolated than any American official
in any part of the world."

Nevertheless, Harris was much occupied in mind,

and sometimes also in actual negotiation, over the important objects he had set himself to carry through. These were, in the words of Roland Morris: " First, to obtain a properly executed convention which would definitely establish his status and rights; second, to adjust the medium of exchange so that purchases by visiting ships might be made on a fairer basis; and Third, to obtain permission to proceed to Yedo and present his credentials to the Shogun's Government as an Envoy duly accredited to the whole Empire of Japan."

The first of these objects was achieved by the *Convention* which was signed on June 18, 1857, after ten months of difficult negotiation; the second was not attained till several years later; and the third was reached, as we shall presently see, when Harris obtained leave to visit Yedo in November 1857.

It is in connection with the negotiations leading up to the signing of the *Treaty of Shimoda* that we find ourselves compelled to notice what, at least on the Japanese side of the ocean, is known as " The Romance of Townsend Harris and Okichi San." There are many Americans, no doubt, who will feel that, since we cannot know all the truth concerning this particular incident, it were better to follow most American accounts of the career of Townsend Harris by ignoring it altogether. Yet, so constant and so open is the reference to it in Japan, and so detailed the account, that such a course does not seem to be quite worthy of the historian. In fact, it leaves the matter open for a more prurient interpretation than seems to be necessary. In history, as in literature, the *motif* of the innocent woman victim employed by destiny for its own purpose is too common a one to be in this case put aside. And while the story of Okichi San, the woman who saved the life of America's first representative in Japan and ministered devotedly both to her master's comfort and the success of his diplomatic task, is a pitiful one, it is not without its heroic side. That a woman, in the supposed interest of international relations, and under pressure of the authorities, should have given up her affianced lover and braved the scorn of her fellow countrymen by more or less surreptitious sojournings in the American Consulate at Shimoda and Yedo, seems to us so pitiful as to be almost incredible. It is all the more so, in that Okichi San ended her days as a drunkard and a suicide, whose last resting-place, in the grave of another, has been discovered only in recent years through the patient researches of Dr. Shunsui Muramatsu.

Not unnaturally there is no reference to *Tojin,* "foreign," Okichi in the annals of American diplomacy. Dr. Cosenza, the editor of Harris' *Complete Journal,* published in 1930, informs me that no reference to the woman appears in any of the diplomatist's surviving papers. We might well dismiss the whole story as a legend or a fabrication, were it not for the explicit discussion of it in Japanese documents connected with the negotiations of 1857. I was in Japan during the celebration of the eightieth anniversary of the signing of the *Treaty of Kanagawa,* held at Shimoda from April 20 to May 3 of 1934, which was attended by the American Ambassador, Joseph C. Grew. One day in this celebration, April 30, was observed as *Okichi Day.* On this day and the preceding, young men and maidens bearing paper lanterns paraded the streets of Shimoda, while Okichi and the Americans concerned in the story, Harris and Heusken, were impersonated in the procession. The entire drama of Okichi and Tsurumatsu, the deserted fiancé, was performed by the geisha, a visit was paid to the grounds of the *Hofukuji*, the temple where Okichi lies buried, and an exhibition of relics was held in the temple known as *Ryosenji*. I need hardly say that this part of the celebration was not attended by the American Ambassador. He confined himself, quite properly, to the program of April 22, on which day he offered branches of the sacred sakaki tree and silent homage at the graves of the four or five American sailors buried on the site of the first American Consulate.

The story of Okichi San is told here, first, because of its genuine human interest; secondly, because of the part it plays in the conduct of the negotiations leading to the signing of the *Treaty of Shimoda;* and thirdly, because the acceptance of the incident as authentic in Japan deprives the historian on this side of the Pacific of any right to ignore it. Nevertheless, Americans are entitled to give the story a quite different interpretation than that which has made it the basis of so many dramas and novels in Japan.

The girl, destined to achieve so strange and dubious a notoriety in her native land, was born at Shimoda on November 10, 1841. Her father was a ship-carpenter, Ichibei by name, and her mother Okiwa. She had one older sister, Omoto. Ichibei was a man of small stature but of passionate temper, for which latter reason he was nicknamed *Fireball*. But, paralyzed at the age of forty, he became unable to work at his calling, so that the support of the family fell upon Okiwa. She, with her two small daughters, earned a precarious livelihood by running errands, and as a street-hawker. Omoto, the elder daughter, married as soon as she reached marriageable age, but Okichi, possessed of her mother's beauty and her father's temperament, remained for a time a somewhat difficult problem.

The turning point in her fortunes was reached in 1847, when the six-year-old girl was taken under the care of an elderly lady of wealth, Osen Murayama. Osen had lived with a family of distinction for thirty years and was regarded in the neighbourhood as a personage of remarkable culture. In order to fill up her abundant leisure, she had cultivated an interest in the children of Shimoda, teaching them gratuitously reading, singing and the playing of the *koto* and the *samisen*. This interest culminated in Osen's practical adoption of Okichi, whose devoted attendance upon her invalid father had attracted the older woman's attention and sympathy.

It was a great opportunity for Okichi San and she availed herself of it to the full. In course of time she rewarded her benefactress by winning wide renown in Shimoda for her singing and her skill with musical instruments. Her rendering of one particular piece, *Akegarasu,* " The Crow at Dawn," led to her being called by her admiring friends Okichi of *Akegarasu.*

But, alas, for the uncertainty of human fortune! On November 4, 1854, several months after the signing of the *Treaty of Kanagawa* by Commodore Perry, came a terrific earthquake, which was universally associated by the Japanese with the intrusion of the foreigner. Shimoda was devastated by the shock and by the tidal wave which followed. Okichi San, clad only in her nightgown, just succeeded in saving herself and her patroness, Osen. But the pair were now left homeless and penniless, except for the shelter afforded them by Okichi's parents. It was a good opportunity for Okichi to show her gratitude to the older woman, and it may be said that she did her part to the full extent of her power, until the death of Osen Murayama in 1855.

Now comes upon the scene another of the principal characters in this little drama, namely, the young ship-carpenter, Tsurumatsu, Okichi's affianced lover, the man whose exemplary fidelity to the girl under the most difficult circumstances is beyond all praise. Tsurumatsu built a simple house for the bereft women, hauled in the kindling wood, and rendered every other service which his own poverty and their need made possible. But this supreme sacrifice was in giving up his beloved to the service of the foreigner, from motives which all alike construed as patriotic.

If the arrangements now undertaken by Mr. Heusken were for the purpose of securing Okichi San as Harris' mistress and another girl, Ofuko San, for himself, it is not to be denied that the episode constitutes a blot upon the otherwise stainless escutcheon of the American diplomat, which it is difficult to excuse. That the Japanese have so construed the incident is undeniable, though in accordance with the standards of social morality prevailing at the time Okichi suffered less in the esteem of her countrymen for a breach of morality than for yielding herself to a foreigner. But the inference that Okichi San was Harris' mistress, however seemingly probable to the Japanese, is not inescapable, while completely foreign to all we know of his rather unbending religious principles. Quite possibly Townsend Harris, sick and low in spirits, craved for the attendance which, from his past experience, he felt only a tender womanly hand could supply, and did not dream of another interpretation being placed upon the relation. Quite probably Heusken, who seems from other evidence to have been himself something of a philanderer, acted in the matter a good deal on his own responsibility, and went much further in the negotiation than his superior was aware. It is even possible that the authorities themselves hoped by the furnishing of women for the Consulate, to soften the hearts of the foreigners and make the progress of the negotiations for the treaty a little less difficult. In this last case, however, it would be hard to explain the evident reluctance of the authorities to consent to Heusken's demands.

So far as the documentary evidence goes, the overtures for the employment of Okichi and Ofuko were initiated by the foreigners. In any case, there can be no doubt as to the unwillingness of Okichi herself to accept the arrangement. Foreigners were at this time the objects of that intense hatred, which several years later brought about the assassination of Heusken. Naturally, too, Tsurumatsu, who was anxious to marry the girl as speedily as possible, objected. For a long time Okichi firmly refused to go to the Consulate, even though the command to do so came from the Governor himself. Then the officials, fearful of the consequences of refusing the American demands, entered upon questionable methods to enforce Okichi's consent. First, they approached her fiancé and by offering him certain compensations, such as that of elevation to the rank of the samurai, persuaded him to renounce his betrothed. Okichi, moreover, was told by one of the officials whom she especially respected and trusted that it was nothing less than her duty as a patriot, to sacrifice herself for the comfort of the American Consul. Important negotiations were proceeding between Harris and the Japanese Government, and her part in the matter was to bridge the gulf with her own body. So, at last, wearied and overborne, she consented as a loyal woman to serve the needs of her country. Everything had worked out contrary to her own desires. Her lover, dazzled with the prospect of a career, had abandoned her. The officials had made her compliance a test of her devotion to the fatherland.

A summary of the proceedings leading to the final decision was drawn up by the Japanese officials and is of such importance that, in spite of its length, I transcribe it here, without in any way associating myself with its implications.

" We wish to report about the question of sending girl attendants to the American officials.

" The American Consul Harris, and his official interpreter Heusken, who are living here, naturally need some person who will faithfully nurse and care for them during times of illness, and since men are unsuited to this task, they have repeatedly asked us to send them two girl attendants, which request we have either ignored or refused in a diplomatic manner.

" However, due to their urgent petition for an immediate and final answer, we authorized our officials to reply that since there were many difficult problems, both official and private, to be solved at this time, we should like to settle these first, before any move was taken concerning the girl attendants.

" Whereupon, they became angry and returned the official document, dated the 18th, pertaining to the two points of agreement, namely, the exchange rate between American coins and Japanese money; the limits prescribed for the American officials in their strolls. This document was returned through Heusken, with Harris' message stating that various promises were made in this agreement with a feeling of reciprocal sincerity, and therefore, considering the importance of this agreement, the Japanese officials on their part should show the same sincerity by sanctioning and sending the girl attendants. This procedure would be considered as natural and proper, he said, but they could not understand the refusal of our officials on this point.

" We received the report that Heusken left this document and went away with the statement that the Consul thought that our officials pretended courtesy and at the same time refused his earnest requests. Therefore, he annuls and makes void the agreement, the so-called Shimoda Treaty.

" If considered carefully, the idea of sending such girls is undesirable and, moreover, professional prostitutes are not as yet sanctioned officially in Shimoda, and so we believe that to maintain our refusal is the best policy. But it seems impossible to continue to do so, since there are other important questions to negotiate.

" Therefore, after careful deliberation among us, we decided to entertain their request. On the 20th, on account of the Consul's illness, Heusken came to our office, representing him, for an interview with us. He stated that, since the Japanese officials show no sincerity and will not accede to their requests, made repeatedly, they have returned the official document. If we should consent to their request for girl attendants he said that we may return this document duly signed by us, and they will again accept it and make it valid.

"Since the Consul's illness made this an urgent matter, for immediate consideration, if this request was not granted, our sincerity would be questioned by them and other great difficulties might arise. The other officials with whom we consulted agreed that we should order the proper authorities to send to the Consul one woman among those who served and accompanied the sailors when they wanted drinks.

"However, since this would set a precedent in our attitude concerning girl attendants for officials of the other treaty nations, and for any future officials who may come here, and since difficulties would arise from similar requests by foreign officials whenever warships and other ships came, we explained that these negotiations and this agreement were special arrangements between us and the American officials.

"They, too, due to their public and official positions as Consul and interpreter, desired the negotiations to be an absolute secret, and promised that while American boats were at anchor in the port, on no account would they call these women to the Consulate.

"After the Treaty is signed, one of us, the undersigned, will go to Yedo and report in detail concerning this negotiation and arrangement.

(Signed) INOUYE, Governor of Shinano.

NAKAMURA, Governor of Dewa.

May 27, 1857.

" Postscript: A girl attendant is to be sent to the interpreter in the same fashion, but since a suitable girl has not been found, this promise is not as yet fulfilled." [5]

In this way was the path smoothed for the famous *Treaty of Shimoda* and the establishment of commercial relations between Japan and the United States. The very length and wordiness of the document, just quoted, reveal but too clearly the embarrassment of the officials and their fear lest compliance might come to be regarded as a precedent in future diplomatic proceedings.

Some light has been thrown upon the final arrangements concerning Okichi San and her companion by the recent discovery, according to a report in the Tokyo *Jiji* of February 23, 1934, of certain documents in a warehouse of the Shimoda town office. These documents include a *diary* which gives a description of Okichi San and the other girl, an account of the manner in which they first attracted the attention of the Americans, and the terms of the contract made. Under these contracts, says the *Jiji,* " the girls were engaged for large salaries and with lavish dress allowance by the year, and the frankness of the documents indicated that in that day, aside from the generosity of the two men, the arrangement was considered a matter of course." The newspaper goes on to say that " Okichi's salary was 120 *ryo* per year, or 10 *ryo* per month. Okichi has a dress allowance of 25 *ryo* yearly and Ofuko was given 20 *ryo*. In those days a *ryo* had the purchasing power of about 50 yen to-day, so that Okichi earned the equivalent of 6,000 yen annually, and Ofuko 4,500 yen." " The agreement," the

Jiji says, " was signed by Okichi, Ofuko, their parents, and the headman of the village; it was stipulated that the girls will not associate with other men and that their parents and other relatives were not to visit the Consulate."

Okichi San went to Townsend Harris at the end of May, or the beginning of June, 1857. Ofuko went to Heusken a few days later. Once at the Consulate, the girl, though she had, as we have seen, entered upon her career with an unwilling heart, did everything in her power to understand and assist the foreigner. Harris, too, on his part, endeavoured to console her in her difficult situation. The two of them made great efforts to carry on conversation, and Harris, at any rate, learned much as to the manners and customs of Japan, the etiquette of dealing with the officials, the price of commodities, and the like. He was kind and tender towards her and she herself became more and more rooted in that affection for him, which she carried to her grave. Harris was at this time frequently ill, suffering still from lack of news from America, and from failure to get replies to his numerous letters, as well as from anxiety over his rapidly diminishing stores. Among other grievances was the discovery that it was practically impossible to obtain cow's milk, which in his weak state of health he quite excusably felt to be a necessity of life. The officials refused him even the privilege of keeping goats within the premises of the Consulate, declaring that " goats belong in the same category as pigs." Okichi San at length found a way out of this difficulty by spending her own money here and there in the purchase, among the neighbouring farmers, of small quantities of milk, which she described as " needed for medical purposes."

About this time, there were many days when Townsend Harris was so desperately ill that only the constant attendance of the devoted Okichi at his bedside kept him alive. But always, twice a day, she stole away to her favourite *judo* (god) in order to plead for the life of her foreign master. Those who see in history no influence of human personality, but only the working out of grim laws of economic determinism, may well reflect upon the thin and uncertain thread of life, which was at this time all that bound America to Japan. Precarious indeed seemed the prospects of the *Commercial Treaty* which Harris was now bent upon negotiating with the Shogun.

As for Okichi San, her position was one of peculiar pathos. On the one hand, in order to avoid scandal, she was not allowed to remain permanently at the Consulate. Yet outside of the Consulate she was regarded as little better than a pariah. The sixteen-year-old girl was to all her former acquaintances *Tojin* Okichi, and *Tojin*, though literally meaning merely " foreigner," carried with it at that time the implication of " an ignorant and beast-like person." From the position of the best-known singer of Shimoda, Okichi had sunk to become a despised outcast. Moreover, it was plain that her connection with Harris was not in any way to be considered a binding one. It would appear that she went with him on the first visit to Yedo, to be presently described, and resided at least for some days in the Consulate established in the *Zempukuji*. But she did not go the second time, probably from fear of attracting notice in diplomatic quarters. The public insults flung at her in Shimoda, with the use of vulgar and contemptuous words, whenever she rode in the elegant palanquin to the Consulate, had now the effect of driving her more and more to the use of strong drink. In this failing there may have been some hereditary influence, since her father had become a drunkard some years before his death.

It is said that it was this increasing addiction to drink which caused Harris to grow more and more indifferent to Okichi San, and it is possible, though we have no knowledge of the actual facts, that this was the reason for the girl's final dismissal from the Consul's service. In any case, the dismissal was followed by a period of miserable and tragic decline.

The rest of the story of Okichi San, which has perhaps too long interrupted our account of Harris' diplomatic work, may here be summarized. When the Consul left Japan in 1862, Okichi rapidly sank into a poverty from which she was quite unable to extricate herself by her talents as a professional singer. The six years of her life, between the age of twenty-one and twenty-seven, remain almost a complete blank. The rumour was even spread that she had followed Harris to America, though another report was that she had been seen on the streets of Kyoto and Osaka. Then, suddenly, at the age of twenty-seven, Okichi turned up as a street-singer in Yokohama where, strangely enough, she met again her old lover, Tsurumatsu. The former estrangement was immediately forgotten, the two were married, and for three years thereafter they lived together happily in their native town of Shimoda. Once again it was possible for Okichi San to enter society, to sing at wedding fes-

tivities and public functions the songs for which she
had formerly been famous. But, alas, the halcyon
time passed, and at the age of thirty-five we find the
woman again as a singer on the streets, this time at
Mishino. Two years later, while following the profession of a hair-dresser at Shimoda, she learned of
the death of Townsend Harris. From this time, whenever it was possible, she found the way to her favourite
shrine on the proper day to observe the ceremonies of
her master's commemoration. All the time her beset-
ting vice was gaining upon her, but it is said she always drink her *saké* from the glass which Harris had
given her.

Then in 1887, when she was forty-six, Okichi became paralyzed, as her father had been before her.
In this condition she soon drifted into the position of
a miserable beggar. In 1890, " when forty-nine years
old, (23rd year of Meiji), burning what few personal
possessions she still retained, and her private documents, including Harris' visiting card, she plunged into
a deep pool of the rivulet called Inubazawa, a mile
from Shimoda, thus ending a life full of sorrows, sufferings and tribulations." [6]

Dr. Muramatsu devoted some forty years to the recovering of the details of this story. After many
labours and disappointments, he finally discovered the
place where the bones of Okichi San lay buried. They
had been hidden in the tomb of another person in the
graveyard of an obscure temple. The remains were
removed from this casual resting-place and now
moulder in a grave of Okichi's own, the tomb to which
I referred as the centre of the celebration of April 1934.

In these last years " the romance of Townsend

Harris and Okichi San " has, in Japan, become the theme of novelist and playwright. Quite recently it was produced as a moving-picture in Tokyo. In Shimoda the pictures of Okichi and the American are not infrequently to be seen on the advertising banners of the popular cinema. Probably the sub-title in Juichiya's novel " *Toki no haisha* " means " the victims of circumstantial forces." Certainly, to Japanese, Okichi at least is that, the victim of forces too great for one poor, unfortunate girl to overcome.

A word may be added as to the *fudo* to which Okichi San so fervently and frequently prayed. Its original owner was Shinjiro Isa, a minor official in the employ of the Shogunate. He, too, was deeply concerned over the fate of the *Treaty*, which depended so much on the frail health of the American representative. He, too, prayed at the lowly shrine for the casting out of the demons of suspicion and distrust. When the treaty was at length successfully negotiated, Isa took back his *fudo* to the family estate at Shizuoka, where it became known as the *Kesazu no fudo*, " the *Perpetually-lighted Fudo*," from the candles which continually burned before it to testify the owner's gratitude. It was eventually brought to Tokyo, and in 1930 was dedicated as the *Black Ship Fudo*, on the site of an old fish-market, near the Mitsukoshi Department Store, just behind the monument to Will Adams. Here it remains to invite those who visit it, to pray still for the exorcism of evil influences, such as may interfere with the peace of the Pacific. It may serve also to remind the passing traveller that, as in the " gorgeous tragedies " of Greece and England, in such examples as an Alcestis or an Iphigenia, an Ophelia, a Desdemona, or a Cordelia, in modern times as in days long passed, no great thing is often achieved except on the "foundation sacrifice" of a woman's devotion.

Now, leaving the reader to make of this strange but all too human story what he will, we may return to the description of Townsend Harris' diplomatic struggles and successes. Of course, there was much more in the negotiations which led to the signing of the Convention of June 17, 1857 than an argument over Okichi San and Ofuko. With the help of the interpreter, Moriyama, whom we met in our last study, Harris had been trying to convince the Governor that behind him were American battleships, if things came to the worst. From the instructions of the Secretary of State, received at the time of his appointment, he passed on the information that "if the Japanese sought to evade the *Treaty of Kanagawa*, the President would not hesitate to ask Congress to give him power to use such arguments as they could not resist." This had its effect, and the Convention was signed after nine days spent in wording the articles. The substance of these was as follows:

"1. The port of Nagasaki, in the principality of Hizen, shall be open to American vessels, where they may repair damages, procure water, fuel, provisions, and other necessary articles, even coals where they are obtainable.

"2. American citizens to reside permanently at Shimoda and Hakodate, and a vice-consul to be appointed by the United States for Hakodate. This to go into effect July 4, 1858.

"3. Weighing of Japanese and American coins,

silver with silver, and gold with gold, and 6% to be allowed the Japanese for recoinage.

" 4. Establishing of consular courts to try Americans and punish according to American laws. Japanese committing offences against Americans to be tried by Japanese authorities and punished by Japanese laws.

" 5. Goods to be exchanged for supplies if no gold or silver possessed by ships resorting to Shimoda, Hakodate or Nagasaki.

" 6. Consul-general given privilege of travelling anywhere in Japan. (But Harris was asked to delay the use of this right and he assented.)

" 7. Purchases for His Excellency the Consul-general, or his family, to be made by himself only, or some member of his family, and payment made to the seller for the same, without the intervention of any Japanese official; and for this purpose Japanese silver and copper coin shall be supplied to His Excellency, the Consul-general."

Following upon the successful accomplishment of this important piece of work, Harris might well have expected things to flow more smoothly, but, as a matter of fact, the summer months of 1857 seem to have been mainly a period of almost unavailing struggle against illness, loneliness, and the opposition of the officials to the plan of presenting the Consul-general's credentials in person to the Shogun at Yedo. It was " quite preposterous," declared the Lord of Shinano, for any such idea to be entertained, and at one time this nobleman even threatened to commit *seppuku* if the credentials were not placed in his own hands. Now and then something relieved the monotony, as, for example, the permission to keep the *Fourth of July* by firing the

proper number of guns. On August 21 we have the
entry in the *Journal:* "Happy day! I get a package
with a dozen newspapers and some China letters from
Mr. Rice." But, alas, there were no letters from
America. On September 8 the highest hopes were
aroused by the appearance of the U. S. Sloop of war,
Portsmouth, under Captain Foote, but there was no
word from Washington. Still the Captain was pleased
to learn of the *Convention* of June 17 and said that the
officials in Washington would "all be surprised" to
hear of it. Harris was too short of provisions to invite the Captain to dinner, but was for that reason all
the more delighted to have a meal or two on board the
ship. During much of these weeks, the Consul was
"wretchedly ill," and more and more convinced that
if he were destined to remain in confinement at Shimoda indefinitely, he might just as well go home.

At last, on September 22, came the good news that
permission had been given for his visit to Yedo "in
the most honourable manner," without any insistence
upon kotowing beyond the "three bows" usual in
the courts of Europe. While these arrangements were
going forward there arrived supplies and letters
(twenty-eight in all) by way of Hakodate, but still
"not one word from the Department of State." In
fact, word was received indirectly that the President
was "for my instant removal."

Yet excitement prevailed above all causes for disappointment, since Harris was now, on November 23,
on the point of starting for this wonderful and long
anticipated visit to Yedo. To-day, the visit from
Shimoda to Tokyo would seem but a short one, made
by sea in a few hours. But for Harris it was a con-

tinuous pageant in which he himself was playing a
leading and picturesque rôle. In front waved the
American flag (Japanese made), carried by a stalwart
officer, and guarded by two of the Consul's guards.
Then came Harris, on horseback, followed by the
norimono, or palanquin, which had been made of
special size to fit the American. This was borne by
twelve bearers, and was followed by Heusken, on
horseback, with his *norimono* and guards behind.
After these came a long train, with packages, bedding,
food and presents, and behind these the Vice-Governor
of Shimoda and the Mayor of Kakizaki. It made a
truly formidable procession of not less than three
hundred and fifty persons, and strung out in single file
for half a mile. The entire journey of a hundred and
eighty miles took seven days, since there were mountains to traverse and a Sunday, the first Sunday in Advent, on which day Harris refused to travel, but " read
the whole service for the day with Mr. Heusken as my
clerk and congregation. . . . This, too, while the law
punishing such an act with death was still in force."

When the Consul came near the residence in the
Azabu ward which had been assigned him, he had
learned enough of Japanese formality to insist on being carried into the house in his *norimono* like a prince,
since only thus could the proper aristocratic seclusion
be maintained.

The entry into Yedo, then, was made in the grand
style and with all due sense of his diplomatic importance. But the following days, too, were crowded with
exciting incidents. Eight men of high rank were
deputed to call on him on the following day, two of
whom had been among those who negotiated with

Perry the *Treaty of Kanagawa*. Soon after, the Shogun's own ambassador was sent to enquire after the Consul's health, and at length, with a due delay to admit of the Shogun's examination of the presents from America, an audience was arranged for Harris with Iyesada on December 7. It was a great historical occasion when Townsend Harris, in " a coat embroidered with gold after the pattern furnished by the State Department; blue pantaloons, with a broad gold band running down each leg, cocked hat with gold tassels, and a pearl-handled dress sword," crossed the bridge leading to Yedo Castle, heard at the doorway of the Audience Chamber the word of introduction, " Embassador Merrican," and found himself bowing before a personage dimly seen upon the dais and presenting his credentials. While all the officials present were prostrate on their faces, Harris gained the courage to look around and received the Shogun's reply, which, translated, was brief and noncommittal: " Pleased with the letter sent with the Ambassador from a far distant country, and likewise pleased with his discourse. Intercourse shall be continued forever." " So ended my audience, when I was reconducted to my original room and served with more tea-gruel." It was learned later that during the ceremony, two young men had plotted to take the life of the American Consul. Fortunately they were arrested and the matter hushed up.

Soon after this historic interview came the delivery of the presents, including much champagne and sherry, which, however, could not be presented until special trays had been made to receive them. Less exciting days succeeded, punctuated, however, with earthquake shocks and illnesses, during which the negotiations over the *Treaty* went forward but slowly. The days even lengthened into weeks and months, in which, to quote Roland Morris, " Japan not only debated but decided her destiny." In this time of patient negotiation, Harris had really to put the Japanese officials through an entire course on international law, in order to make clear that the President was not asking a favour but only seeking to bring about an exchange of the customary international courtesies.

The *Preamble* to the *Treaty* was accepted by January 25, 1858, but the tug-of-war between the negotiating parties was by no means over. There were so many things that had to be fought over. One was the need for more open harbours, more conveniently situated than Shimoda. Another was the right of the Consul to travel without restriction into other parts of the Islands. Still another was the necessity of providing a proper residence for a Minister at Yedo. It was the wish of the Shogun's ministers that the American representative should reside between Kanagawa and Kawasaki, and only come to Yedo when there was special business to transact. Kanagawa and Yokohama were offered as ports instead of Shimoda, but Americans were on no account to travel outside of the strict limits imposed upon them.

In reference to the difficulties of these days J. H. Gubbins rightly draws attention to the trouble caused by language. There was " the incubus of two languages (Japanese and Chinese) disguised as one," " rendered still more irksome from the fact that the borrowed Chinese written language never became thoroughly assimilated with the Japanese spoken language to which it was joined, but preserved a more or less separate identity. Moreover, there was the necessity of rendering this Sino-Japanese into Dutch, not the correct Dutch spoken by the interpreters, but a mercantile patois, which had again in the written agreements to have every word standing in the exact order of the Japanese. This alone was enough to drive a diplomat crazy."

It is probable, too, that at this time Harris did not sufficiently appreciate the difficulty of the Shogun's position. Iyesada was, as we have already noted, between the necessity of placating, on the one hand, the Powers, who with their fleets had already shown in China their ability to break through the barriers which had hitherto guarded the Orient, and, on the other, the Imperial party, supported as it was by the anti-Tokugawa clans, such as the Satsuma, Choshu, Hizen, and others. These last had been urging the Shogun to expel the foreigner instead of making further treaties with him. Harris certainly did not realize at this time the strength of these forces, and was even disposed to question the existence of the *ronins*, whose presence even in Yedo made the guarding of him by the Shogun a considerable problem. As for Kyoto, such things as came to the ears of the Consul tended to make him more or less incredulous of dangers from that quarter. Kyoto, he said, was " comparatively a poor place," " merely a city of priests and temples," and so on. He reports of the Emperor according to the hearsay of Yedo. " They spoke almost contemptuously of the Mikado and roared with laughter when I quoted some remarks concerning the veneration in which he is held by the Japanese. They say he has neither money, political power, nor anything else that is valued in Japan. He is a mere cipher."

Under such circumstances, Harris may be excused for believing that his negotiations with the Shogun's ministers were being dragged out unnecessarily. But the delay made him seriously ill towards the end of February, and from this point on, the *Journal,* which had been so carefully kept from the day of his arrival, breaks off. What follows is only to be gathered from *Fragments,* preserved here and there, and from the account given by the first British representative, Sir Rutherford Alcock.

The forces of England and France were at this time beginning to threaten war with China, which resulted in compelling the Chinese to receive the Foreign Ministers in the capital of the Manchu Empire. With the collective strength of the Western world at the gate, the self-chosen isolation of the Orient was shaken as never before in all its history, and the shock of the impact naturally reached even to the ears of the Japanese ministers. All this proved of considerable assistance to Townsend Harris, in the effort to hurry up negotiations with the Shogun, for by making terms with the intruders quickly, Iyesada saw a way by which he might save himself the humiliation which had been the ill-fortune of China.

So at length the draft treaty was agreed upon and, with no more to do than fill in the date and affix his signature, Harris returned to Shimoda in the month of May. Even now there was discernible a disposition to procrastinate, but in July the *U. S. S. Mississippi* arrived at Shimoda, with the news that the Chinese treaties had been exacted at the mouth of the cannon.

This news made a great sensation and immediately thereafter Harris went on the *Powhatan* to Kanagawa with the blunt advice to the Shogun's ministers: " Conclude your treaty without delay." So critical was felt to be the situation that three days after the coming of the Consul, the *Commercial Treaty* was signed on board the *Powhatan,* and the long struggle brought to a happy conclusion. Perhaps the word " conclusion " is still a little premature, since it was not ratified in the United States till May 22, 1860, and in Kyoto it was signed without having received the Imperial approval. The consent given by the famous Ii Naosuke Kamon no Kami, Lord of Hikone, and the Shogun's Prime Minister, was regarded by many as a defying of the conservative element and even, metaphorically speaking, a snapping of the fingers of the swaggering Prime Minister " in the face of the Emperor himself." This action of his was destined presently to bear bitter fruit. Of this we shall have to say something later. It is sufficient at present to say that Harris' work had paved the way, or, as Sir Rutherford Alcock puts it, *macadamized* it for all the other Treaty Powers. The treaty became the model on which later Conventions were framed, until the revision of these in 1894. Great Britain and France followed immediately along the path which had been opened by the patient and far-seeing efforts of the American Consul.

The main contents of the *Commercial Treaty* of 1858 may be summarized as follows:

1. Peace and friendship. The status of the Diplomatic agent and Consul-general. Privileges of residence in Japan. The right to travel beyond the treaty limits. The right of Consuls to reside in the open

ports. The Consuls to have privileges like to those of the corresponding Japanese officials.

2. The Mediation of the United States in differences between Japan and the European Powers. Assistance to be given by American warships to Japanese vessels on the high seas and by the United States Consuls in foreign ports.

3. Additional ports, namely, Kanagawa and Nagasaki, to be opened July 4, 1859; Niigata to be opened from January 1, 1860; Hyogo (Kobe) from January 1, 1863. American citizens to be permitted to reside in these cities. Rules and regulations for such residence. Provisions as to residence of Americans in Yedo and Osaka. Regulations as to trading. These provisions to be made public by the Japanese Government. Rice and wheat not to be exported from Japan. Copper surplus to be sold at auction. Americans to be allowed to employ Japanese.

4. Duties to be paid according to tariff. Proceedings to be taken where a difference exists as to the values of duties. Regulations as to supplies for the U. S. Navy. Opium to be prohibited. No higher duties to be levied than those fixed by the treaty.

5. Foreign coins to be current in Japan.

6. Jurisdiction over offences. Provision for adjudications where Americans appear against Japanese in Consular courts, and where Japanese appear against Americans before the local authorities.

7. Limits of right to travel from the open ports, namely, 10 *ri* in any direction. American criminals, that is, those convicted of felony, to lose the right of permanent residence in Japan.

8. Religious freedom. Religious animosity not to be excited.

9. Japanese authorities will, upon the request of the Consul, arrest deserters and fugitives from justice.

10. The Japanese Government may purchase or construct vessels of war, etc., in the United States. The Government may also engage from the United States the services of scientific men and advisers.

11. Regulations appended (pertaining to trade) are made part of the treaty.

12. Conflicting provisions of the treaty of March 31, 1854 and the Convention of June 17, 1857 are hereby repealed.

13. Revision of the treaty and trade regulations may be made upon one year's notice at any time after July 1, 1872, if desired by either party.

14. The Treaty to take effect July 4, 1859. Ratification to be exchanged at Washington. Signed in the English, Dutch and Japanese languages. In case of dispute, the Dutch version is to be considered as the original.

It was in the June of 1859, on the eve of the treaty coming into operation, that there arrived in Japan the first British envoy, Sir Rutherford Alcock, who, in his *Three Years in Japan*,[7] has given a very illuminating account of the events of this period. It was a great puzzle to Sir Rutherford, after he had obtained a little insight into Japanese affairs, to account for Harris' success. " No force," he writes, " apparently had been used. It was indeed the peculiar pride and boast of Mr. Harris, that he had effected his object with no material means of support or coercion; the triumph of reason, argument and diplomacy! This seemed very

incomprehensible to me, and I confess very doubtful."
Yet, when the British envoy had, as he thought, "un-
ravelled the mystery," and had made all due allowance
for the preparatory work of the Dutch, the pressure
of the fleets, and the difficulties of the Shogun, he is
obliged to sum up the matter in the words: "Throughout the negotiations, apparently single-handed, and
without any material support from his Government,
the American diplomatic agent thus surmounted all
difficulties and proved himself equal to the occasion.
How such success was secured, with the knowledge
since attained, it is easy to see; but it detracts nothing
from the credit due to the strategic skill with which
the negotiator turned the weakness of the Japanese,
the strength of his neighbours, and even his own want
of material support from the Government he represented, all equally to account for the success of his
mission. Where others might have seen only motives
of discouragement, he found all the elements of victory."

The signing of the *Treaty*, however, gave Mr. Harris little or no time to rest upon the credit of his accomplishment. The "bitter fruit" which some had
predicted as the outcome of this submission to the
overseas foreigner was not long in coming to ripeness.
First of all there was the popular feeling that the signing of the treaties had brought upon the nation the
anger of the gods. As the Shogun Iyeyoshi had died,
somewhat mysteriously, eight days after the departure
of Perry, on July 27, 1853, so now we have, soon after
the signing of the *Treaty* of 1858, the death, "with or
without medicine," of the physically incompetent Iyesada. It very much impressed the imagination of the

Japanese that each of the Shoguns responsible for negotiations with the outsider had been thus mysteriously removed. In addition, as there had been the great earthquake following the acceptance of the *Treaty of Kanagawa,* so now there was the great visitation of cholera, a disease probably introduced by the *Mississippi* in August 1859.

Meanwhile, the *Jo-i,* or " barbarian-expelling " party, was busy in Kyoto. The minister, Lord Hotta Masahiro, who had in vain ~~tried~~ to induce the anti-foreign Emperor Komei to agree to the *Commercial Treaty,* had been compelled to resign and his place had been taken by the great statesman to whom allusion has already been made, Ii Naosuke Kamon no Kami. The latter was fated to endure much, and to suffer assassination for the odium incurred by making terms with Harris.

As you change street cars to-day in Tokyo, in going from the Hibiya Park towards Aoyama, you pass the spot where on March 24, 1860, Lord Ii paid the penalty for his complaisance at the hands of a band of *ronin,* supposedly under the influence of their former master, the Lord of Mito. In the Sakurada Affair, as this incident is known, the attackers, disguised in straw raincoats to present the appearance of innocent bystanders, took advantage of a snowstorm to get near the Lord of Hikone's palanquin and carry out the object of the vendetta. It is said that the head of Lord Ii was taken to Kyoto and there exposed with the inscription: " This is the head of a traitor who has violated the most sacred laws of Japan—those which forbid the admission of foreigners into the country." Then the grisly trophy was carried back to Yedo and one night thrown into the grounds of the Hikone yashiki. The assassination of Ii was an irreparable blow to the Tokugawa Government and, as J. H. Gubbins says, " after his death the fall of the Shogunate was only a question of time." [8]

The resentment of Japanese super-nationalism was brought home to Harris still more directly in January 1861 by the murder of his interpreter and secretary, Heusken. Long before this event, it was clear that in some respects the signing of the treaty had made matters worse instead of better for the foreigners then in Japan. There was a new Shogun, Iyemochi, the thirteen-year-old son of Nariyuki, of the Kii branch of the Tokugawa family, though the more liberal side of Japanese statesmanship had fought hard for the succession of Keiki (Yoshinobu), son of Nariyaki, of Mito, a man of matured convictions. The new appointment played directly into the hands of the *Jo-i* party, whose cause, moreover, was strengthened by the premature arrival of many foreigners to take advantage of the commercial provisions of the new treaty. This had provided that on July 1, 1859, there should be opened for the residence of foreigners the shipping port of Kanagawa, a place about sixteen miles from Yedo and on the western side of the Bay. But the Japanese officials seemed determined to place the settlement at a fishing village called Yokohama, on the opposite side of the Bay, and out of the direct line of traffic. They claimed that Yokohama was actually the same as Kanagawa, since the two places were in the same district. But it is clear that the main purpose of the authorities was to keep the foreign traders under more direct surveillance than would have been possible

at Kanagawa. Harris, together with the British representative, Sir Rutherford Alcock, found the settlement
of this question almost as difficult as the wresting from
the Shogun of the *Treaty* itself. It was much complicated by the impatience of the foreign pioneers of
trade, who came hurrying over from Nagasaki and
China, to secure a prior claim to the most advanta-
geous locations. In vain Harris and Alcock protested
that the Japanese Government was bent on creating
another *Deshima;* the foreigners saw that the diplomats were only hindering their start in business. They
became furiously angry at what they deemed "the
unrelenting hostility and perversity of the Foreign
Representatives at Yedo." So the two years of con-
troversy ended, as was natural, in a victory for the
Japanese authorities, though some concessions were
won by the diplomats, such as the extension of the site
of foreign settlement to the foot of the bluff. It was
under these circumstances that Yokohama was
founded, where, significantly enough, a statue of the
famous Lord Ii Kamon no Kami was erected in 1909.
Up to the time of the earthquake of 1923, a sign of
the haste with which the site of Yokohama was seized
upon was visible in the odd numbering of the houses.
The first foreigner who came called his place No. 1
and the next followed with No. 2, in whatever part of
the town he settled.

Another difficulty in which the foreigners were involved was that of the currency question. By the
Treaty it had been agreed that foreign coins were to
be exchangeable for Japanese coins, weight for weight.
But at the time it had not been remembered that
whereas the ratio of silver to gold in Japan was 5 to

1, in Europe and America the ratio was 15 to 1. This difference did not long escape the eye of the foreign trader. When merchants found that they could buy up the gold coinage of Japan, ship it over to China, and realize a profit of cent per cent, the desire to traffic in currency reached the point of delirium. " Who would look at tea and silk, with all the risks of falling markets, in face of a steady and certain exchange of silver against Japanese gold, with never less than 100% gain? " [9] Nor was the craze confined to merchants. When an American frigate came into port, " one officer resigned his commission, and instantly freighted a ship and started a firm; and nearly every other officer in the ship, finding by the favour of the customhouse an unlimited supply of Aziboos, as they were about to take the embassy over to America, entered largely into profitable operations for converting silver into gold." It is obvious that all this added vastly to the worries of Harris and his colleagues. Especially when the Japanese Government took the only possible course of changing the relative weights of gold and silver coins, this action was denounced by the traders as a " gross violation of treaty right." Sir Rutherford Alcock expressed in all probability the views of Harris as well as of himself, when he wrote to his Government that " in estimating the difficulties to be overcome in any attempt to improve the aspect of affairs, if the ill-disguised enmity of the governing classes and the indisposition of the Executive Government to give partial effect to the treaties be classed among the first and principal of these, the unscrupulous character and dealings of foreigners, who frequent the ports for purposes of trade, are only second and scarcely inferior in importance, from the sinister character of the influence they exercise."

It is no wonder that the Foreign Representatives, between the upper and lower millstones of official and commercial suspicion and hostility, found their position at this time a difficult one. Moreover, the temper of the Kyoto party, hostile from the first both to the diplomatists and the traders, was at a dangerous degree of tension. This tension it was which found its expression in the murder of Heusken, already alluded to, on January 15, 1860. A meeting had just taken place at the residence of Count Eulenberg, the Prussian Envoy, for the signing, after five months of wrangling and delay, of the Japanese-Prussian Treaty. In the arrangement and distribution of the customary presents, Heusken had taken a prominent part. After dinner, he mounted his horse and was returning to the American Legation, accompanied by the ordinary escort, when he was set upon by a band of six or seven swordsmen, who wounded him so savagely that he died an hour or two after his removal to the Legation. The event cast a pall of gloom and apprehension over the whole of Yedo. Harris wrote, four days after the assassination: " I am suffering deeply from this sudden and awful catastrophe. Mr. Heusken was associated with me over five years and he was the companion of my lonely solitude at Shimoda. Our relations were rather that of father and son than of chief and employé." It was a tremendous blow to his faith in the ultimate triumph of patience and forbearance. But in such a crisis Townsend Harris stood the test. All his colleagues, misappreciating the difficulties of the Shogun's Government, were now of the opinion that the time had come for the Foreign Representatives to withdraw to Yokohama and from thence appeal to their respective Governments. The Dutch Diplomatic Agent went first, followed presently by the French and English Ministers, and Count Eulenberg went a day or two later. Only Harris was left, "disapproving entirely of the course thus unanimously followed by all his colleagues." His explanation is contained in a private letter, dated February 12, quoted by Roland Morris: "We have lived in Yedo about nineteen months in safety, and this fact is proof of the desire and ability of the Government to give us efficient protection. . . . In judging of the acts of this Government it is of importance that the political antecedents be taken into consideration. For more than two hundred years this country was completely closed against foreigners: this barrier so rigidly maintained is suddenly removed and the country opened to foreign intercourse. It is well known that a large party of men of high rank are opposed to the new order of things initiated by the treaties, and in this city that opposition is concentrated and felt in its greatest intensity. . . . It is unquestionable, in my mind, that the enormous enhancement of prices on articles of general consumption consequent upon the admission of foreign commerce has intensified their feelings of opposition. A government may make treaties and observe their stipulations, but it is beyond the power of any government to control public opinion. . . . It is only time, patience and forbearance that can procure this most desirable result." He writes again, in a mood of much sadness: " I had hoped that the page of future history might record the great fact that in one spot in the Eastern World, the advent of Christian civilization did not bring with it its usual attendants of conquest and bloodshed. This hope, I fear, is to be disappointed."

The fear was well grounded, especially since the new Shogun, in receiving the Emperor's sister in marriage, in the same year, was obliged to give a pledge that within ten years he would expel the foreigners from the land on account of the " insufferable and contumelious behaviour " of the strangers who had forced their way into the Empire. Before ten years had passed a very different attitude had been adopted in Kyoto as well as in Yedo. But in the interval many outrages upon the persons and property of the foreigners, including their diplomatic representatives, unhappily took place.

The Ministers, perhaps a little ashamed and annoyed at their precipitancy, returned to Yedo on March 6, 1861, two days, as Roland Morris reminds us, after the inauguration of Abraham Lincoln as President of the United States. They put a good face on their temporary departure from the Shogun's capital, employing the time in studying the situation at Yokohama. On their return, they demanded, and received, the honour of being conducted to their respective Legations by two Governors of Foreign Affairs in person, with a salute of twenty-one guns to each of their reinstated flags. They marvelled a little at Harris' particular style in diplomacy, but I fancy were not a little envious of his unshaken calm and faith.

Harris, unfortunately, did not stay long enough in Japan to see this faith completely vindicated, for the country's internal turmoil did not cease till the actual resignation of the last Shogun at the end of 1867.

But he was privileged to behold many changes from
which a prophetic eye might have anticipated the accomplishment of a good deal of that for which he had
so strenuously fought. The Government was already
maturing plans to meet the new era of international
relations by the establishment of a school for instruction in foreign languages. Though it was not till 1862
that the Shogunate inaugurated the policy of sending
students abroad for instruction, a few were sent by the
Satsuma clan, and some, like Ito and Inouye, went
overseas on their own account and at their own risk.
One interesting and immediate result of the new
treaties was the sending abroad of missions to foreign
lands, bearing copies of these epoch-making documents.
The first of these missions visited the United States in
1860, in the last year of President Buchanan, and has
been but lightly touched upon in the histories. To
quote from my *Outline History:* " The envoys and
their suite came in the *U. S. S. Powhatan,* and at the
same time came the Japanese steamship, *Kanrin Maru,*
under Captain Katsu, the organizer of the modern
Japanese navy. Landing at San Francisco, on March
9, the envoys were warmly received, the Board of Su-
pervisors of the City taking occasion to express ' the
earnest wish that the amicable relations happily exist-
ing between the Imperial Government of Japan and
the United States of America and their people, may be
perpetuated and productive of great and mutual advantages.' " The envoys went to Washington by way
of Panama, were received by the President and Secretary Cass, and entertained in various ways. They
were much amused at a " group dance of both sexes "
(a ball) at Washington, and gratified by the presenta-

tion to each of a handsome watch by the Walton Company of New York.

Other changes of the time include the foundation in 1858 by Yukichi Fukuzawa, " the Sage of Mita," of the educational establishment in the compound of the Okudaira mansion, now known as Keio University.

In truth, Harris had at this time, in spite of manifold disappointments, much reason to feel gratified with the achievements of his six years as the American representative. He was trusted now where formerly he had been hedged around with suspicion. His sympathy with the difficulties of the Shogunate enabled him to secure the postponement of the opening of the ports of Yedo, Osaka, Kobe and Niigata, a postponement which did much to assuage the excitement in Kyoto. He also persuaded Mr. Seward, the Secretary of State, to abandon the plan he had conceived for an international display of naval force in Japanese waters. Unlike many of his contemporaries, Harris felt that a rapid westernization of the long secluded Empire, at a time when the fate of the Shogunate hung in the balance, might be productive of evil rather than good.

But he was beginning to feel his work done, and in the July of 1861 he sent a request to his Government, asking to be relieved on the ground of advancing years and an unsatisfactory state of health. The Japanese Government now awoke to the fact that the possession of such a friend, as Townsend Harris had proved himself to be, was an asset not lightly to be lost. On May 1, 1862, when, however, Mr. Pruyn, Harris' successor, had already arrived, a letter was received from the Japanese Government which ran, in part, as follows: " We have to state to Your Excellency as follows:

During the time of your residence at this Court, since the exchange of the first *Treaty*, you acquired a perfect knowledge of the real circumstances of our country and offered us your kindly aid in every respect. . . . The merits of Your Excellency are so great that we wrote a letter to your Government in the 11th month of our last year expressing the wish that you might remain here for some years longer. No reply to that letter has as yet been received. We are very sorry to learn, however, that Your Excellency's successor has arrived. You will shortly return to your country. But in our opinion it is still uncertain what decision may be taken by your Government in regard to that wish, and we therefore beg to enquire from Your Excellency whether you could not arrange so to postpone your departure until the said reply be received by us." Well does Morris conclude his quotation from this letter with the words: " Reward indeed to the faith that never faltered."

This testimony to the work of America's first representative in Japan is amply confirmed from other sources. Not to multiply these, we may quote the words of Marquis Okuma, one of the greatest of the statesmen who contributed to the making of the New Japan. He says: " We can never be too grateful towards Townsend Harris, who always assisted Japan with open-hearted friendship in the days of her infancy. Other European countries that have sent their missionaries could not at all compare with the United States in the number of their agents and the grandeur of their ideals. Therefore it is never unjust to say that Japan is indebted to the United States in the highest degree for her progress and advancement in the path of modern civilization." [10]

There is not much more that we need say of Harris. When he left Japan for America, the United States was in the throes of a rending and devastating civil war. During these years the same faith which had won its victories in the troublous civil conflicts of Japan was called into action in the cause of the Union. For a while, Harris lived in Florida and thence went north to end his days in his old environment of New York. Here he passed away, after a short illness, February 25, 1878, at the age of seventy-four. He lies buried in Greenwood Cemetery, Brooklyn.

But as we gaze at the coloured crayon picture which is, or used to be, on the walls of the American Chancellery in Tokyo, or as we muse under the great ginko tree in the courts of the *Zempukuji,* where the first American flag fluttered to the breezes of Yedo, or, again, as we stand before the *Black Ship Fudo,* before which Okichi San prayed for the recovery of her foreign master, we are more inclined to think of Townsend Harris as the embodiment of American faith in the peace of the Pacific and of the patience which looks beyond the clouds of doubt for the sunshine of understanding and accord. " I would sooner," he wrote, " see all the treaties with this country torn up and Japan return to its old state of isolation than witness the horrors of war inflicted on this peaceful people and happy land."

NOTES

[1] See *An American Shrine in Tokyo,* Memorial Meeting for Townsend Harris, held at Zempukuji. Tokyo, 1931.

[2] See H. H. Gowen, *An Outline History of Japan* (1927), p. 294 ff.; I. Nitobe, *The Japanese Nation,* p. 278 ff. (1912).

[3] *Outline History of Japan,* p. 298 ff.

[4] Townsend Harris' memory, after all, is not infallible. He writes "1853," but was probably thinking of the great earthquake of November 4, 1854.

[5] Translation furnished me by Mr. Aisaku Nakajima, of Tokyo. Mr. Nakajima has given me his kind permission for this and other quotations in this study.

[6] From an unpublished MS. by A. Nakajima.

[7] See Sir Rutherford Alcock, *Three Years in Japan,* 1877.

[8] On the *Sakurada Affair* see Walter Dickson, *Japan,* p. 437 ff.; E. W. Clement, T. A. S. J., December 1920.

[9] On the Currency Question see Alcock's *Three Years in Japan,* I, 146 ff.

[10] When Viscount (then Baron) Shibusawa was the guest of the Japan Society of New York the President (Dr. John Finley) mentioned the report that the Baron had sent a wreath for the grave of Townsend Harris. "Not so," replied Shibusawa, "I took it myself and laid it on the grave. And I wrote two poems in memory of Townsend Harris and hung them in the branches of a Japanese maple-tree overhanging his resting-place."

[11] On the subject of the Okichi San episode I owe much to material in my hands from the pen of A. Nakajima, of Tokyo. Other sources used for this sketch are as follows: Roland Morris, *Townsend Harris;* J. H. Gubbins, *The Making of Modern Japan,* 1922; W. E. Griffis, *Townsend Harris, the first American Envoy,* 1895; Captain F. Brinkley, *History of the Japanese People,* 1912; Payson J. Treat, *Japan and the United States,* 1921; James Murdoch, *A History of Japan,* 3 volumes. I am permitted to use the quotations from *The Complete Journal of Townsend Harris,* with Introduction and Notes by Professor Mario Emilio Cosenza, 1930, through the kindness of the Japan Society of New York, and the quotations from the study by Mr. Roland Morris through the kindness of the author.